NATIONALISM AND RACISM IN THE LIBERAL ORDER

Nationalism and Racism in the Liberal Order

Edited by

BOB BRECHER
University of Brighton

JO HALLIDAY
Anglia Polytechnic University

KLÁRA KOLINSKÁ
Charles and J.E. Purkyně Universities

Ashgate

Aldershot • Brookfield USA • Singapore • Sydney

Published by
Ashgate Publishing Ltd
Gower House
Croft Road
Aldershot
Hants GU11 3HR
England

Ashgate Publishing Company
Old Post Road
Brookfield
Vermont 05036
USA

British Library Cataloguing in Publication Data
Nationalism and racism in the liberal order. - (Avebury
    series in philosophy)
    1. Liberalism 2. Nationalism - Europe - Congresses 3. Racism -
    Political aspects - Europe - Congresses 4. Post-communism -
    Europe - Congresses 5. Violence - Political aspects - Europe
    - Congresses
    I. Brecher, Robert II. Halliday, Jo III, Kolinská, Klára
    320.5'1'094'09049

Library of Congress Catalog Card Number: 98-70988

ISBN 1 84014 148 4

Printed and bound by Athenaeum Press, Ltd.,
Gateshead, Tyne & Wear.

Contents

Preface

This book contains a selection of papers originally prepared for a conference on Nationalism and Racism in the Liberal Order, held in July 1997 at J.E. Purkyně University in the Czech Republic. Following on from two earlier conferences – also jointly organized by Brighton, Anglia Polytechnic and J.E. Purkyně universities – the conference brought together some 70 people, from a considerable variety of disciplines and countries, and students as well as more established academics, to discuss a twin spectre that seemed to many of us to be haunting post-'communist' Europe.

Across the continent, and not least in the countries of central and eastern Europe, the Romani, Turkish, south Asian and many other minority subjects – if all too rarely full citizens – of Europe's nation-states, new and old, are being subjected to a level of harassment, hatred and violence which one had hoped would never again be seen in Europe. At the same time, and even if in many cases in effect if not by intention, the varieties of objections and alternatives to the allegedly imperialistic universalism of the Enlightenment commonly described as postmodernism seem not so much to be freeing us from the shackles of intolerance as to be pitching us against those very 'Others' it had berated the Enlightenment – and liberalism in particular – for refusing to recognize. Historical racisms and fascisms, which liberalism had at least sought in principle to counter, even if perhaps at considerable theoretical cost and even if only sporadically in practice, seem to be finding new allies – however inadvertent and however unrecognized – among the postmodern moral and political relativists who herald liberalism's intellectual demise. Of course, that the putative intellectual demise of liberalism as a universalizing theoretical construct should coincide historically with its alleged political triumph might seem another of the odder features of the 1990s – but perhaps we should expect just these sorts of contradiction to arise in the circumstances in which we find ourselves … .

In the face of the erosion of its pretence to neutrality, does liberalism still retain the intellectual resources needed to combat the horrors that racism consists in and that nationalism so often leads to? Or, in response to a recognition of the hopeless pretensions of any universalism, is the flight to the local and to the inner all that we can hope for? What other than personal or communal distaste – hardly anything reliable or resilient, and historically all too clearly no match for racism's insidious advances, whether now or in the recent past – might we be able to marshal in the face of Europe's new-found freedoms to hate? Might notions of national identity, far from necessarily furthering such hatreds, and far from being inimical to the liberalism as against which nationalism has so often identified itself, serve as a means of defence? Or is 'national identity' itself too fluid a notion, and too dependent upon that as against which it defines itself, to play such a role? Might the idea of multiculturalism, for all the problems it causes for liberal conceptions of neutrality, disinterest and equality, prove a more fruitful direction to take? Or are its inevitable and illiberal relativisms too close to those of the postmodern pragmatists to constitute a bulwark against the neo-Nazi's 'Why not?', effective though it may be against the liberal's complacent 'Why?' And what of the notion of identity itself? How is that to be theorized, and how might it help in building conceptions of the self – whether individual, social or national – which do not work by defining themselves as *against* others, while yet recognizing them *as* others?

These are some of the questions which were addressed in Ustí by philosophers, sociologists, political scientists, educationalists, linguists and lawyers, and which constitute the background against which the following more specific discussions are conducted. Beginning with a presentation of what is arguably Europe's biggest contemporary scandal, its attitude to and treatment of the Romani, the book moves through considerations of multiculturalism and nationalism, via two case studies, to somewhat broader problems and contradictions both of liberalism – vis-à-vis racism and postmodernism – and of the communitarianism posed as its alternative. Finally, it considers a variety of understandings of, and problems about, the 'identity' which is both cause and outcome of the problems with which the volume deals.

Bob Brecher
Jo Halliday
Klára Kolinská
Brighton, November 1997

Acknowledgements

We should like to thank Anglia Polytechnic University, the University of Brighton and J.E. Purkyně University for their continuing support of the series of conferences, the third of which constitutes the basis of this book; and, most importantly, all the participants in the 1997 conference, whether or not contributors to this volume.

1 Introduction: Towards a Typology of Violence against Roma in Central and Eastern Europe

CLAUDE CAHN

Introduction: Violence

Violence, according to the *Cambridge International Dictionary of English* (1995), is 'actions or words which are intended to hurt people'. Physical violence is manifested by beating, kicking, punching, shooting, stabbing, torture, arson, rape, pogrom and genocide. The set of phenomena collected under the heading 'violence' is a break from the civilized order, a failure of other forms of interpersonal mediation. Social actions and events which can be regarded as 'violence' are viewed, in cultures which espouse the rule of law, with a deeper gravity than others.

Violence is distinct from coercion. The CIA 'Human Resource Exploitation Training Manual – 1983' explains coercion as follows:

> The purpose of coercive techniques is to induce psychological regression in the subject by bringing a superior outside force to bear on his will to resist. Regression is basically a loss of autonomy, a reversion to an earlier behavioural level. As the subject regresses, his learned personality traits fall away in reverse chronological order. He begins to lose the capacity to deal with complex situations, to cope with stressful interpersonal relationships or repeated frustrations (United States Central Intelligence Agency, 1997, pp. 23–5).

Coercive pressure is exerted by governments and majority populations on minorities and on problematic individuals (see Bauman, 1991) to conform, integrate and assimilate. Modern state-building depends, at least in part, on coercion. The traumas and repeated failures of the project of coercion has characterized Central and Eastern Europe throughout its modern history. In

1

Eastern Europe, coercion has been known repeatedly to fail; and in the wake of its failure, violence has commonly appeared. In modern European history, the two phenomena, violence and coercion, are inextricably linked, for where coercion fails – as it so often does – so violence follows. Although the subject of this essay is violence against Roma, coercion must be regarded as its thematic partner and silent precursor. Its effect on the nature of the violence that follows it will be apparent throughout the course of this discussion.

Classic Anti-Romani Violence

There are two forms of anti-Romani violence which commonly appear in various combinations throughout the history of Roma in Europe: police brutality and community violence. The two are probably related, although we understand only very vaguely how. Police brutality against Roma can be seen almost everywhere that Roma live. In recent years, instances of police brutality against Roma have been documented in Albania, Austria, Bulgaria, the Czech Republic, France, Greece, Hungary, Italy, Macedonia, Romania, Slovakia, Spain, Turkey, Ukraine and the United States. Many of these cases have led to fatalities, such as deaths by shooting in Albania, Bulgaria, the Czech Republic, France, Greece, Hungary and Romania, and deaths by beating by the police in Albania, Bulgaria, Macedonia and Turkey.

Police brutality against Roma can be seen in two ways. One possibility is that it is a response by police to a destabilized law enforcement atmosphere; where officers believe that they have lost control of the public order, they may be more inclined to become violent. This is especially noticeable, at present, in places like Ukraine. Since the late 1980s, the police all over the former Soviet Union have had to face the fact that they are much less in control than they were previously and to come to grips with this. In response to high levels of organized crime, corruption and white collar crime and the intersection between the three – cowboy capitalism – police have responded with violence, and generally against weaker members of society. Field research conducted by the European Roma Rights Center (ERRC) in 1996 revealed, for instance, that the incidence of police brutality against Roma in Trans-carpathia is, at present, extremely high;and the Uzhorod Roma organization *Romani Yag* reports four cases of extreme police brutality in Uzhorod alone between 1 January and 1 May 1997. The second explanation is racism. The police may simply be more likely to become violent when dealing with Roma, or may believe that Roma need special treatment in order to make them behave.

On 9 May 1996, for example, a police officer in southern Romania shot and killed a Rom who had refused to pull his wagon over to the side of the road. It is highly doubtful that resort to the firearm is typical in cases of traffic infractions by non-Roma in Romania. Similarly, the Sofia-based non-governmental organization (NGO) Human Rights Project reports that the shooting of petty Roma criminals who steal copper wire for resale has become increasingly common since 1989. Still another example of racist practice among the police is the development of so-called 'prophylactic' policies of crime prevention which specifically target Roma as a group, in countries such as Turkey and Ukraine (see European Roma Rights Center, 1997a). In cases such as these, ideological hatred of Roma may not really be at issue. More likely, a larger societal racist discourse has manifested itself in the behaviour of individual officers or in the formulation of law enforcement policy.

Racism may, however, appear in its overt form in instances of police brutality against Roma. That is, individual police officers may simply be racists and may exercise their racist beliefs while in uniform. In 1994, for example, police in Horšovský Týn in the Czech Republic shot and killed a Rom in police custody. None of the three officers involved was removed from the police force, and the investigator's office concluded that there was 'no suspicion of criminal offence' in the case. A letter to the regional government from the family of the victim protesting against the investigator's decision received a hostile response.

The second form of 'classic anti-Romani violence' is community violence. Here, whole communities of non-Roma gather and harass, attack, expel or kill Roma. Such attacks have been documented in Albania, Bulgaria, Hungary, Romania, Slovakia and Ukraine since 1989. Between 1990 and 1993, following the fall of the Çeauşescu regime, pogroms of this sort occurred all over Romania. These were usually triggered by a crime by a Rom or a bar fight between Roma and non-Roma and they received international attention, not least because the villagers were usually summoned by the picturesque means of ringing the village church bells. In one particularly gruesome episode in 1993, a mixed mob of ethnic Hungarians and Romanians burned 14 homes of Romani families and demolished a further five houses in the village of Hădăreni in Mureş County and then chased their inhabitants out of the village. Three Roma were killed in the attack (see European Roma Rights Center, 1996a).

One way of explaining community violence against Roma in Eastern Europe is to see it as a creation of traditional culture. It is particularly recognizable to those familiar with the well-documented phenomenon of anti-Jewish violence. And there are concrete parallels. Scholars of the so-called 'blood libel' against Jews are familiar with the fact that it commonly arises around Easter, with the accusation that Jews have killed Christian children to use their blood in the baking of the ceremonial bread of the Jewish Passover holiday.[1] It is therefore noteworthy that one of the most gruesome community attacks on Roma to have taken place since 1989 took place on Easter Monday, 1996, in the village of Zalistie in Central Slovakia. In that incident, villagers attacked a house inhabited by Roma three times in the course of one evening. During the third attack, villagers set it on fire and then hounded the Roma who were trying to escape back into the fire. One Romani man died in the blaze (see European Roma Rights Center, 1997b).

Another explanation for community violence against Roma relates to the elusive idea of societal stability. Research conducted by the ERRC in Romania in 1996 revealed that community violence had largely been replaced by police raids on Roma communities, as well as by a rise in shootings by individual police officers. One might therefore explain community violence in Romania as a series of convulsions resulting from the breakdown of the previously stable society of the Çeauşescu era. Following this period of instability, as the state reasserted control, episodes of police violence became more likely and instances of community violence decreased. This idea is lent weight by the fact that community violence has been extremely rare in postwar Western Europe. That is, where state power does not come radically into question, acts of racist violence are either individual or are acts of the police who, in the Weberian scheme, legitimately monopolize violence. 'Instability' is among the best, or at least most tidy, explanations available,[2] although one would not want to overvalue it, since community violence has not entirely vanished from Romania: on 9 March 1997, the Bucharest-based Roma NGO *Romani CRISS* reported that on 16 and 17 January 1997, groups of between 50 and 100 ethnic Romanians armed with pistols and shotguns gathered in the village of Tăngănu near Bucharest, chased out the Roma and vandalized their homes. The phenomenon of community violence, like that of racism or, indeed, that of violence itself, is not likely exhaustively to be defined by one or another theory, and one should be wary of any attempt to do so. Nevertheless, what is important is that these are, at the very least, different *emphases* or *modulations* of violence.

Racially-Motivated Violence: The Czech Republic

Police brutality and community violence are timeless[3] (see Fraser, 1995). Roma have known them for centuries. Racially-motivated, ideological targeting of Roma for violent acts is, on the other hand, a modern phenomenon. This type of violence against Roma is presently at its worst in the Czech Republic.

The Czech Republic is unique in Europe for having a political party that has made hatred of Roma the centrepiece of its political programme. The 'Republicans' *(Republikanská Strana České Republiky* or, popularly, *'Republikáni'),* who claimed approximately 8.5 per cent in the last national elections, place the 'resolution of the Romani problem' high on their party agenda, and the party leader, Miroslav Sládek, has stated publicly that his followers believe that the act of being born a Rom should be criminalized. The Czech Republic is also noteworthy for a vibrant skinhead movement whose rhetoric is very largely obsessed with Roma. According to the Prague-based NGO HOST, attacks by skinheads since 1989 have claimed the lives of nine Roma and one Turk mistaken for a Rom; the Czech Press Service claims that there have been over 35 racially motivated deaths in the Czech Republic over the same period. Gangs of skinheads have killed Roma by stabbing, drowning and immolating them. One Rom was killed in 1995 by skinheads who broke into his house and beat him to death in front of his family with a baseball bat. The *U.S. Department of State Czech Republic Country Report on Human Rights Practices for 1996,* published in January 1997, observed that, since 1994, there had been a sixfold increase in the incidence of skinhead violence against Roma.

The Czech court system, however, has not treated the wave of skinhead violence with the gravity it merits. Despite the preoccupation of Czech skinheads with Roma, law enforcement and judicial bodies have turned a blind eye to evidence of racial motivation when attacks have taken place. One example of a failure by the prosecution to invoke the articles of the Czech Criminal Code concerning racially-motivated crime took place in late 1996. The case involved skinheads who had assaulted a group of Roma and then forced them off a train, on the pretext that the train was 'for whites only'. The reasoning of the judge was that the crime was not racially motivated since both the skinheads and the Roma belonged to the 'Indo-European race'. Tortured judicial reasoning has been matched by undue delay in acting on complaints of discrimination or incitement, even where the alleged abuses are gross. In one well-publicized case, a Roma family was forcibly evicted from flats which they legally occupied in the northern Bohemian city of Ustí nad Labem, their rental contracts were confiscated, and, under continuous police escort, they were put on a train to Slovakia. Although a complaint was filed at Ustí nad Labem District Court on 19 May 1993, the court did not address the claim for three and a half years. During this period, the plaintiffs lived in parks and abandoned garages around the city. It was only when the Czech Constitutional Court interfered, in late 1996, that legal action was resumed.

Czech prosecutors have also shown a propensity for using the relatively new racially-motivated crimes provisions of the Criminal Code against Roma. In one recent incident in the northwest Bohemian town of Louny, five Roma were convicted of defamation of nation, race or belief (Article 198 of the Criminal Code) after they insulted and attacked police officers who had arrived to break up a fight in a flat. This is hardly the spirit of such provisions: Article 198, like similar provisions in most European jurisdictions, is designed to protect weak minorities. Its invocation against Roma charged with violence against representatives of the state is especially cynical.

Manipulation of the legal system for anti-Roma ends in the Czech Republic does not take place only at the level of the individual before the law: Roma have also been directly targeted by discriminatory legislation. In 1993, following the division of Czechoslovakia by peaceful means, a law on citizenship was effected in the new state: tens of thousands of Roma were suddenly designated foreigners, and were accordingly denied all of the rights they had previously enjoyed as Czechoslovak citizens. This wholesale divestiture of rights was made possible by the decision of the Czech legislature to base the new law on a previously meaningless designation under the 1969 citizenship laws, one added following the Prague Spring of 1968 to appease Slovak nationalists. The purely symbolic 'second-level citizenship' that the 1969 law had created suddenly became the sole criterion for legal belonging; people who could be determined to be 'Slovak' because of a series of fixed attributes such as place of birth had to apply for citizenship regardless of where within the Federation they had resided, while people discovered to be 'Czech' in a similarly arbitrary fashion were automatically granted citizenship in the successor state. This procedure constituted the first act of forced mass statelessness in Europe since the second world war. All of this was carried out by a parliament and government chosen in elections in which these Roma had participated; and was signed into law by President Havel, erstwhile warrior for human rights. The application procedure for citizenship, moreover, was deliberately obfuscatory. In addition to a number of complicated administrative stipulations, the 'Slovaks' which the Czech state had just created were – among others – expected to demonstrate a clean criminal record for the previous five years. Legislative amendments to the law, which posed as proper responses to international criticism, allowed the Ministry of the Interior to waive the five year criminal record if they so desired: although this procedure has been applied in individual cases, both the fact that inadequate effort was made to inform affected people of its existence and the inherent arbitrariness of its application render it unacceptable as a remedy to the injustice of the law itself.

Thousands of Roma residing in the Czech Republic are currently *de facto* stateless as a direct result of this recent citizenship law. It deprives them of access to a range of benefits open only to Czech citizens: those denied citizenship are unable to vote or run for office, and many non-citizens have difficulty obtaining permanent residence, which is a necessary condition of receiving social benefits from the state. Additionally, as non-citizens, Roma can be and often have been sentenced to the punishment of expulsion for committing a crime. This penalty leads to their compulsory 'return' to a country – Slovakia – which many do not know and to which they lack effective ties. According to the Prague-based NGO Tolerance Foundation, 663 'Slovak citizens' were sentenced to expulsion by the Czech courts in the period 1 January 1993–30 June 1996. Tolerance Foundation states that of the first 120 cases they were able to document, in 118 cases the sentenced individual was a Rom. One expulsion, handed down as part of the sentence of a man convicted of the theft of 140 crowns' (approximately five US dollars) worth of sugar beet, was quashed by the Supreme Court in May 1997. At a recent hearing of the United States Commission on Security and Co-operation in Europe on 13 May 1997, the Czech Ambassador to the United States, Alexandr Vondra, branded as 'a lie' the Human Rights Watch report that there was a substantial number of *de facto* stateless (Roma) children in Czech orphanages. He also claimed that, following last year's amendment to the citizenship law, 'the Council of Europe [now] considers this law satisfactory and that is also the opinion of the various NGOs, both abroad and in my country'. This assertion is false: many organizations have continued to criticize the amended Czech citizenship law, noting that the amendments have not removed the substantive defects of the law which to this day place Roma – having lived for years in the Czech Republic – at risk of expulsion to another country. Nor was the Council of Europe statement to which Vondra referred a categorical endorsement of the present state of the law.

The drastic effects of the citizenship law and of the judicial tolerance of racially-motivated violence constitute only the most egregious examples of Czech failure to uphold international human rights standards in cases concerning Roma. In every area of life in the Czech Republic, Roma face a daunting array of discriminatory practices and hindrances to their ability to live with dignity. A disturbing proportion of Romani schoolchildren are placed in schools for the mentally handicapped, according to criteria which are at best dubious and subjective. Figures published by the Ministry of Education for the school year 1990–91 revealed that of 17,901 students in so-called 'special schools for problematic children' 11,682 were Roma.[4] Helsinki Watch found that Czech school officials send Romani children to schools for the mentally retarded for a whole range of reasons, many of them cultural or behavioural and not at all related even to standardly accepted notions of intelligence. Many Roma reported that Czech schooling officials place Romani children in special schools without bothering to test them. This over-representation in schools which afford little education and no life prospects is mirrored by a similarly high number of Roma in jails and in institutions for the mentally disabled.

The results of this veritable onslaught against personhood in the Czech Republic have shown themselves in the periodic attempts of Roma to flee the country. Most recently, in August 1997, following the broadcast of a television programme about the comfortable lives of Roma in Canada, thousands of Roma attempted to escape *en masse*. As the event reached crisis proportions, the mayors of several towns in the northeast of the country proposed that municipalities would pay two thirds of their air fares if Roma gave up the tenancy agreements on their flats.

Modern Czech political culture was formed in the crucible of national conflict.[5] Nationalist rhetoric remains a possible locus for political organization, but there are no minorities left in the Czech Republic to scapegoat besides Roma. Jews, for the most part, did not survive the second world war and the massive German minority was expelled. Roma in the Czech Republic are therefore the one large, exposed focus for populist mobilization. The engine of exclusionary nationalism, reborn all over Central Europe following 1989, has in the Czech Republic fixed on Roma as its object.

The Exception: Hungary

Hungary is characterized by lower levels of anti-Romani violence than other Central European countries. This is to say that, despite a large Roma minority, Hungary does not have the pervasive and intense anti-Romani atmosphere of countries such as Bulgaria, the Czech Republic, Romania or Slovakia, and although there have been episodes of police violence and community violence, there have been no episodes on the truly gruesome scale witnessed in those four countries. A skinhead movement exists, but most observers agree that the height of its popularity was somewhere around 1993, and that since that time it has been fairly marginal. One Rom has been killed as result of skinhead violence – a 32 year-old Romani man was beaten to death by two underage skinheads in 1992 in the northern industrial city of Salgótarján. Attacks by Hungarian skinheads are often directed not against Roma, but against dark-skinned foreigners. I will offer here three possible reasons why Hungary appears to be exceptional.

Hungary has, on paper at least, the most favourable minority legislation in Europe. The 1993 Minorities Law grants a series of positive rights to 13 recognized minorities. Roma have set up over 400 'Minority Self-Governments' as afforded under the provisions of the Minorities Law; by far and away the most of any minority in Hungary (see Kovats, 1997). It is important to emphasize, however, that it has done little to enfranchise Roma: the law itself is unclear as to the nature and role of the local minorities' self-governments; financing is complicated, and much of it is dependent upon local communal authorities, not all of whom have been convinced of the necessity of Roma self-governments; there are few links between the Gypsy National Minority Self-Government and the local Roma minority self-governments, and few are envisaged; and, finally, a Romani elite is being simultaneously created and diverted into technical and powerless roles on advisory committees. In fact, Hungarian minority legislation has acted like a black hole into which the energies of Roma and right-wing extremists alike have vanished. On the one hand, a generation of Romani activists has been persuaded to seek its political empowerment, not on the streets, but in the gently corrupting back rooms of government; powerless Roma advisory boards; and a stream of subsidies to loyalist Romani intellectuals. On the other hand, the very existence of both minority legislation and its associated real or perceived costs has drawn political energy away from attacks on minorities and toward attacks on a government perceived to be 'liberal-bolshevik' and dominated by cosmopolitan Zionists.

The favourable treatment of Roma, as of its minorities in general, by the post-1989 Hungarian government is no accident: Hungarian foreign policy is obsessed with the issue of Hungarian minorities in the neighbouring states of Romania, Slovakia, and the Federal Republic of Yugoslavia. The 1993 minority legislation, enacted while Prime Minister József Antall was still in office, was viewed at the time of its adoption into law as a legislative stick with which to beat Romania and Slovakia in the international arena, rather than as evidence of an enlightened attitude *per se*. Nevertheless, it is also the case that Hungary has distinct advantages over other Central and Eastern European states, having the experience of minority policies of the 1867–1918 period upon which to draw, pragmatically or otherwise. In this sense, Hungary may have the richest state resources in Europe for positively addressing domestic minorities of a significant size while not yet fully satisfying aspirations for autonomy (see Kann, 1983).[6]

There are two other possible reasons for the relatively lower levels of anti-Romani violence in Hungary, both of them cultural. The first and less demonstrable of these has to do with cultural space: Hungary is, with Spain, one of two countries in Europe where Roma have played a visible and active part in the development of national culture. Roma arguably contributed heavily to the development of the various distinctive styles of Hungarian folk music, similar to their role in the development of the flamenco style in Spain. Travel literature by non-Hungarians in Hungary during the 1930s, for example, documented favourable cultural images of free-spirited Gypsies (see, for example, Starkie, 1933 and Morris). In a day of debate devoted to Roma issues in the Hungarian parliament on 27 March 1996, speeches made by rightist/national parties emphasized that the Hungarian Roma were an intrinsic part of the nation. So, for example, the Young Democrats' *(Fidesz)* speaker Tamás Tirst told the assembly that '[T]he history of the Gypsy community is entwined with that of the Hungarian majority.' Lower levels of anti-Romani violence may be in part explained, then, by the existence of a positive cultural space for Roma in Hungary. (By contrast, Roma in the Czech Republic have no place in the national cultural space, and are often regarded as foreigners; most Czechs are aware that few Czech Roma survived the second world war and most Roma living in the country today are regarded as Slovaks.)

Secondly, as noted above, the revival of anti-Semitism as a force for populist political mobilization diverts the focus of extremist rhetoric and extremist violence away from Roma. Hungary is distinctive in retaining the prewar popular tendency to equate both liberalism and communism with Jews. In marked contrast to the Czech situation, the neo-liberal Alliance of Free Democrats *(Szabad-Demokraták Szovetségé)* in Hungary is widely perceived as 'a Jewish party', while both comparable parties in the Czech Republic *(ODA* and *ODS)* are not only seen as Czech, but also regularly command a far higher proportion of the electorate's approval. Roma are therefore far less prominent in the rhetoric of the Hungarian Right than in that of the Czech Right, while international finance and a takeover of the government by local 'foreigners', whose devious plans include cross-pollination of Hungarians with Africans, feature front-and-centre in the nightmares of the Hungarian populists. It is, therefore, perhaps not surprising that levels of community violence have been low in Hungary, by Eastern European standards – even though, according to Parliamentary Ombudsman for National and Ethnic Minorities, Dr Jenő Kaltenbach, one of the greatest problems faced by minorities in Hungary is prejudicial treatment by the police, a phenomenon which concerns mainly, though by no means exclusively, Roma.

It is worth remembering in this context that this difference in the expression of xenophobic sentiment as between Hungary and the Czech Republic is already reflected in prewar legislation. Hungary adopted the first modern anti-Jewish laws in 1920, while the then Czechoslovakia passed anti-Gypsy legislation in 1927 – in both cases well before the Nazi legislation in Germany that is typically held up as Europe's bogey.

Conclusion: Roma and Nationalism

In the past 15 years, the number of publications dealing with nationalism has multiplied dramatically (see especially Anderson, 1983; Brubaker, 1996; Gellner, 1983, Hobsbawm, 1990, Smith, 1986). Given the historic allegiance between nationalism, state-building and violent racism, it seems appropriate to weigh some of the theoretical approaches which have recently been articulated against the actual experience of Roma in the European states discussed here. The first and most obvious conclusion I would draw is that, as might be suspected, there is a continuum which proceeds from nationalist discourse, through racist views to racist violence. This continuum is not often called into question by people hostile to nationalism; but what is significant is that many moderate nationalists question or deny nationalism's tendency toward racism, the facts notwithstanding.

Second, Benedict Anderson's (1994) contention that nationalism is not an ideology in the same way that liberalism, communism and socialism are ideologies, but is rather something which inheres in (or at least adheres to) modern identity in a much more intimate way is also, I believe, vindicated by the outline of the position I have given here. For while nationalism is at present more dynamic in Eastern than in Western Europe, there is no way of avoiding the fact that Roma face similar forces all over the continent. In fact the more historical an approach one takes, the more one is forced to conclude that while Roma presently face more violence in Eastern than they do in Western Europe, the contemporary Western European quietude seems to have been purchased at the cost of both the exclusionary forces exercised by the European

Community, and earlier episodes of intense violence against Roma (Acton, 1995).[7] This second point will certainly be more unsettling to those hostile to nationalism, particularly theorists such as Eric Hobsbawm, who writes in the introduction to his *Nations and Nationalism Since 1780* (1990, p. 12), that hostility to nationalism is a *sine qua non* for its study. This seems disingenuous; those of us not presently nationalists may live in the luxury of not having to be.

This leads to the third and most emphatic conclusion that I believe may be derived from the material presented above: nationalism is not a unitary phenomenon, but is rather a form of potential energy available in society. The forms it takes and the preoccupations and obsessions which particular nationalisms hold dear, however, are highly historically contingent, almost to the point of being mutually unrecognizable. For it is clear that, although anti-Roma tendencies are present everywhere, the situation in the Czech Republic is at present markedly worse for Roma than that in Hungary. Nevertheless, one could not plausibly maintain that the present Hungarian discourse is less nationalistic than its Czech counterpart. And while I have given only one account of why this may be so, it remains the case that Czech nationalism is preoccupied with Roma in a way which Hungarian nationalism isn't. As such, Ernest Gellner's (1983) portrait of the Ruritanians in the Empire of Megalomania – 'The Course of True Nationalism Never Did Run Smooth' – while graceful, turns out to be a portrait of a specifically Slovak nationalism and its particular preoccupations, rather than of nationalism *per se*. There is no simple correlation, that is to say, between the degree of nationalism present in a country and that society's treatment of any of its particular minorities: in order to defend the latter, therefore, is will not do merely to castigate nationalism.

The marked contrast between Hungary and the Czech Republic notwithstanding, however, even comparatively less violent countries like Hungary provide little reason, at present, for real optimism about the future of the Roma. Living in a political and social terrain where state-building has and continues to be fraught with trauma, partial failure and the legacy of failure, Roma all over Eastern Europe find themselves exposed to community, police and ideological violence. The levels and forms this violence take are dependent on domestic particularities, accidents of the political terrain and the role Roma play in the public imagination. Everywhere, however, Roma are a weak minority whose fate depends more on the whim of the states in which they live and the sentiments of the majority population than on any factors within the Roma community itself.

Notes

1 On anti-Semitism generally, for example, see Langmuir (1990a and 1990b). The most famous incidents of the modern blood libel in Central Europe – the blood libel trial at Tisza-Eszlár, Hungary in 1882 and the so-called 'Hilsner Affair' in Bohemia in 1899 – both concerned accusations of ritual murder in connection with alleged uses of Christian blood at Passover. (See Červinka, 1968; Fischer, 1988, especially pp. 42–77; Nussbaum, 1947; and forthcoming comparative literature by Hillel Kieval.) Kieval in particular is keen to see episodes such as alleged ritual murders as modern phenomena related to societal transition. The Zalistie attack's proximity to Easter also suggests Mikhail Bakhtin's exposition of the carnival/*mardi gras* as a time of social inversion in which the normal order and customary restraint are suspended. See Bakhtin (1994).

2 This conclusion is reached also by Klier (1993) in explaining 'The Pogrom Tradition' in Eastern Europe. Klier finds that pogroms occur precisely at moments of weakened state power.

3 At least one scholar of Roma has denied that Roma are an ethnic group and has asserted that they are solely a police category created by the modern state-building process: see Lucassen (1996).

4 *Ustav pro informace ve vzdělaní, Statistika Školství (1990/91, ČR)*, reprinted from Helsinki Watch (1992, p. 44).

5 On the national conflict and its impact on identity politics, see Cohen (1981) and Kieval (1988).

6 Debate continues among historians today over whether it was internal minority policy or external meddling which caused Austria-Hungary to collapse, but the fact remains that during the whole of the period from *Ausgleich* to Trianon, Hungary attempted all available methods, from promotion to repression, in dealing with its huge population of non-ethnic Hungarians.

7 Acton's version of Romani history is of 'Genocide' in Western Europe in the 16th century and pre-modern slavery in Eastern Europe. In Acton's memorable terms,

> When the Rom of Eastern Europe face Travellers of Western Europe, it is the survivors of slavery facing the survivors of genocide. [...] slavery and genocide were the differing keys to the catastrophe wrought among Gypsies in East and West in 16th century Europe. As from the 19th century there was renewed international migration of Gypsies, the survivors of slavery and the survivors of genocide faced a common fate in the renewed anti-Gypsy and anti-Traveller persecutions and genocides of the 20th century.

References

Acton, T. (1995), 'Introduction: Unwriting History' in McCann, T. et al., *Irish Travellers*, Queen's University Institute of Irish Studies, Belfast.

Anderson, B. (1983), *Imagined Communities*, Verso, London.

Anderson, B. (1994), CEU lectures, October, Budapest, Hungary.

Bakhtin, M. (1994), 'Carnival Ambivalence: Laughter, Praise and Abuse' in Morris, Pam (ed.), *The Bakhtin Reader: Selected Writings of Bakhtin, Medvedev and Voloshin*, E. Arnold Publishers, London.

Bauman, Z. (1991), *Modernity and Ambivalence*, Polity Press, Cambridge.

Brubaker, R. (1996), *Nationalism Reframed: Nationhood and the National Question in the New Europe*, Cambridge University Press, Cambridge.

Cambridge International Dictionary of English (1995), Cambridge University Press, Cambridge.

Červinka, F. (1968), 'The Hilsner Affair', *Leo Baeck Institute Yearbook,* Vol. XIII, pp. 142–57.

Çinar, D., Hofinger, C. and Waldrauch, H. (1995), *Integrationsindex: zur rechtlichen Integration von Ausländerrinen in ausgewählten europäischen Ländern*, Institut für höhere Studien, Vienna.

Cohen, G.B. (1981), *The Politics of Ethnic Survival: Germans in Prague 1861–1914*, Princeton University Press, Princeton.

European Roma Rights Center (1996a), *Sudden Rage at Dawn: Violence Against Roma in Romania,* September.

European Roma Rights Center (1996b), *Divide and Deport: Roma and Sinti in Austria*, September.

European Roma Rights Center (1997a), *The Misery of Law: The Rights of Roma in the Transcarpathian Region of Ukraine*, April.

European Roma Rights Center (1997b), *Time of the Skinheads: Denial and Exclusion of Roma in Slovakia*, January.

Fischer, R. (1988), *Entwicklungsstufen des Antisemitismus in Ungarn 1867–1939: die Zerstörung der magyarisch-jüdischen Symbiose*, R. Oldenbourg Verlag, Munich.

Fraser, A. (1995), *The Gypsies*, Blackwell, Oxford.

Gellner, E. (1983), *Nations and Nationalism*, Blackwell, Oxford.

Helsinki Watch (1992), *Struggling for Ethnic identity: Czechoslovakia's Endangered Gypsies*, Human Rights Watch, New York.

Hobsbawm, E. (1990), *Nations and Nationalism Since 1780: Programme, Myth, Reality*, Canto, Cambridge.

Human Rights Watch/Helsinki (1996), *Roma in the Czech Republic: Foreigners in Their Own Land*, Vol. 8, No. 11, June.

Kann, R. (1983), *The Multi-National Empire*, Octagon Books, New York.

Kieval, Hillel (1988), *The Making of Czech Jewry: National Conflict and Jewish Society in Bohemia 1870–1918*, Oxford University Press, Oxford.

Klier, J.D. (1993), 'The Pogrom Tradition in Eastern Europe' in Bjorgo, Tore and Witte, Rob (eds), *Racist Violence in Europe,* New York: St. Martin's Press.

Kovats, M.(1997), 'The Good, the Bad and the Ugly: Three Faces of "Dialogue" – the Development of Roma Politics in Hungary', *Phralipe*, January–February, pp. 23–34.

Langmuir, G. (1990a), *Towards a Definition of Antisemitism*, University of Califonia Press, Berkeley.

Langmuir, G. (1990b), *History, Religion and Antisemitism*, University of Califonia Press, Berkeley.

Lucassen, L. (1996), *Die Geschichte eines polizeilichen Ordnungsbegriffes in Deutschland, 1700–1945*, Böhlau Verlag, Cologne.

Morris, E.K. (date of publication unknown), *Hungary: Land of Enchantment*, Henry Hartley Publishers Ltd, London.

Nussbaum, A. (1947), 'The "Ritual Murder" Trial of Polná', *Historia Judaica*, Vol. IX, pp. 57–74.

Smith, A. (1986), *The Ethnic Origins of Nations*, Blackwell, Oxford.

Starkie, W. (1933), *Raggle-Taggle: Adventures with a Fiddle in Hungary and Roumania*, Albemarle Library and John Murray, with Frome and Tanner Ltd, London.

United States Central Intelligence Agency (1997), 'Human Resource Exploitation Training Manual – 1983', reprinted in *Harpers*, April, pp. 23–5.

2 Liberalism, Multiculturalism and the Principles of Community

DAVID ARCHARD

The phenomena of nationalism and racism in the liberal order confront political philosophers with particular and pressing problems. It is no longer enough to dismiss them as unworthy of rational scrutiny. The claim by the editors of the *Blackwell Companion to Contemporary Political Philosophy* that '[n]ationalism – still less racism, sexism or ageism – does not figure [in the Companion], on the grounds that it hardly counts as a principled way of thinking about things' (Goodin and Pettit, 1993, p. 3) has been often critically cited as an instance of political philosophy's apparently blithe disregard for the realities of modern political life. Moreover, one of the volume's contributors, Will Kymlicka, makes the surely plausible claim that the liberal picture of the political world just does not and seemingly cannot accommodate the fact that people are – whether one likes it or not – divided by race, culture and nation (Goodin and Pettit, 1993, pp. 376–7). The communities to which people actually belong, and to the membership of which they attach so much importance, can not simply be dismissed as beneath philosophical contempt.

Political philosophy must then begin to devise and refine the theoretical apparatus with which it can scrutinize the normative significance of community in our political lives. What follows is a modest contribution to such a process which takes as its context the problem that multiculturalism poses for liberalism. I first identify the problem of multiculturalism and then try to distinguish four interrelated strands in any satisfactory and comprehensive account of multiculturalism. I seek to show what is involved in the evaluation of any community and to expound five plausibly liberal principles by which communities might be differentially evaluated. I sketch these principles and suggest, without offering a full-blown defence, what sorts of issue need to be addressed in defending them.

16

The Problem of Multiculturalism

The problem which multiculturalism presents for any political philosophy arises from the existence within a society of stable, well-defined, historically durable communities whose identity and defining characteristics are determined by some combination of institutions, practices, ways of life, values, shared history and ethnicity.[1] The problem is to what extent a society should, consistent with its central values, tolerate a presently given diversity of communities. Toleration should be understood as extending from doing nothing to diminish that diversity to taking positive steps to preserve (or even enhance) it. The terms and forms of toleration or intolerance can be legal, financial or social.

The issue of consistency as it is relevant here can be raised in two distinct ways. Imagine that a society has a set of central defining values, P. Any organized practice or activity which takes place within that society might be judged according to P. The question here would be whether it is consistent with a society being regulated by P for that society to tolerate what can be judged as wrong or without value in terms of P. Or it might be appropriate to ask as a separate question whether some of the society's constitutive activities and practices prevent or make it difficult for that society to reproduce itself over time as one regulated by P. To take a particular illustrative example: say that the society is one organized according to some recognizably liberal principles of justice. Should such a society tolerate a community whose organizing precepts are unjust by those principles? Should it, for instance, be tolerant of a culture whose defining ideals and practices are explicitly discriminatory towards its women members? That is the first way in which the issue of consistency might be raised. But one might also ask whether such a liberal society can tolerate communities which bring their children up in such a way that, as adult citizens, they are unable to accept or live in a society regulated by these principles of justice. They might, in consequence of the education they receive within their community, come to lack the sense of justice needed to sustain a willingness to have their social existence regulated by the principles of justice in question. That is the second way in which the issue of consistency might be raised. It is the way, for instance, in which Rawls's 'political liberalism' has been criticized for its failure to address the need to restrict religious fundamentalism in the private sphere (Exdell, 1994) or to reform the family in ways indicated by feminism (Okin, 1994).

It is also important to note that communities may be weakly consistent with P if they do not violate the terms of P, or do not make it impossible for a society to be regulated by P. Or they may be strongly consistent with P in so far as they realize the values of P or contribute positively to the reproduction of the society regulated by P. There is, thus, a distinction to be made – if the context is a liberal society – between cultures or communities which are illiberal and those that are non-liberal; between those whose defining way of life is inconsistent with, because it violates, liberal values and those whose defining way of life is weakly consistent with those values but is recognizably other than a liberal way of life.

Evaluating Multiculturalism

Any evaluation of multiculturalism according to some set of political values must address at least four kinds of interrelated question. There is the matter of the significance of communities and of communal membership. Why is it valuable, if it is, for there to be communities as such? Second, there is the question of how to evaluate particular communities. Why is it valuable, if it is, not just to have some different communities but to have these specific ones? And how should a comparison between the various communities be made? Third, there are the questions surrounding the facts of community identity, reproduction and change. Communities cannot be created *ab initio* and it is a brute fact about our world that communities with their particular characters and histories already exist. But do they stay as they are; or if they do change, how do they do so? There are, in fact, two sorts of issue to be considered here. The first concerns the criteria for the identification of a community. When has the same community evolved over time and when has one community simply disappeared or been replaced by another distinct community? Clearly the continued existence of every present feature of some community cannot be a necessary condition of its staying the same community. Yet for each and every community there must be some essential characteristics such that it could not lose these and be regarded as still the same.[2] The second issue is about *how* communities change, both in their essential and their non-essential character. What kinds of factor bring about significant changes in their nature? And what role – whether economic, political, legal, educational, cultural or whatever – can be played by the society of which they form a part? Fourth, and finally, there is the question as to how cultural diversity or plurality as such is to be evaluated. By 'as such' I do not mean to express the intrinsic value of diversity, since diversity may also – or indeed perhaps only – have instrumental value. Rather I mean by 'as such' the value of diversity which is not reducible to the summed value of the constituent elements of that diversity. There are those who have believed that the existence of a plurality of communities poses a danger of reduced social solidarity and consequent support for the polity. J.S. Mill, for instance, thought that ' free institutions are next to impossible in a country made up of different nationalities' (Mill, 1975, p. 382). More recently, David Miller, in defending the value and significance of a shared national identity in sustaining support for principles of justice, has argued that such support is weakened by the existence of plural cultural identities (Miller, 1988–9; 1995, ch. 5). Lord Acton famously criticized Mill's view, maintaining that plurality, not homogeneity, is the best guarantor of individual liberty (Acton, 1907). Similarly, contemporary friends of multiculturalism would argue that a society is the stronger and not the weaker for having a rich diversity of cultural identities (Parekh, 1990, pp. 68–70).

The four sets of issues identified above are interrelated in the following kinds of way. The manner in which communities can be expected to change constrains the plausibility or reasonableness of any demand that they should change. Again, it is likely that different communities will be more or less consistent, in both the weak and the strong senses, with the central values of their host society. But the imperative to tolerate only those which are maximally consistent with these values will be constrained by a recognition of the value of diversity as such. In the present context the interesting relationship is between the first and second issues, between the reasons for valuing communal membership as such and those for valuing the existence of particular communities. Defences of multiculturalism by liberals have urged that the existence of distinct cultural communities is valuable to their individual members in the following kinds of way. Their value may lie in providing a context of meaningful options for living (Kymlicka, 1989); or in supplying the ground for deep, rewarding interpersonal relationships through a sharing of values, beliefs and ends; or in providing the individual with a major determinant of her sense of identity and thus supplying a key constituent of any meaningful good life (Raz, 1994, pp. 175–8).

If communities are valuable for promoting some end, then it seems that we may ask whether particular communities promote this end to a greater or lesser degree. In that way a comparative evaluation of different communities appears to follow from a valuation of community as such. But some ends promoted by communal membership are not realized to a greater or lesser extent, whereas others clearly are. Take the contrast between the values of ' membership' and ' contexts of choice'. I shall take ' membership' here simply to denote the fact that one belongs to some group and that this fact is recognized by other members of that group. Now, of course, there are at least two ways in which there might be thought to be varied degrees of the good, if it is a good, of membership. First, membership can be full or partial. One can be a part-time or half-member of some group. The rules of clubs and societies frequently allow for associate or occasional membership. Let me stipulate, then, that membership is here understood as full. Membership is all or nothing: either you are a member or you are not. Second, there are goods associated with membership which may be graded. Thus being a member of certain groups will carry with it a higher social status than is the case with other groups. Or a well-endowed group may be in a position to provide better goods and services to its members than other groups can. The associated goods of membership might also, clearly, vary in line with degrees of membership. Let me then stipulate further that the good of membership is the good simply of belonging to a group which is exclusive of such associated goods.

Understood in this way the good of membership is either possessed or not. You either belong to some group and enjoy the good of membership or you do not. The valued end of membership is not subject to further variation. On the other hand, if membership of a community is valuable for providing its members with a context of choice, then it makes sense to ask of particular communities how rich, extensive, meaningful or varied is the context of choice provided. It makes sense differentially to evaluate communities as contexts of choice.

Particular communities may be differentially evaluated according to the extent to which they realize or promote what it is that is valued in membership of communities as such – so long, that is, as what is valued in membership of some community can be realized in varying degrees. However, it is also possible to evaluate communities in terms of what I shall call their particular constitutive values. What follows in the rest of this piece is an attempt to consider what principles should be used to evaluate a community's constitutive values. This consideration of possible principles is done within the context of broadly liberal values. This is for the following reasons. Multiculturalism is currently perceived as a problem for Western liberal democratic societies. Moreover, most work done within contemporary political philosophy on the subject of multiculturalism displays broadly liberal sympathies. Nevertheless, some at least of the values which configure philosophical liberalism, such as for instance that of equality of respect, ought to be shared by any defensible political doctrine. In sum, liberalism supplies an excellent example for political philosophy of why there is a problem of multiculturalism – to what extent a society should, consistent with its central values, tolerate a presently given diversity of communities – even though that problem is not unique to liberalism. Having said that, my approach to the topic does not presuppose a full endorsement of liberalism.

To resume the foregoing. Addressing the problem of multiculturalism requires a recognition of the following: that different cultures may be consistent with a society's defining values in a weak and strong sense; that evaluating these different cultures, in their specificity, can be done both by the terms of what makes communal membership as such valuable and by an appraisal of their particular constitutive values; that toleration of communities, judged in these various ways, must be constrained both by a recognition of how they can be changed and by an acknowledgement of what is valuable in the very fact of diversity. Let me now say more about the constitutive values of a community.

Evaluating Communities

These values are both ideological and structural. First, a community may profess a set of values, ends, beliefs and goals. These may be professed explicitly or expressed implicitly in its various practices. These are its ideological constitutive values. A community is also constituted or organized as a community in ways that realize structural constitutive values. For instance, how a community regulates the admission or expulsion of members, how it changes its character over time, what mechanisms it has for identifying and resolving internal conflict, realize its structural constitutive values.

This distinction allows us to see that a community might be illiberal in at least two ways – ideologically and structurally. Imagine that a community is identified, in part, by the subscription of its members to a belief that there should be no such thing as free speech. That belief, as well as the membership itself, are sustained by denying the members any opportunity to discuss or criticize the defining constitutive value of the community. Thus the principle of unfree speech is both an ideological constitutive value of that community (what it professes as a common belief) and a structural constitutive value (organizing the terms of enduring membership by regulating internal debate).

Let me now suggest five liberal principles of community by which the constitution of particular communities might be differentially evaluated. First, there is a 'principle of internal equal regard', whereby all members are accorded the same basic respect. A necessary condition of a group's being a community is that its members should be bound together by some significant and relatively enduring set of shared bonds or ties. The question of *what* these bonds must be is left to one side. Clearly they may be determined by, among other factors, religion, culture, ethnicity, nationality, territory, class or gender. But the bonds, whatever their source, must be significant and enduring. The principle of internal equal regard requires that such bonds, whatever they might be, should at least be between persons mutually acknowledged as equals. Such a principle of equal mutual regard is arguably foundational for liberalism itself where the scope of the community is the society as a whole (Dworkin, 1978).

The principle displays similarities to the terms of the condition which, it is argued by Andrew Mason, is necessary for a group to be a community 'in the moral sense': that the group of people are '*mutually concerned* and refrain from systematically exploiting each other' (Mason, 1993, p. 217). However, Mason's condition is stronger than the principle of internal equal regard. Whilst this principle will rule out systematic exploitation by some members of others, it does not require mutual concern. I can surely be indifferent to the life of someone even whilst I acknowledge her as deserving of the same respect as any other. Indeed it is very likely that I will be unconcerned with how the lives of many others in a large community go; but not, of course, have to deny that each and every one of them is my equal. The bonds that constitute a community do not have their source in regular 'face-to-face' contacts between the members. It is a mistake to think that significant and substantial ties of community require intimacy and physical proximity. The mistaken assumption is that only if relations are direct, unmediated and grounded in personal familiarity can there be the degree of mutuality which a community must realize (Young, 1990, pp. 312–17). When Benedict Anderson famously described the nation as an 'imagined community' (Anderson, 1983) he intended 'imagined' to be the contrary of 'real' where this means that there is regular physical contact, 'face-to- face' relations, between the members, which sustains its sense of community. For Anderson modern large scale communities – of which the nation is the most striking example – are so large scale as not to be able to be 'real' in this sense. The sense of community is real in the sense of strongly felt even in the absence of 'real' community, that is, actual physical closeness.

The principle specifies that the equal regard is 'internal'. The ties which bind a community give its members the sense that they should show a special regard for and owe particular duties to one another that are not appropriate for non-members. A community is, in short, a source of moral partiality. It is of course a matter of deep contention whether such partiality is consistent with the impartiality required of the moral point of view (Archard, 1996).

However, it is consistent with showing a special regard for the members of one's own community that one should show a basic or minimal moral regard for non-members. That one should come to the rescue of a community member before that of a non-member does not mean that one should do nothing for the non-member in circumstances where assisting her was possible and morally required. Writing about nationalism, both David Miller and Yael Tamir think that preferential regard for one's own co-nationals is perfectly consistent with showing a minimum moral regard for non-nationals (Miller, 1995, ch. 3; Tamir, 1993, ch. 5). The principle of internal equal regard does not require that one see those outside the community as undeserving of any moral status, nor as not being, like those within one's community, equally human beings. The principle simply constrains a community member's display of a special regard for her fellow members with the requirement that all of these members should be seen as equally deserving of such regard. For instance, a community violates the principle of internal equal regard if either its ideological or structural constitutive values discriminate against women. This might be the case if a community professed the belief that women are inferior to men, or if women were systematically excluded from playing the same role as men are accorded in the central, defining practices of that community.

The second principle of community is that of 'warranted exclusion', whereby the grounds of non-membership can be shown as justifiable to those who are excluded. At the limit, membership of the community of humanity is co-extensive with that of the species. However, actual communities are bounded entities with limited membership. Indeed, membership of a community is valued in significant part by its members because it is not open. If belonging to a group (and being acknowledged by the other members as belonging) matters to me it is in part because it is not the case that anyone at all can belong.

The issue is how the closure can be justified to those excluded. Let me call that property whose possession is sufficient to qualify some individual for membership of a community the 'entrance qualification' for that community. At a minimum the principle of exclusion must be impartially administered. It would be arbitrary and unfair, other things being equal, to exclude someone from a community who possesses that community's entrance qualification. Exclusion is warranted if an individual cannot reasonably complain at their lack of an entrance qualification.

The principle applies to non-membership of some particular community. It is of course possible that someone should belong to no community and have no reasonable complaint at her exclusion from each and every community.

She does not have a further ground for complaint, namely that she is excluded from belonging to *any* community, unless there is some reason to think that the range of communities to which she might belong has been constituted in a morally inappropriate way. Similarly someone who has been fairly denied each and every available opportunity of employment can object to lacking a job only if the number and character of such opportunities open to her has come about in some immoral way.

Membership of some communities is accorded by contingencies of birth which no individual is in a position to alter. I cannot complain that I cannot be French, even though I might regret that I was born English.[3] Membership of some other communities is accorded by subscription to a way of life, set of principles or participation in a set of practices. I cannot complain if I do not myself subscribe to these constitutive ends. An atheist cannot feel unreasonably excluded from a religious community.

Cause for warranted complaint at exclusion is given if the principles underpinning an entrance qualification or the conditions which must be satisfied for an entrance qualification to be obtained unfairly discriminate against individuals with otherwise good reason to be included in a community. Similar reasoning applies to cases of people already members who are then excluded. A citizenship test would be unfairly constructed if it were made especially difficult for some particular group to pass. A good example here is the citizenship tests which blacks in the Southern states of America were forced to pass in order to be registered as voters. Such tests asked unreasonably difficult questions about America's constitution and history and were not required of Southern whites.

The test of what is and is not, in this sense, a proper entrance qualification will depend on the nature of the community, its constitutive values and ends. For example, since an academic community is plausibly defined as one whose purpose, in significant part, is the acquisition and dissemination of knowledge, it is reasonable to argue that its entrance qualification should properly be determined in terms of a capacity to contribute to the realization of that purpose. Of other communities, such as those constituted by some unchosen contingency of birth, it seems inappropriate to describe the entrance qualification as proper or improper. One cannot say that it is wrong to be counted as English only because one was born English.

However, it may be correct to say that the entrance qualification to some communities should not be based upon unchosen and unalterable endowments at birth. Whilst I cannot complain at not being French, I might reasonably complain if French citizenship were denied to me because I was not French. I could do so if it is plausible to argue that the entrance qualification for a polity should properly be fixed by such things as residency, productive contribution to the commonweal, willingness to abide by its laws and so on. Guest workers (*Gastarbeiter*) in Germany have a good claim to be allowed to be naturalized citizens of that state in respect of the burdens they have borne in service to that society over time. Excluding them from full political membership on the grounds that such membership is accorded only on the basis of being ethnically German is unfair. It is all the more so in that ethnic Germans – who have long lived outside the state, cannot speak German, have done nothing for German society, have no connections with it other than their ethnic identity – do qualify for German civic status.[4]

The third moral principle of community is that of 'external tolerance', whereby the community's constitutive values, both ideological and structural, are consistent with the existence of other communities which also fulfil the morally required principles. A community need not be tolerant of a second community which is itself intolerant of the first. An instance of external tolerance is provided by the characterization of 'polycentric' nationalism. This, according to Anthony Smith, is a nationalism which combines loyalty to and special valuation of one's own nation with a toleration of other members within a world family of nations (Smith, 1971, pp. 158–60).

Toleration of the other, it should be said, is weaker than respect for or recognition of the other. The former requires only that one do nothing, even whilst disapproving of the other, to make it more difficult for the other to exist.[5] The latter requires some form of positive endorsement of the other.[6] Community A tolerates community B when it does not contribute to circumstances which make B's continued existence harder. A's beliefs and ideals may nevertheless be such that, by their lights, B's way of life or constitutive values have to be judged as fundamentally mistaken. A's values respect or recognize B when B's defining way of life is viewed as equally deserving of respect as A's own.

The fourth principle of community is a principle of 'individual autonomy', whereby the exercise of sufficient individual choice consistent with the continued identity of both the group and its individual members is permitted. This would be a crucial principle for many liberals. It is now conventional, following the recent work of John Rawls (Rawls, 1993), to distinguish between political liberalism and comprehensive liberalism. The former is committed only to support for regulative principles of political and social cooperation which remain strictly neutral on the question of what constitutes the good life for individual citizens, including whether or not a more autonomous life is preferable to a less autonomous one. The latter endorses a familiar, classically liberal picture of the individual good life as one led freely and autonomously.

Earlier it was said that a liberal society should perhaps tolerate communities whose constitutive values are consistent with its own defining values, and that one sense of 'consistency' required that the communities should educate their own members so that they could be the citizens of such a liberal society. It is arguable that an education for citizenship in a liberal democratic polity will require that adult individuals be able to think for themselves, deliberate judiciously on issues, and choose appropriately in the light of such an exercise. That is just to say that even political liberalism, sensitive to the conditions for the successful reproduction of a liberal society, will be committed to encouraging its members to be autonomous. Thus Amy Gutman (1995) argues that comprehensive and political liberalism converge in this manner on the question of a desirable civic education.

We may take it, then, that liberalism values individual autonomy and is committed to supporting those environments which are themselves supportive of autonomy.[7] The degree of autonomy which someone enjoys is specified in terms of an 'internal' capacity – to deliberate rationally, acquire information, and choose independently – and an 'external' context of sufficient choice – meaningful, worthwhile, plentiful and feasible options.[8] Environments are thus supportive of autonomy when they encourage the development of autonomous characters and supply contexts of sufficient choice within which autonomous lives can be led. Communities can offend against this principle of individual autonomy in ideological or structural ways. In the former way a community may explicitly disavow individual autonomy when its defining values, for instance, privilege obedience to inherited tradition or authority. In the latter way a community may socialize its members to be conformists, deny them the opportunity to dispute its identifying doctrines or severely limit the range of significant choices a member can make.

In general terms a community may sustain its particular identity over time by limiting, to some degree, the choices of its members. Indeed, it is likely that a community can sustain itself only by constraining both the members' freedom to exit and the range of internal choices open to them. The problem for the liberal derives from recognizing that this is so and wishing to minimize the limitations imposed. Will Kymlicka thus displays a characteristically liberal multiculturalist desire to combine 'external' protection of communities with a concern to minimize any community's imposition on its members of 'internal' restrictions (Kymlicka, 1995, ch. 3).[9] We need to acknowledge that choices can be limited in a variety of ways – from explicit physical coercion through to ostracism and disgrace within the community for a failure to comply – and that choices can concern both what one can do within the community and whether or not one stays within the community.

Take as an example the practice of arranged marriages. Let us imagine a community within which the young have their marital partners selected for them by their elders. It is further assumed that the culture outside the community enables and endorses the familiar contemporary Western practice of freely choosing one's own partner. Now consider a number of possibilities. A young person within this community might feel able, having carefully and rationally considered the respective merits of arranged and free marriages, to support her own community's way of doing things. She knows that she lacks a choice open to her contemporaries who are not members of the community but she does not think of this as a loss of autonomy because she judges such a choice to be valueless. She values arranged marriages but not freely chosen ones.[10] Second, she might judge marital freedom to be preferable in itself to a system of arranged marriages, yet believe the latter, and her subjection to this system, to be an acceptable price to pay for the continued existence of her community and her membership of it. She prefers staying in the community with its practice of arranged marriages to leaving that community. In turn her preference for continuation of communal membership may arise in a number of ways. It might derive from a positive endorsement of her own community (if she could freely choose which community to live within she could think of no better one than her own) or, more negatively, from an acknowledgement of the costs of exit. When the surrounding culture is hostile – in circumstances, most obviously, of institutional and social racism – continued membership of one's birth community may supply a haven of support, defence and understanding whose loss would be enormously grave and possibly irrevocable. Third, someone may, on balance, choose to repudiate the community which endorses a practice of arranged marriages yet be subject to pressures to remain within that community and accept the marriage which has been arranged for her. These pressures may range from physical coercion through to social and psychological sanctions against her nonconformity.

A young woman accepts the partner which her elders have chosen for her. Is her choice autonomous? Clearly so if the case falls into the first category listed above; clearly not if her 'agreement' falls into the third category; and less clearly one or the other if her compliance is for the second kind of reason. The principle of individual autonomy acknowledges, without attempting to resolve, the difficult issues raised by this tension between individual autonomy and communal stability. That is why it speaks of 'sufficient' choice which is 'consistent with' a continued communal identity. It recognizes that it is difficult enough to agree what is and is not autonomous without even broaching the further question of counts as 'enough' autonomy. The further matter of what is and is not 'consistent' with a given communal identity can be satisfactorily answered only by broaching the issues of community identity, reproduction and change – issues which were identified above as falling under the second of the four interrelated questions needing to be addressed under the problem of multiculturalism.

The principle of equal regard accords equality of moral regard to all within a community . The fourth principle of community accords members sufficiency of individual choice consistent with continued communal identity. One important area of choice is the determination of the community's character. One might thus take as an implication of these two principles when conjoined something which merits explicit statement as a fifth principle: that of 'democratic self-determination'. This might be expressed as the claim that each member of a community should have the same opportunity as any other to play their part in determining the nature of the community. There need not be formal mechanisms for allowing everyone to do this, and, in this sense, talk of democratic self-determination is perhaps overly and unnecessarily formal. The basic idea is that the community's practices, institutions, customs, habits of interaction and so on should not be such as to preclude any member or subgroup of members from playing their part alongside the others in shaping the community's identity. The principle does not say that everyone should have the same opportunity or chance actually to determine the community's character, only that they should have the same chance to play their part in doing so. A familiar feature of democracy proper is that equality of input, such as is guaranteed by universal franchise, does not mean equality of outcome, that is each voter having the same chance as everyone else of seeing their preferred choice become law or policy. I may be in a permanent minority on some issue or range of issues. This is a problem for democracy only if one's minority status is associated with some structural feature of the society within which the democratic procedures operate and which associates one's status with habitual disadvantage.

The adjustments made within democratic theory to accommodate these difficulties might also be made to apply to the ways in which a community can determine its own character for itself without excluding some of its members from that self-determinative process. One wants to be able to say that a dissident minority who, in effect, wish for their community to become a totally different kind of community are not wronged in failing to see their wishes realized. And yet one wants to add that it is also wrong that a subgroup – identified in some salient manner by age, gender, sexual preference, for instance – should persistently fail to make their mark in shaping their community's identity.

Conclusion: The Proper Place of Evaluation

What has been offered are plausible liberal principles which might be used to evaluate the constitutive values of any individual community within a society. They are offered as a way of beginning to address the second set of issues identified as constituting the problem of multiculturalism – the value of particular communities. But three cautions are in order. First, these principles should not be seen as operating in isolation from the other three sorts of consideration which derive from the value of communal membership, the value of diversity as such and the conditions of communal identity and change. Second, it should not be forgotten that communities can be either weakly or strongly consistent with the defining values of a society. Third, the principles do not provide stern threshold requirements which must be met if a community is to be of any value. Rather they supply the various terms in which we might differentially evaluate various communities as more or less valuable.

Some communities might fail by these principles to be considered of any value and thus appear to merit the intolerance of a liberal society. At an extreme, a liberal society might be prepared to tolerate only those communities which realized liberal values to a maximal degree. That would, perhaps, only be to say that the liberal could envisage merely a single community coextensive with liberal society. However, due acknowledgement of the following – that diversity is valuable, that any society comprises an already existent plurality of communities whose conditions of change and existence are complex, that non-liberal cultures may be morally worthy and that the value of communities is not all or nothing but more or less – ought to lend support to the view that the feasible, and desirable, options lie somewhere between the two extremes of tolerating no diversity and tolerating any diversity.[11]

Notes

1   Will Kymlicka has argued that 'multicultural' diversity within a society can take the forms of 'multinational' and 'polyethnic' diversity (Kymlicka, 1995, ch. 2). Insofar as the first

form raises particular issues of secession, irredentism and federalism this paper is more concerned with the second form of diversity, that is where an expression of cultural integrity need not be linked to demands for independent political self-determination within some territory.

2   Kymlicka draws a distinction between 'the stability of a cultural community and its character at a particular moment' (Kymlicka, 1989, p. 169). He does so in order to avoid the implication that any defence of the value of some community must be a defence of its presently given character.

3   We should note that a state may determine nationality either by the principle of *ius soli*, wherein birth on the national territory suffices, or that of *ius sanguinis*, whereby birth to a parent who is already a national is sufficient (Dummett and Nicol, 1990, ch. 1).

4   Michael Walzer (1983, ch. 2) offers an excellent discussion of the principles of justice that should determine the distribution of the good of 'membership' and, within that context, discusses the case of guest workers.

5   This is the core idea of toleration as forbearance of that which one could and would otherwise wish to change. It is of course possible to argue that toleration requires more than forbearance and that merely 'leaving alone' is a necessary but not sufficient condition of toleration. See Mendus (1989), especially ch. 1.

6   Charles Taylor is the source of the influential idea that it is crucial that one's own particular identity – whether as an individual or as a group – be recognized by others as equally deserving of respect, and that much contemporary politics is dominated by the needs and demands of such 'recognition'. See especially Taylor (1992).

7   Joseph Raz argues for the particular claim that if persons live in an autonomy-supporting environment then they can flourish only by leading autonomous lives (Raz, 1986, ch. 14).

8   Good studies of what autonomy means are supplied by Richard Lindley (1986) and Gerard Dworkin (1988).

9   The tension between these two has been identified as a debilitating weakness of Kymlicka's specifically liberal defence of groups rights. See the exchange between Kymlicka and Kukathas (Kukathas, 1992a and 1992b; Kymlicka, 1992).

10   This is because, as Raz has observed, a cultural change from prearranged to freely chosen marriages represents not the imposition of free choice onto a fixed social relation but rather a profound change in the understanding of the marital relationship itself and what is valuable about it (Raz, 1986, p. 392).

11   This final version of the paper benefited greatly from many constructive comments offered by various people on the occasion of its first delivery at Ustí. I should, however, particularly like to thank Alison Assiter, Ann Bousfield, Keith Graham and Ross Poole for their questions and suggestions.

References

Acton, Lord (1907), 'Nationality' in Figgis, J.N. (ed.), *The History of Freedom and Other Essays*, Macmillan, London.

Anderson, B. (1983), *Imagined Communities: Reflections on the Origin and Spread of Nationalism*, New Left Books, London.

Archard, D. (1996), 'Moral Partiality' in French, P.A., Uehling, T.E. Jr, and Wettstein, Howard K. (eds) *Midwest Studies in Philosophy*, Volume XX, 'Moral Concepts', University of

Notre Dame Press, Notre Dame.

Dummett, A. and Nicol, A. (1990), *Subjects, Citizens, Aliens and Others: Nationality and Immigration Law*, Wiedenfeld & Nicolson, London.

Dworkin, G. (1988), *The Theory and Practice of Autonomy*, Cambridge University Press, Cambridge.

Dworkin, R. (1978), 'Liberalism' in Hampshire, S. (ed.), *Public and Private Morality*, Cambridge University Press, Cambridge.

Exdell, J. (1994), 'Feminism, Fundamentalism, and Liberal Legitimacy', *Canadian Journal of Philosophy*, Vol. 24, No. 3, September, pp. 441–64.

Goodin, R.E. and Pettit, P. (eds) (1993), *A Companion to Contemporary Political Philosophy*, Blackwell, Oxford.

Gutman, A. (1995), 'Civic Education and Social Diversity,' *Ethics*, Vol. 105, No. 3, April, pp. 557–79.

Kukathas, C. (1992a), 'Are There Any Cultural Rights?', *Political Theory*, Vol. 20, No. 1, February, pp. 105–39.

Kukathas, C. (1992b), 'Cultural Rights Again: A Rejoinder to Kymlicka', *Political Theory*, Vol. 20, No. 4, November, pp. 674–80.

Kymlicka, W. (1989), *Liberalism, Community, and Culture*, Clarendon Press, Oxford.

Kymlicka, W. (1992), 'The Rights of Minority Cultures: Reply to Kukathas', *Political Theory*, Vol. 20, No. 1, February, pp. 140–6.

Kymlicka, W. (1995), *Multicultural Citizenship: A Liberal Theory of Minority Rights*, Clarendon Press, Oxford.

Lindley, R. (1986), *Autonomy*, Macmillan, London.

Mason, A. (1993), 'Liberalism and the Value of Community', *Canadian Journal of Philosophy*, Vol. 23, No. 2, June, pp. 215–40.

Mendus, S. (1989), *Toleration and the Limits of Liberalism*, Macmillan, London

Mill, J.S. (1975), *Considerations on Representative Government* [1861] in his *Three Essays*, Oxford University Press, Oxford.

Miller, D. (1988–9), 'In What Sense Must Socialism be Communitarian?', *Social Philosophy and Policy*, Vol. 6, pp. 51–73.

Miller, D. (1995), *On Nationality*, Clarendon Press, Oxford.

Okin, S.M. (1994), '*Political Liberalism*, Justice, and Gender', *Ethics*, Vol. 105, No. 1, October, pp. 23–43.

Parekh, B. (1990), 'Britain and the Social Logic of Pluralism' in *Britain: A Plural Society. Report of a seminar organised by the Commission for Racial equality and The Runnymede Trust, October 1989*, Commission for Racial Equality, London.

Rawls, J. (1993), *Political Liberalism*, Columbia University Press, New York.

Raz, J. (1986), *The Morality of Freedom*, Clarendon Press, Oxford.

Raz, J. (1994), 'Multiculturalism: A Liberal Perspective' in *Ethics in the Public Domain, Essays in the Morality of Law and Politics*, Clarendon Press, Oxford.

Smith, A.D. (1971), *Theories of Nationalism*, Duckworth, London.

Tamir, Y. (1993) *Liberal Nationalism*, Princeton University Press, Princeton, NJ.

Taylor, C. (1992), 'The Politics of Recognition' in Gutman, A. (ed.), *Multiculturalism and 'The Politics of Recognition'*, Princeton University Press, Princeton, NJ.

Walzer, M. (1983), *Spheres of Justice: A Defence of Pluralism and Equality*, Basil Blackwell, Oxford.

Young, I.M. (1990), 'The Ideal of Community and the Politics of Difference' in Nicholson, L. (ed.), *Feminism/Postmodernism*, Routledge, London.

3   Ethnic Pluralism and the Liberal Virtues

JOHN EDWARDS

Introduction

One of the ironies of 'celebrating' the values of ethnic pluralism in liberal societies is that to do so is, at one and the same time, to practice that key liberal value of tolerance but also, seemingly, to abrogate that other central liberal value – of individualism.

When we acknowledge the importance of a variety of ethnic cultures and values in a society and promote their equal worth (a form of ethical pluralism),[1] and when we embrace all members of all ethnic or social groups in common and equal citizenship, we are exercising one of liberalism's highest ideals. But when we also promote the interests and welfare of minority ethnic[2] groups by the use of policies that focus on whole (ethnic) groups (as opposed to individual members of groups), then we are likely to transgress that other liberal virtue, namely that the proper object of public and social policies is either the individual or individuals who are defined as members of a group that is itself defined in terms of moral relevance. When the proper object of state policy *is* a group, that group must again be defined by its moral relevance. In these terms, ethnic groups do not have moral relevance (or at least they do not *prima facie* have moral relevance) and to treat them or their members as objects of state welfare appears to do harm to key liberal values. Much will depend, of course, on how we define 'moral relevance' (and its counterpart, 'moral arbitrariness') and we shall have more to say about this in subsequent paragraphs. However, we can put down a marker here by saying that the morally relevant group (of people in the population of, say, a local authority) having priority in the allocation of state (public, social) housing is that group defined as being in greatest housing need. 'Need' is the morally relevant criterion. We would not think it right, therefore, to give housing priority to Afro-Caribbean people *as a group* just because they are Afro-Caribbean. For the purposes of housing allocation they represent a morally *arbitrary* group.

32

(If it turned out that priority *was* being given to Afro-Caribbeans because they had disproportionately high housing needs, there would be no arbitrariness. The relevant criterion would still be need, not 'being Afro-Caribbean'). As ever with markers, the full treatment will serve to show that the matter is considerably more complex than is allowed here, but hopefully the sort of thing that is at issue is clear. As a point of departure, however, it is uncontroversial to assert that to give standing, public resource and welfare to a group that is identified solely by its peculiar ethnic status (or *de facto* to benefit individuals because they are members of such a group) sits uncomfortably with such values of deontological liberalism as justice, individual autonomy, individual freedom, tolerance, equity (and some versions of equality), 'relevant reasons' and the elevation of the right over the good (see Sandel 1982; Gutmann 1980).

Now, these contradictions between the values of liberalism and the recognition of the standing of *prima facie* morally arbitrary groups are more problematic in some multicultural societies than others. Indeed, in some multi-ethnic countries they are not (or are hardly) problematic at all and it will be necessary, to avoid confusion, to note why this is the case. The most convenient way to illustrate such variations is to use the dichotomy outlined by Gordon between 'liberal pluralism' and 'corporate pluralism' (Gordon, 1994, p. 188). By the former he means the sort of value plurality we have described above – one in which there must be morally relevant reasons for treating ethnic groups differently. Corporate pluralism, on the other hand, exists where a nation or country gives explicit recognition or standing to different groups.[3] Thus countries such as Belgium, the Netherlands, India and Switzerland give formal recognition to ethnic groups (often linguistically different groups) within their boundaries in such matters as education provision and in the polity, where a certain proportion of seats in the legislature may be 'reserved' or set aside for one or more minorities. This is not to say that such recognition or the relations between minority and majority groups is unproblematic in all senses; but it is unproblematic to the extent that in such circumstances liberal societies have made some form of accommodation to the value contradictions we are concerned with here.

Where formal (and often constitutional) recognition of ethnic differences exists it will often be the result of a need (perhaps for the purpose of maintaining civil peace) to accommodate the strongly felt *interests* of different groups rather than to give legal or constitutional standing to different *values*, and conflict over the latter may persist. But values and interests are closely linked; values feed and sustain interest and interests acknowledged help to strengthen values. Conflict over value differences, therefore, whilst not being the immediate target of constitutional or legal recognition, will in all probability be reduced when valued interests are recognized. It is where corporate pluralism does *not* exist in a multi-ethnic society that conflicts are more likely to arise, therefore, between the characteristic values of liberalism and the ways in which the liberal state tries (often with the best intentions) to cope with multiculturalism, to acknowledge a plurality of values and to meet the social and economic needs of minorities, or – at least – of minority group members. And one of the first victims of states' attempts to bend liberal values in order to make some accommodation will be the liberal value of tolerance itself (see Glazer, 1994; Fullinwider, 1980).

This, then, is the context within which two broad themes arise which will be my concern in this chapter. They are different but connected and both come into being – and are a matter for concern – because of the value conflicts that seem inevitably to arise when liberal states accommodate value pluralism. The first theme revolves around the difficulty of promoting a plurality of cultures in a society when this may compromise social, educational and economic progress for some minorities or minority group members because 'success' and the reward system are grounded in the single 'dominant' value system. The second theme centres on the question of moral relevance and moral arbitrariness and how groups identified by a morally arbitrary characteristic can (if they can) become the proper objects of public policy.

What is thus at issue when there is a conflict between value plurality and a single set of values, pursuit of which is at least a very important condition of economic success, is how tolerant a liberal state should be in promoting diversity and the values of multiculturalism if[4] the pursuit of multicultural values serves to compromise the 'success' chances of minorities (and some majority members). Should value pluralism be 'celebrated' or even tolerated if it damages its supposed beneficiaries? And what is at issue when liberal states promote the welfare of disadvantaged minorities (or disadvantaged members of minority groups – a different thing) by adopting group-based policies, or recognizing the standing of whole groups, or acknowledging group rights, is that to do any of these things appears to contradict the key values of liberal individualism.

These are broad topics and we can only hope to provide some pointers within the span of a single chapter: but if any defence is needed for what must inevitably be a fairly shallow philosophical treatment, it is that pragmatically, these are matters of immediate and pressing policy importance in many liberal states. Multicultural policies are 'going wrong' – or at least seen not to be delivering equality of diversity – in many countries some of which have struggled to find the path of least resistance, and others, such as the United States, which seem on occasions to have embraced the demands of a 'diversity culture' which itself sets its teeth against tolerance and curiosity.

Tolerance, Value Pluralism and Success

I shall assume for the purposes of the present argument that 'success' in some form or another is valued by most people at least to the extent that it is thought to be better than failure.[5] People think of and measure success in different ways and many would much rather aspire to no more than half the way up the ladder in their chosen field, preferring for their quality of life (or a 'good life') to find fulfilment in other domains such as family life, voluntary activity, religious devotion or artistic enterprise. There is, in other words, no systematic or close association between economic or professional success on the one hand and the preferred good life on the other. It is important to note, therefore, that in what follows I am not concerned with conceptions of the good life but only with the more orthodox idea of success in the educational, occupational and, more generally, economic spheres. It is in respect of this kind of success that liberal societies promote the idea of equality of opportunity and in terms of which they often measure the relative disadvantage of members of different ethnic groups. We do not, however, need to acquiesce in the view that economic success has to be of value for the good life to recognize that *de facto* it is considered to be of considerable importance (if only in a relative sense) in liberal societies.

The Domain of Success

For most people the domain of success is a fairly limited affair and few would admit to having achieved it (with the exception, it seems, of those who inhabit the entertainment world where claiming already to have it is a necessary precondition of actually getting it). But success is a social value in itself, quite apart from how people feel about their own achievements. Success is 'good', it is what people should strive for. And the more people are successful, the better off is society.[6] In short, we value success.

To say this, however, is insufficiently precise: what we need for the purposes of our argument is a specification of how sentiments about success translate in practical terms in those parts of society where success is generated and measured. These will be principally the education and occupational systems. It is easier to measure success than precisely to provide a working definition. Reaching the ranks of certain professions (law, medicine, accountancy, academia – but not school teaching) are some measure of success, but financial reward is probably its single commonest metric. The route to success (so we pretend) is through hard work in education, dedication, some deferred gratification and more hard work and competitiveness in one's chosen occupation or profession. (The argument here *is* theoretical.) There are two practical components to success that it will be helpful to identify. The first is the process of gaining success that we note above; the second is the structure of the reward system or how 'success' becomes manifest in a pattern of jobs, occupations, professions and statuses about which there is a broad consensus. The connection between these two components is that there is an acknowledged route through education, training, self application and so on (the first component) in order to achieve a desired position in the reward system (the second). And the key to this part of our argument is that both of these depend on a unitary value system. Neither acknowledges or allows for value pluralism.

Now, to say that neither the path to success nor the manifestation of success in the form of the reward system allows of a plurality of values is not to assert that there is one and only one route to achievement in the reward system. But it is to say that the processes of education, training, and the getting of and progress within jobs are fairly circumscribed and leave little scope for those who do not wish to follow the orthodox path. Thus, in the first component we have identified, the education system at all levels is geared to taking examinations and gaining qualifications, and each set of qualifications acts as a passport to the next set. Entry to the professions almost always requires some formal certification and this is becoming increasingly the case across the entire spectrum of jobs and occupations if only, in some instances, in the form of having had some previous experience.

The important thing about all this is that the curricula to be followed, the examinations or tests to be taken, what opportunities are opened or shut off by success or failure at the various hurdles are all firmly embodied in the values that predominate in the society in question. They are designed to be consistent with, to reinforce and to serve these values. It would be unthinkable were it otherwise. And so it is with our second component, the structure of the reward system itself. There may appear to be little logic or functional relevance to the sorts of professions and occupations that attract high financial rewards and status but the arrangement is integral to and reflects the core values of society and – most germane to our present arguments – it is relatively inflexible and not open to a plurality of values or cultures. If liberal societies welcome and 'celebrate' a diversity of cultures and values, therefore, it would appear that the way they organize success does not.

Promoting Pluralism and the Liberal State

Most liberal societies – and almost all of those that contain minority ethnic groups within their population – promote some form of multiculturalism or cultural value pluralism as a value in itself. Value and ethnic pluralisms are seen as 'good things'.[7] This often manifests at a minimum level in legislation designed to prevent inferior treatment of people just because they belong to a minority; and then, in varying degrees in different countries, in more active policies such as affirmative action to promote minority interests or wellbeing. These kinds of policy might function (among other things) – or at least if successful and if they do not create unintended consequences – to establish a climate in which policies and activities more directly concerned with multiculturalism or cultural pluralism can flourish.[8] Among the most common of these in the United States and Britain (but not, it should be added in all European countries) are the promotion and 'celebration' of diversity most usually found on US campuses, and more specifically, the use of multicultural curricula in schools, colleges and universities (see Ravitch, 1994; Asante, 1994).

The last of these is perhaps of most immediate relevance to the present argument, that there appears (to put it no more strongly) to be an inconsistency between on the one hand wishing, in the interests of equality, to promote the success of minority group members in what we have identified as a unitary 'success' value system and on the other, promoting a plurality of cultures and values the effect of which might be to compromise those chances of success. Now, the impact of the ethic of multiculturalism may be superficial and indirect across society as a whole, but in one respect it is more direct and specific. This is the case of multicultural curricula in schools. It has to be said that in none of the arguments being aired here is any case made for or against the value, wisdom, function or morality of multicultural curricula. Our concern is *only* to point up what appears to be a value inconsistency. Multicultural curricula are designed to enable minority children to use familiar materials and histories in their studies. For majority children the purpose is to raise awareness of other cultures, values and histories – usually those of minority cultures that are represented by other children in their school and neighbourhood. Clearly, there is no inconsistency between such activity and other cherished values of liberalism; the inconsistency is largely a practical one. Time spent on multicultural studies may leave too little space in the curriculum for the sorts of basics that *all* children will require on the path to success. Both Glazer and Ravitch, for example, have noted that for both majority and minority children in multi-ethnic schools in America, less time is spent on basics such as mathematics, English and the sciences because of the increasing amount of multicultural studies (Glazer, 1994; Ravitch, 1994). And whatever we think about multicultural education, it will not contribute in the same measure as curriculum basics to the achievements necessary for success. As we have already seen, the unitary value system that drives the path to success and which underpins the reward system is unforgiving about cultural pluralism. In short, by teaching multiculturalism, we are probably reducing the chances of success of its recipients.

There is another, less direct, way in which promoting multiculturalism through school (and college) curricula may do harm. It lies in the pretence that in *functional* terms, all cultures are of equal value (because a society is multicultural). Whilst any liberal will agree that all cultures and cultural values are of equal intrinsic and moral worth, it is to live a lie to think that in countries like the United States and Britain, with market economies, they are of equal *functional* worth. That this is so has been demonstrated above in our discussion of the unitary value system of success. It really comes down to the difference between the society we would like to think we are and the rather harsher one we in fact inhabit.

Some of what has been said must be speculative: we know too little about the impact of the value inconsistencies we have identified and the data that would help us do not (yet) exist. That there *is* value inconsistency, however, is more than plausible and to the extent that its effects are deleterious, we must ask whether the liberal virtue of tolerance requires that the costs be allowed to lie where they fall. Should a liberal state, in the interests of tolerance, promote cultural and value pluralism in the knowledge that to do so may compromise the chances of success of minority, and some majority, children? Should it, in the interests of tolerance, promote the idea of cultural and value equality, when it knows that, functionally at least, it is not true? And should it, in the interests of tolerance, and of multiculturalism itself, allow some of the costs to fall on those majority children who happen to be in multicultural schools and are taught multicultural curricula? In respect of this last question, there are many white American parents who think not; they have removed to white areas or send their children to private schools. It is an irony, therefore, that the multicultural curriculum has resulted in recent years in *increasing* levels of school segregation in the United States (see Hacker, 1995).

Equality of Opportunity in a Plural Society

The idea and practice of equality of opportunity is an endorsement of the liberal value of fairness and, like fairness, it has little to do with equality.[9] It is, in effect, the way in which liberal societies try to increase the chances that inequalities are distributed according to 'relevant' criteria – primarily (and supposedly) that of merit (see Edwards, 1990). We should all have a fair chance to achieve our position in the (highly unequal) reward system.

Given this conception of equality of opportunity (it is by no means uncontroversial – see Frankel, 1983, Coleman, 1983 and Shaw, 1989 for different views), there are two matters that arise for our concern with multiculturalism; and to the extent that they reflect policy and policy consequence, they appear to pull in opposing directions. The first is that we see it as right and proper to give children (and adults) from ethnic minorities additional or compensatory education when necessary, to enhance their opportunities in education and subsequently in the world of work. The second follows from what we have already argued and it is that time and effort spent on multicultural curricula (sometimes allegedly in the *interests* of equality of opportunity) may reduce chances of succes. and mislead its consumers into a belief that the ways to success are more plural than in fact they are. The first point is common ground and we need not retread it; the second is another perspective on arguments we have already exercised and we need not dwell on that either. What is important to dwell on is the fact that the success of equal opportunities practices and policies will be affected by these two apparently opposing types of action, both seemingly reflecting the same liberal values of tolerance and fairness. But just to assert this is to raise a greater dilemma about equality of opportunity in multicultural societies. To argue that two types of equal opportunity practice may have countervailing impacts on the effectiveness of the strategy of equality of opportunity supposes that we know (or ought to be able to find out) how to measure 'effectiveness', or at least, what 'effectiveness' consists in. The purpose of equal opportunity policy is, as we have noted, to make fairer the chances of being unequal; and 'fairer' in this context must mean that only morally relevant characteristics (such as merit) should count in the contest and that arbitrary characteristics such as race, ethnicity and gender should play no part in the distribution of inequality. In all this, however, the structure and legitimacy of the reward system and the paths to find a position in it are taken as 'given'. Whatever else we might say about equal opportunity policy, it acknowledges the unitary nature of success. It may pay obeisance to multiculturalism but at the end of the day the idea of equality of opportunity is firmly grounded in the unitary value of success in the reward system.

Nowhere is this plainer than in the way we measure the effectiveness of equal opportunity policy (or more generally, how 'real' equality of opportunity is).[10] When examining the effectiveness of such policies in a multicultural context, standard practice is to examine the representation of minority groups across the spectrum of jobs, statutes, occupations and professions and to compare this representation with some baseline such as representation in the population, the labour force or labour draw area (see for example Levin-Epstein, 1987; Edwards, 1997). It is in such measurements of output that we find the idea of equality of opportunity firmly welded to a notion of success that both in itself and in its necessary connection to a relatively inflexible reward system is defined by a unitary, or at least confined, value. And the inconsistency that we are trying to articulate is nowhere starker than when we promote a multicultural ethos and instigate multicultural curricula – only then to measure the extent of equality of opportunity for minorities by counting their representation across a distinctly non-multicultural reward system.

There is one further inconsistency about our attitudes to equality of opportunity that we should touch on here because it reflects our sometime unwillingness to accept the consequences of multiculturalism – even among those who profess it most strongly. We have noted that the most common way we measure the extent of equality of opportunity between different ethnic groups (majority and minority) is to compare the relative representations of each group in a range of occupations, professions and so on and to look for inconsistencies between such representations and respective representations in the population or workforce or labour draw area. At the crudest level we might then say that if (for example) X per cent of the male labour force is Afro-Caribbean but only X-Y per cent of doctors are from this group then there is under-representation and a *prima facie* inequality of opportunity. Indeed, it is frequently the case that such an example of under-representation would call forth explanations in terms of discrimination and – more frequently because of its totemic status – of 'racism', an approach not infrequently adopted in publications of the Commission for Racial Equality. Now it is not necessary to deny the crucial impact of discrimination in all its forms to see the inconsistency of promoting the values of multiculturalism on the one hand and then attributing all differences in representation in the reward system to racism and discrimination on the other. If a society is multicultural (as the United States most certainly is and Britain is marginally), and if it celebrates diversity and a plurality of cultures, why should it believe that cultural differences will have no effect on the occupational structure? Amidst a plurality of values, cultural styles, life path preferences, religious devotions and so on, why is it only occupational and job choice that remain immune to a plurality of cultures, preferences and choices, so that any differences *must* be attributed to 'racism'? Explanations for ethnic differences in occupational structures are multifactorial, as Gudgin and others have shown (see Gudgin and Murphy, 1991; Gudgin and Breen 1994), and the reductionism of the 'racism' argument in the context of celebrating diversity flatters dogma more than curiosity.

Liberal Individualism and Group Rights

Where different ethnic groups coexist in a society, it is not infrequently the case that there will be observable and measurable socioeconomic differences between them. In some countries the differences are extreme (the United States – see Hacker, 1995), in others (Britain) moderate but sufficient to command attention (see Modood et al., 1997). Most countries, though of course in varying degrees, are mindful of such differences and will wish (in theory at least) to reduce them. The difficulty for the liberal society is how to effect an evening-up of ethnic differences whilst at the same time upholding the values of individualism. In fact, the 'difficulty' is multiform but for present purposes we shall consider it in two necessarily related parts: the moral component and a practical component. The argument will be kept at a general level but we cannot avoid making more than usual reference to the case of the United States, where the debate has been more thoughtfully conducted than anywhere else.

The heart of the difficulty is this. Can you (if you can at all) correct ethnic imbalances in education, status, occupations, professions and unemployment[11] by policies that recognize only the standing of individuals; or is it necessary to use practices that recognize and are aimed at whole groups? And if the latter, can they coexist with the value of liberal individualism?

Groups and Individuals

We have noted that, generally speaking, in liberal societies with a strong value of individualism, the only proper object of public policy is the individual (see for example, Sher, 1987; Thurow, 1979). Groups, other than those defined in a morally relevant way, do not have standing. And for most purposes, the sort of group that causes difficulties in this regard is either an ethnic group or a gender group. Our concern here is with ethnic groups.[12] An uncontentious way of illustrating these points is the example we have already given in the introduction. The groups defined as African-American in the United States or as Pakistanis in Britain do not have moral standing in the sense that neither of these groups has a right to, or could be considered as due, welfare provision *qua* group. Nor does membership of these groups give any individual any standing in relation to welfare provision or any other activity by or on behalf of the state.[13]

The dilemma then is this. Inequalities in multi-ethnic societies are not ethnically random. One or more minority groups will be manifestly worse off (on average) than the majority and other minority groups. But apparently ethnically conscious solutions to this inequality problem are ruled out because we cannot acknowledge ethnic minority groups *qua groups* to be the proper recipients of state attention. There are two principal resolutions of this difficulty. The first is to reduce inequalities by policies that do recognize only the standing of individuals. Thus, for example, as we have already noted, in principle, if we concentrate welfare resource on the most needy (a morally incontestable notion) and if most of the needy belong to a minority ethnic group, or a disproportionate number of a minority group is needy, then some equalization will be effected. This might work (in a practical sense) if welfare resource for the needy were redistributive – which is the case in neither the United States nor Great Britain (see Glazer, 1988; Le Grand, 1982). In addition to this, policies designed to put right the wrongs of racial and ethnic discrimin-ation at the level of individuals could be implemented. This is in effect what was attempted in Britain with the Race Relations Act 1976. It has succeeded in eliminating some of the more explicit and blatant manifestations of discrimination, but as a means of doing away with institutional discrimination and the culture in which it thrives, the Act has, not surprisingly, been less than revolutionary. The second strategy is to give ethnic groups standing by making them relevant from a moral point of view. This has been achieved, as we have noted, in those cases where a whole group can be said to have been caused harm, where the harm is palpable (such as deprival of property or lands) and where in consequence a case can be made that the whole group is owed compensation.[14] In cases other than this, however, the translation of a group from 'arbitrary' (having no standing) to 'relevant' is complex and morally contentious. We shall say more about it shortly but it will be helpful first to give an example of policies that do appear to give ethnic groups moral standing (and which are contentious). This may help to make the arguments more concrete. The example we use is that of affirmative action policies and practices in the United States,[15] which operate principally in the areas of education and employment and which in essence are concerned to increase numbers and proportions of minority group members in areas where they are 'under-represented', for example in medical and law schools, other university faculties and in employment areas such as certain professions (again law and medicine primarily) and upper levels of business.

The history of affirmative action in the US is a long and tortured one and had some of its roots at least in the 'Griggs Doctrine' which evolved from the findings of the *Supreme Court in Griggs v. Duke Power Co.* (1971) (see Davis and Graham, 1995, pp. 304–6). The Court handed down a majority decision that established the principle that in order to show discrimination (in this case by Duke Power Co. against black employees) you did *not* have to prove intent on the part of the discriminator. Activities, therefore, on the part of an employer or university which were 'facially neutral' (apparently nondiscriminatory) but which had a *de facto* discriminatory affect *were* discriminatory (see Belton, 1981; Edwards, 1995, pp. 103–7). What counted now was 'disparate impact'. Thus, if a test used for recruitment or promotion purposes appears to be perfectly nondiscriminatory (as, facially, would the average intelligence test) but is passed by a lower proportion of minority testees than of the majority, then it has 'disparate impact' and is discriminatory. The same could equally well apply to a battery of interview techniques and it does not matter why the disparate impact occurs.

There is no necessary causal connection between the constitutional confirmation of disparate impact and the establishment of affirmative action; but the former changed the landscape of discrimination in a way that provided fertile ground for the latter. Disparate impact spread the domain of discrimination to an extent that made calls for stronger remedies that recognized racial groups as legitimate recipients of state assistance almost irresistible. The principal instruments by which affirmative action could be implemented (Titles VI and VII of the Civil Rights Act 1964 and Executive Order No. 11246 1965) were already in place and the affirmative action wagon had begun to roll, but it was with *Griggs* that momentum really picked up. And it has continued to roll without much hindrance until the mid-1990s, when a white majority backlash, assisted by a conservative Supreme Court, has helped to put the brakes on, and, in California at least, to reverse two decades of activity, resulting in major reversals in the ethnic composition of entrants to law and medical schools at the University of California at Berkeley for 1998.

To understand what all the fuss is about we need to know a little about how affirmative action (or what many of its opponents call 'preferential treatment') works. All companies in the United States, other than construction firms, which have government contracts over a certain dollar value and more than 50 employees, and all but some private universities and colleges, have to monitor the ethnic (and sex) composition of their workforce on a regular basis and at every level[16] and compare all minority representations at all levels with their 'availability' (an estimate of minority group members' availability for work, taking into account qualification levels, availability for work — i.e. not already in employment — location, travel to work distance, and so on) (for a detailed analysis see Edwards, 1995, p. 32). If the availability figures suggest that one or more minority groups are under-represented at particular levels in a company then it must institute an 'Affirmative Action Plan' designed to increase minority representation wherever it falls short of what might be expected. The plan will include such 'affirmative action' measures as checking all recruitment procedures (including all tests) for disparate impact, advertising job vacancies in the minority press, aggressive outreach to minority schools and colleges, fast track promotion for minorities, special and compensatory training, mentoring programmes and so on. In implementing the plan, a company or university must make 'every good faith effort' to reach the levels of representation that the 'availability' analysis suggests are appropriate[17] (token efforts will incur the wrath of the Office of Federal Contract Compliance Programs); but by the same token, the target representation levels must not be treated as quotas that *have* to be reached. Failing to reach the target does not matter, providing that 'every good faith effort' has been applied.

These are the barest bones of what is a complex set of processes that operate on a vast scale in the United States, and at enormous expense. How then does it illustrate our theoretical arguments about the moral standing of individuals and groups and (what we shall presently consider) the distinction between morally relevant and morally arbitrary groups? Well, the first thing to note is that were the affirmative action process prosecuted in the manner described above, it would *not* be contentious, and I doubt that it would offend any of our concerns over the proper standing of groups for policy purposes (or, indeed, any doubts we may have about whether we are treating morally relevant groups). What an affirmative action plan would strive to do would in effect be to search strenuously for more minority group members who could be applicants for a job (or could be made to be so with a little help) and to encourage them to apply. (Parallel processes would operate for applications for places in university.) *But* once they had applied they would (in a pure affirmative action model) be treated like all other minority and majority applicants and whether they were appointed would depend solely on their merit and whether they were the 'best person for the job'. Now there may be many reasons why fewer minority group members apply for jobs than could do so (expectations of rejection or prejudice or discrimination, educational qualifications that are just below what is required – and would be much higher had they been able to go to a decent school – family and peer pressures and so on). We need not rehearse the evidence for this multiplicity of reasons or for the likelihood that, were they to be compensated for, there would be many more minority applicants who would compete on equal terms with those from the majority. There can be nothing exceptional, therefore, in a process that targets some compensatory assistance at minority groups[18] but then makes minorities compete equally on merit. At the crucial point, the prizes are competed for and won or lost by individuals, not groups, and since therefore the 'group' is not at issue, neither is its status as a morally relevant or arbitrary matter of contention.

However, affirmative action does not work, and has not worked, in the way described here. And if it had, it would not have been nearly as successful as it has been. For a number of reasons that I have described elsewhere (Edwards, 1991, 1995) much affirmative action has become preferential treatment. Targets have become quotas, entry standards for universities and colleges have been set lower for minorities, qualification criteria for professions have been changed or abandoned and minorities have been preferred in promotions. The uniform application of the criterion of merit[19] has been abandoned where affirmative action has turned into preferential treatment. Instead, one or both of two things has happened: individuals have been treated in particular ways by the state or others 'promoting' state policy *because of* their race or ethnicity rather than their merit; or whole groups (minority ethnic groups) have been treated in different ways *because of* their defining characteristic (ethnicity, race, etc.), but the effects of such group treatment have fallen on some individual members of the group (those who gain positions on preference criteria) rather than on all members — and would not have fallen on them had they not been members of the group.[20] We shall deal with the 'group' issue below. What is of immediate concern is whether the situation we have described is one that overrides the value of liberal individualism or whether, because not all members of an ethnic group benefit, this is not group treatment, so that on this score at least we need not fear for one of liberalism's key values.

The point at issue becomes clearer if we consider another case of group treatment. Suppose a Native American Nation, such as the Lakota, is granted reparation payment because of the historical theft of their lands.[21] Suppose further that reparation payment will be in the form of a dollar settlement to every living member of the nation (plus perhaps a trust fund for future generations). In this case every living member of the Lakota Nation would benefit and we can reasonably say that what has happened is a group action. The difference as against the preferential treatment case is clear: there, only a minority of a given ethnic minority will benefit. Does that mean that preferential treatment is not a group practice? Despite the dissimilarity to the Lakota case, I think it is. This is because the individual beneficiaries of preference procedures have no standing *as individuals*. The fact that 'A' got a place in law school on lower grades than 'B' is a consequence of her belonging to a particular minority group and the purely serendipitous facts of being in the right place at the right time. The only thing that can account for her treatment is that she is African-American/Hispanic/Native American etc.[22] What has occurred has been a *group* practice which happens to have impacted on particular individual members of the group for no obviously good reason.

Morally Relevant and Morally Arbitrary Groups

Our final concern is with the moral standing of groups. Liberal individualism obviously does not proscribe all group policies and practices. It could not make sense to do so. What matters in a liberal state is whether groups so recognized can be justified in being identified for policy purposes on morally relevant grounds. And as we have seen, a group the identity of which is defined only in terms of its ethnicity, race or sex does not appear *prima facie* to fulfil the relevance criterion. To reiterate what we said at the beginning: there seems no justification or logic in allocating social housing (or any other public good) solely on the grounds of race.

   What then makes a group or a collectivity 'morally relevant' in the sense that it does become thereby the proper object for state action? It turns out that most (perhaps all) morally relevant groups are *not* also identified by any other morally arbitrary criterion. Thus, if for welfare purposes we define the group that is the proper object of concern, it will be the group defined by the concept of 'need' in one of its forms. The relevant group for social housing provision will be that group of people defined as having particular housing needs. Now, members of other (arbitrarily) defined groups such as young people, single mothers, Afro-Caribbeans, may be highly represented among the need group but there is no characteristic common to all members of the need group, other than their neediness.

   There have been a number of attempts to derive criteria of moral relevance for groups *ab initio* (see for example Feinberg, 1973; Campbell, 1988) but none have been flawless and we shall, for the sake of brevity, simply assert the most likely candidates and then see what relation, if any, they have to groups defined by ethnicity. We have assumed 'need' to be a defining characteristic of a morally relevant group. 'Need' justifies (but does not necessarily command) state action. Compensation will also define a group with standing, insofar as if a group as a whole has been harmed then the group as a whole ought to be compensated. A third and more general defining criterion would be 'rights', so that if a group has a right to something or a right that something not be done to it, then the group as a whole can call in what is its due. And so far as group-defining criteria are concerned, there are probably few, if any, other criteria of moral relevance than these three.[23]

The difference between a morally arbitrary and a morally relevant group should now be clearer. The question that remains is whether the moral standing for policy purposes of a morally arbitrary group can be established by showing that at the same time it can be defined as morally relevant. This is the second strategy that we noted above for making the treatment of ethnic minority groups congruent with the demands of liberal individualism.

Is it possible to argue that an ethnic group (such as those in the United States members of which benefit from preferential treatment) can be defined as a morally relevant group thus removing (some) moral doubts about the use of preference practice? The question has been long debated in the US (see for example, Nickel, 1972; Nunn, 1973; Taylor, 1973; Goldman, 1975) but the nub of the argument, it seems, has to be a claim that since *all* members of a minority such as Hispanics or African-Americans or Native Indians have been harmed by past discrimination and prejudice, then all (or all descendants) are owed compensation – such as preferential treatment – and since the debt is to *all* members then it is the group as a whole that is the relevant object. At this point, the argument seems to become a factual one. The claim carries far more weight in the context of the harm done by slavery to black Americans than it does for the Latino population, the majority of whom, particularly in the West, are relatively recent arrivals. And perhaps the most compelling group-harm claim is in respect of many of the Native American Nations against some of whom policies of virtual genocide were operated.

Are such arguments plausible? That harm has been done by slavery, oppression, prejudice and discrimination is indisputable. But have all members of all minorities suffered? Are we to attribute the relatively depressed status of black males today to the effects of slavery? And certainly not all members of any particular minority appear to have suffered equally.[24] What we require, but do not have, is a set of criteria and accompanying cogent arguments for determining the circumstances under which we can reasonably argue that a morally arbitrary group can, for the purposes of public policy, be counted as morally relevant. At present we have more uncertainties and questions than we have answers.

But there is one final point at which liberal individualism may well baulk. Any translation from arbitrary to relevant group requires that a myriad of individual circumstances translate into a group characteristic. It requires that many sacrifice their individual status as black, Hispanic, etc. to that of a member of a group. And in the process, as we have noted in respect of preferential treatment, there can be little semblance of just distribution *within* the group. Those chosen are chosen serendipitously and individual claims must be sacrificed to the moral relevance of the group.

Notes

1   My concern in this chapter is less with the usual notion of pluralism – as a variety of often competing values among the population of a liberal society – but in a more limited sense with the variety of values and ethical beliefs (and contingently, cultures) that come to exist in a liberal society because of the presence within it of one or more ethnically distinct groups. Most works in ethical pluralism give little emphasis to value pluralism that arises *because of* ethnically and culturally different groups: but of course much of what is important in arguments about ethical pluralism will remain the same irrespective of *how* value plurality arises. (See for valuable treatments of value or moral pluralism Kekes, 1993; Rescher, 1993; Mackie, 1977; McIntyre, 1988.)

2   I use 'ethnic' in the now common shorthand to include groups which distinguish themselves from other minority groups and from the majority in virtue of their race, ethnicity or religion. I am not concerned here with groups that claim identity through gender or sexual preference.

3   The reasons for such recognition in liberal societies with a plurality of ethnic groups – and why it happens in some countries but not others – is relatively poorly researched and beyond the scope of this chapter.

4   The 'if' is of course contestable.

5   This has as much to do with the inescapable expectations of others as with self-interest. Something of what I mean is captured by Walzer (1983, chs 4–6) in his discussion of spheres of justice.

6   Success, of course, is not confined to market economies. In the Soviet Union the collective had a duty to be successful in achieving its quotas.

7   This says nothing about their motives for doing so, however. For most such societies it may be a matter of promoting the liberal value of tolerance itself. But there may be some in which it is seen as an irritating but functional necessity.

8   Space does not permit a detailed analysis of the idea of multiculturalism and the cognate ideas of value and cultural pluralism: but for useful coverage see Rex (1996), chs 1 and 3; and for a vivid picture of America as a multicultural society and how it became one, see Dinnerstein, Nichols and Reimers (1996).

9   A detailed analysis of equal opportunity practice and theory is beyond the scope of this chapter, but see Edwards (1987, 1990); Blakemore and Drake (1996); Jewson and Mason (1992); Gibbon (1992).

10 I have discussed this elsewhere and provide only a summary argument here; see Edwards (1990).

11 Other areas of inequality such as health, housing, wealth, criminality and so on are beyond the scope of this chapter.

12 In order to forestall immediate objections, there will be circumstances in which an ethnic group will be recognized as having standing (Native Americans, Jews in Europe) but it will be in respect of a morally *relevant* reason that attaches to the whole group – such as grounds of compensation or reparation. This will be the subject of subsequent paragraphs.

13 In this regard, it is worth noting that when the state in Great Britain makes a ruling by its judicial apparatus in favour of a minority ethnic group member in a discrimination case, and awards compensation, it is to the wronged (morally relevant reason) individual that the award is made, and *not* to the individual qua minority group member, nor in any proxy sense to a minority group.

14 This may mean in practice that compensation is made to the descendant members of the group, the antecedent members of which suffered the harm.

15 They are of course used elsewhere, but nowhere to the extent nor with the same sophistication of debate as in the United States.

16 In universities and colleges, monitoring will include students, faculty and administrative and manual staff.

17 The process of matching representation to availability is known as the *utilization analysis*.

18 This is not entirely accurate. A case could be made that it is wrong to target assistance on minorities when the numbers of very poor (but, it has to be added, not racially discriminated against) whites is as great or greater (see Capaldi, 1985; Mosley and Capaldi, 1996; Glazer, 1975).

19 In fact the merit principle itself is very flawed and we pretend too much if we think that it justifies the allocation of inequalities in the reward system. I have discussed this elsewhere – see Edwards (1997).

20 Our argument has concerned the moral standing or otherwise of ethnic or racial groups in the context of state provision or assistance. It could be argued that the perpetrators of preferential treatment are private sector companies (or universities) which in so doing have perverted the true intent of state affirmative action policy. And whilst it is true that the Supreme Court has reined in on preferential treatment whenever the opportunity has arisen over the past eight years or so, I do not think it plausible that the federal government did not know that affirmative action had turned to preference and had not acquiesced in it. And it is probably true that it did so for the best of motives – preference was delivering results in a way that affirmative action never could.

21 Those familiar with the history of Indian claims will recognize parts of this vignette to be factual.

22 This is not strictly true because she would have had to have reached *some* level of qualification.

23 We might wish to consider 'merit', which has featured in our earlier discussion, but I take this to be a quality that attaches only, or mainly, to individuals.

24 Similar difficulties arise on the reverse side of the coin – who pays the costs? And are all whites equal in their culpability for past harm?

References

Asante, M.K. (1994), 'Multiculturalism : An Exchange' in Pincus, F. and Ehrlich, H. (eds) *Race and Ethnic Conflict*, Westview Press, Boulder.

Belton, R. (1981), 'Discrimination and Affirmative Action : An Analysis of Competing Theories of Equality and "Weber"', *North Carolina Law Review*, Vol. 59, No. 1, pp. 531–98.

Blakemore, K. and Drake, R. (1996), *Understanding Equal Opportunity Policies*, Prentice Hall, London.

Campbell, T. (1988), *Justice*, Macmillan, London.

Capaldi, N. (1985), *Out of Order : Affirmative Action and the Crisis of Doctrinaire Liberalism*, Prometheus, Buffalo, NY.

Coleman, J. (1983), 'Equality of Opportunity and Equality of Results' in Letwin, W. (ed.), *Against Equality,* Macmillan, London.

Davis, A. and Graham, B.L. (1995), *The Supreme Court, Race, and Civil Rights,* Sage, Thousand Oaks.

Dinnerstein, L., Nichols, R. and Reimers, D. (1996), *Natives and Strangers*, Oxford University Press, Oxford.

Edwards, J. (1987), *Positive Discrimination, Social Justice and Social Policy*, Tavistock, London.

Edwards, J. (1990), 'What Purpose Does Equal Opportunity Serve?', *New Community*, Vol. 16, No. 2, pp. 19–35.

Edwards, J. (1991), 'US Affirmative Action Alive and Well Despite Supreme Court', *Equal Opportunities International*, Vol. 10, No. 1, pp. 11–13.

Edwards, J. (1995), *When Race Counts*, Routledge, London.

Edwards, J. (1997), 'On What "Ought" To Be : The Flaw in Employment Equality Practice for Minorities', *New Community*, Vol. 23, No. 2, pp. 233–48.

Feinberg, J. (1973), *Social Philosophy*, Prentice Hall, Englewood Cliffs.

Frankel, C. (1983), 'Equality of Opportunity' in Letwin, W. (ed.), *Against Equality*, Macmillan, London.

Fullinwider, R.K. (1980), *The Reverse Discrimination Controversy*, Rowman and Littlefield, Totowa, New Jersey.

Gibbon, P. (1992), 'Equal Opportunities Policy and Race Equality' in Braham, P., Rattansi, A. and Skellington, R. (eds), *Racism and Anti-Racism*, Sage, London.

Glazer, N. (1975), *Affirmative Discrimination, Ethnic Inequality and Public Policy*, Basic Books, New York.

Glazer, N. (1988), *The Limits of Social Policy*, Harvard University Press, Cambridge, Mass.

Glazer, N. (1994), 'Multi-culturalism and Public Policy' in Aaron, H., Munn, T. and Taylor, T. (eds), *Values and Public Policy*, Brookings, Washington DC.

Goldman, A. (1975), 'Reparations to Individuals or Groups?', *Analysis*, No. 35, pp. 168–70.

Gordon, M. (1994), 'Models of Pluralism: The New American Dilemma' in Pincus, F. and Ehrlich, H. (eds), *Race and Ethnic Conflict*, Westview Press, Boulder.

Gudgin, G. and Breen, R. (1994), *Evaluation of the Ratio of Unemployment Rates as an Indicator of Fair Employment,* Northern Ireland Economic Research Centre, Belfast.

Gudgin, G. and Murphy, A. (1991), *The Labour Market Context and Potential Effectiveness of Fair Employment Legislation in Northern Ireland,* Central Community Relations Unit, Belfast.

Gutmann, A. (1980), *Liberal Equality*, Cambridge University Press, Cambridge.

Hacker, A. (1995), *Two Nations*, Ballantine Books, New York.

Jewson, N. and Mason, D. (1992), 'The Theory and Practice of Equal Opportunities Policies: Liberal and Radical Approaches' in Braham, P., Rattansi, A. and Skellington, R. (eds), *Race and Anti-racism*, Sage, London.

Kekes, J. (1993), *The Morality of Pluralism*, Princeton University Press, Princeton, New Jersey.

Le Grand, J. (1982), *The Strategy of Equality*, George Allan and Unwin, London.

Levin-Epstein, M.D. (1987), *Primer of Equal Employment Opportunity* (4th edn), Bureau of National Affairs Inc., Washington DC.

MacIntyre, A. (1988), *Whose Justice? Which Rationality?*, Duckworth: London.

Mackie, J. (1977), *Ethics: Inventing Right and Wrong*, Penguin, Harmondsworth.

Modood, T. et al. (1997), *Ethnic Minorities in Britain*, Policy Studies Institute, London.

Mosley, A. and Capaldi, N. (1996), *Affirmative Action*, Rowman and Littlefield, Boulder.

Nickel, J. (1972), 'Discrimination and Morally Relevant Characteristics', *Analysis*, Vol. 32, No. 4, pp. 113–14.

Nunn, W. (1973), 'Reverse Discrimination', *Analysis*, Vol. 34, No. 5, pp. 151–4.

Ravitch, D. (1994), 'Multiculturalism : *e pluribus plures*' in Pincus, F. and Ehrlich, H. (eds), *Race and Ethnic Conflict*, Westview Press, Boulder.

Rescher, N. (1993), *Pluralism*, Clarendon Press, Oxford.

Rex, J. (1996), *Ethnic Minorities in the Modern Nation State*, Macmillan, London.

Sandel, M. (1982), *Liberalism and the Limits of Justice*, Cambridge University Press, Cambridge.

Shaw, J. (1989), *Equal Opportunities: The Way Ahead*, Institute of Personnel Management, London.

Sher, G. (1987), 'Predicting Performance', *Social Philosophy and Policy*, Vol. 5, No. 1, pp. 188–203.

Taylor, P. (1973), 'Reverse Discrimination and Compensatory Justice', *Analysis*, Vol. 33, No. 6, pp. 177–82.

Thurow, L. (1979), 'A Theory of Groups and Economic Redistribution', *Philosophy and Public Affairs*, Vol. 9, No. 1, pp. 25–41.

Walzer, M. (1983), *Spheres of Justice*, Blackwell, Oxford.

4 Liberalism, Nationalism and Identity

ROSS POOLE

Identities

Humans are, as Charles Taylor (1985, ch. 2) has suggested, 'self-interpreting animals'. I take this to mean that the selves which we are – and which each of us is – are formed through the ways in which we interpret (and misinterpret) ourselves. Of course, we do not create for ourselves the conceptual resources we employ in these self-interpretations. They are provided for us by the forms of life within which we live. These self-conceptions – these *identities* – give us a perspective on the world, a sense of the past and the future – and in particular a sense of *our* past and *our* future. They provide us with the values and standards on which we judge and act. An identity defines a perspective on the world and our place in it. It is because we understand the world in a certain way that it has a certain pertinence to us. It calls upon us – or those who have the appropriate identity – to act in one way rather than another. It is because an identity defines a world that it is also a mode of agency.

As we are called upon to participate in different forms of social life, we acquire different identities. This means that we live in different worlds, are subject of different standards and are required to act in different ways. For much of the time, these worlds coexist in happy complementarity, symbiosis or indifference. But sometimes they conflict, and the demands that they make can be neither denied nor satisfied. Where the identities define more or less distinct social groups, the clash between identities is the stuff of politics; where the identities compete for the same individual commitment, it is also the stuff of tragedy.

Persons, Utility Maximizers and Citizens

Personhood is a fundamental category in modern societies, and it is often

52

conceived – especially by philosophers – to be written into the nature of human existence. We are, it is assumed, essentially persons; all else is accretion. However, this assumption is probably not much older than the 17th century. Indeed, it may well be that when John Locke (1975, Book II, ch. xxvii) provided his famous analysis of personal identity, he was not so much explicating a pre-existing concept as creating a new one (see Poole, 1996a). Be that as it may, the pervasiveness of the concept since Locke is testimony to the hegemony of liberalism in mainstream Western thought. For personhood is the form of identity appropriate to a liberal political and legal order. We are persons insofar as we engage in certain legal and moral practices (I here follow Hegel, 1991, Part I). In part, this is because these practices have a performative function. We are *deemed* to be persons, i.e. the bearers of certain rights and duties, when we participate in the relevant practices. But it is also because we *become* persons as these practices and the expectations associated with them enter into our own self understanding. For example, as persons we are held responsible for what we have done in the past (promises made, acts performed). Insofar as we understand ourselves as persons, we appropriate those past acts as ours. While Locke was right to see that a certain kind of memory was essential to personal identity, he was wrong to conceive of this as if it were a natural condition of personhood. It is rather, as Nietzsche (1967, Essay Two) argued, that we have to learn to remember things in this way. As we participate in certain forms of social life, we learn to appropriate certain facets of the past as a past for which we are *now* responsible; and we learn to act with the knowledge that a future self will appropriate what we now do as a past for which it will *then* be responsible. Acquiring memories of this appropriative kind is part and parcel of becoming a person. Associated with this conception of self is a certain conception of the world. In learning to be persons, we also learn to perceive others as persons, i.e. bearers of rights and duties, and this mode of perception informs us as to how we must act with respect to these others.

We are not just persons. Another pervasive identity in the modern world is that of *rational utility maximizer*; and this exists in uneasy symbiosis with our identity as persons. Almost all economic theory and a good deal of social science works on the assumption that rational utility maximizers is all that we are. This assumption provides a good approximation of our behaviour in a wide range of social transactions, more especially those involving market behaviour: and not surprisingly. For as we are inscribed into the social practices constitutive of the market, we have little choice but to learn to calculate the outcomes of the various transactions that are available to us and what their effect on us will be, and then to select that transaction which has the best outcomes for the least expenditure. A not inconsiderable amount of ink has been spilt by philosophers attempting to show that a reasonable simulacrum of a social morality can be derived from the assumption that we are – or ought to be – calculative utility maximizers (see, e.g., Gauthier, 1986). But all these attempts have been unsuccessful. For an individual who is solely concerned to maximize, the past would exist only as a source of data on how best to satisfy current and future desires. Such an individual would not appropriate the past as one which he or she was responsible for, and thus could not be *bound* by past commitments. If we were like this, then, as Nietzsche observed, we would not have 'the right to make promises'.

On these matters, Kant is much a better guide than Bentham. The social morality required to regulate market behaviour must constrain the operations of desire. As we learn to conduct ourselves in terms of calculative desire, we must learn also to place limits on the scope of these desires. The social practices surrounding the market are one form of education; the complementary legal and moral practices, the other. As we become utility maximizers, so we also become persons.

There is, however, a tension between the demands of utility maximization and of personhood; and it is an irresoluble one if these identities merely compete with each other. As Kant recognized, there needs to be a third and containing identity. For Kant himself, this was supplied by the Christian narrative of immortality and redemption (see Kant, 1956, Book II, ch. II). For Hegel, who in this matter stands at the end of the classical republican tradition, membership of the state – *citizenship* – provides that term. Hegel argued that on its own, personhood is too empty and formalistic a category to provide a genuine constraint on the operations of self-interest (or any other form of interest for that matter). Perhaps even more significantly, it fails to offer a fulfilling form of identity. Personhood does not provide us with a narrative through which we can live our lives. It merely expresses the minimal claims which we make on the world and should recognize in others. The category of the person expresses what we have in common with every other bearer of rights, and abstracts from the specific forms of life which give meaning to our lives. To treat someone *merely* as a person is to suggest that there is little else of significance to them, and it is for this reason that 'the simple abstraction "person" has something contemptuous about it, even as an expression' (Hegel, 1991, Part I, Section I, §35).

Citizenship is another story. For philosophers, it is redolent with a past in which individuals expressed themselves as soldiers, leaders and makers of their political destiny. The republican tradition identifies commitment to one's fellow citizens and service to the public with freedom (see Skinner, 1990; Poole, 1996/97). Insofar as it provides the individual with a role in the story of the state, it allows him (though rarely her) to identify with its triumphs and tragedies. Patriotism – the first virtue of the citizen – was not exemplified merely in the self-sacrifice required in war, but also in the day-to-day interactions of social life. For modern republicans, it is our identity as citizens which provides the commitment to the state and to the rule of law and an appropriate recognition of the claims of fellow citizens. It might well be that one should also be a person and treat others as persons; but personhood is not a self-sufficient form of identity. We can be persons only if we (or most of us) are also prepared to act as citizens.

Hegel knew all too well that the glories of Greece and the Roman Republic were not for the modern world; yet he hoped that modernity might sustain a practice of citizenship which would provide individuals with reason to identify their own aspiration with those of the state and their fellow members. Yet even as Hegel wrote, the chances of a revival or recreation of a practice of classical citizenship world were diminishing. As the category of citizenship was expanding, it was also increasingly becoming a formal affair. Modern citizenship was becoming, not a way of life engaging the best energies of citizens, but rather a framework of rights which allowed citizens to busy themselves with their private affairs (see Walzer, 1989). In this context, it becomes a moot point whether there is in the end a clear distinction between the concept of citizenship and personhood.

Hegel was aware of these problems, but argued that modern social life provided the institutional framework within which individuals might be educated into a practice of citizenship. However, while he envisaged a series of mediations between the self-interested calculations characteristic of commercial life and the expressive commitment required by a practice of citizenship, he allowed little participatory role for citizens in the affairs of the state. In practice, all that individuals could do was to recognize the overriding rationality of the political order to which they belonged. There is a deep problem here. Unless there is a meaningful link between the individual's activity and political life, the concept of citizenship is in danger of becoming as formal, abstract and ultimately empty as the concept of personhood. In these circumstances, it is likely that individuals will pursue purely private goals and will not sustain the legal and political structures on which they ultimately depend. As Hegel (1977, pp. 290–4) himself recognized in his account of the Roman Empire, unless there is an active practice of citizenship, the state will lapse into arbitrary despotism, and the legal and moral category of personhood become an empty shell. Private interest will subordinate questions of right on the one hand and political commitment on the other.

National Identity

There is a historical connection between liberalism and nationalism, insofar as liberal institutions and practices developed within the framework of the nation state. The burden of my argument here is that there is a conceptual connection as well.

Our identity as persons presupposes a more encompassing identity. However, if citizenship is to provide that identity, then it will not be citizenship on the classical republican models, in which property owners engaged their best energies and gained fulfilment in the life of politics. For in the modern world, politics and associated activities are subject to the same division of labour as other activities: they involve special skills and have become the responsibility of specialized workers. The very size of the modern state has stood in the way of any meaningful practice of political participation and self-government. However, if the relationship between citizens and the modern state is not one of formation, it can nevertheless be one of *mimesis*. If the republican ideal is one of citizens making the state through their own activity, and thus being subject as individuals to what they themselves have collectively made, the national ideal involves citizens finding themselves in the public culture of the state and thus being subject, as individuals, to a collective embodiment of their own identity. The nation state claims an identity between the culture which informs the operations of the state, that which is expressed in everyday social life and that which constitutes the self-conception of its members. In the nation state, individuals find their identity expressed and confirmed in the rituals through which state power is exercised, whether or not they play any role in that exercise.

The nation exists in the culture through which individuals learn who they are. Language is a key component. Insofar as the nation has appropriated the language through which we identify ourselves and others, national identity has become a second nature to us. Insofar as the nation identifies a land which is ours, it defines the place of our belonging and its ground in a near literal sense of our existence. Insofar as it provides us with a past and a future, it gives us memories and aspirations far richer than those of our individual existence. One should not underestimate the strength of this identity, even –

or especially – now, when, as I shall argue, the nation form is in terminal decline. The cultural resources which have formed or been appropriated by the nation are immensely rich, and the needs which they answer are deep-seated ones. The nation – its language, place, history and culture – has earned its place as the foremost of the identities which compete for our allegiance.

All too often the nation state takes an illiberal form. But this should not lead us to suppose that the liberal state can easily do without its national frame. As Yael Tamir (1993) and David Miller (1995) have recently argued, many liberal practices presuppose the cultural and political environment provided by the nation state. If liberal rights are to be secure, then the practices of law and politics which define these rights must be accessible to all persons. If citizens are to contribute to public debate and to understand the positions at stake, then a common public language is all but essential. If we are to feel committed to the results of political decisions and the outcomes of political debates, then some identification with the form of the political process is necessary. If we are to contribute to the wellbeing of other citizens, then some fellow-feeling is required. If we are to take some responsibility for past injustices and for the future wellbeing of our state, some sense of historical continuity is essential (Poole, forthcoming 1998). A national culture provides a national memory and projects a national future, and as we acquire a national identity we acquire this memory and this future. To be sure, abstract principles of liberal right and democratic process may provide reasons for some of the commitments required for a healthy political life. But political commitments also require a sense of community, history, tradition, and place, and these are precisely the domain of the nation.

For too long, liberals treated nationalism as an irrationality, a pathology unworthy of serious attention. Thus, Robert Goodin and Philip Pettit explained their exclusion of the concept from their *Companion to Contemporary Political Philosophy* with the remark that 'nationalism hardly counts as a principled way of thinking about things' (1993, p. 7). This dismissive attitude has meant that liberals ignored one of the conditions of a viable liberal practice. In recent years, however, the tide has turned, and nationalism has begun to receive attention from liberal theorists (see, e.g. Tamir, 1993; Margalit and Raz, 1995; Miller, 1995). However, it may well be that philosophers have recognized the importance of the concept only at a time when it is ceasing to represent a lived practice and is becoming a relic of an irrecoverable past.

The Owl of Minerva

The cultural unity affirmed by the nation state was always more imagined than real; nevertheless, it has operated as a plausible ideal in much social and political life. There can be no doubt that it has legitimated the exclusion or maltreatment of those defined as other, and that it has fuelled some of the more unpleasant conflicts in the contemporary world. However, it has also played a not altogether pernicious role in sustaining liberal and democratic political practices, and it continues to sustain some sense of social responsibility and commitment. The nation has been a profoundly ambiguous presence in the history of the past 200 or so years. But it also has been an inescapable one. However, the nationalist imagination is the product of a very specific moment in world history, and there are reasons to suppose that this moment is over.

Three movements coincided to create the ideal and the actuality of the nation. First, the development of market relations broke up the self-contained and culturally isolated agricultural communities which had formed the social environment of the vast mass of the population in the pre-modern world. For a long period, the most intensive development of the market – both of commodities and of labour – was territorial. Capitalist enterprises characteristically located themselves within a given territory, and used that territory as the base for their larger ambitions. Second, the modern state was able to claim a more or less absolute sovereignty within a given area, and has been remarkably successful in making that claim good. It developed new forms of power, and became a continuing presence in – rather than an occasional intrusion on – social life. Third, forms of popular culture (the novel, the broadsheet, the magazine, the political and religious tract) developed which made use of the new technology, especially the printing press, and which was addressed to the growing audience of those who were literate in the vernacular print languages. A conception of a common national life was formed and disseminated.

These three developments provided the space within which the nation was imagined as the foundation of sovereignty and the source of political identity. In the contemporary world – 'late modernity' – the economic, political and cultural changes which are taking place point away from the nation state. Market relations now have the most tenuous relationship with existing state borders. Capitalism has become more visibly transnational than ever before. State sovereignty is increasingly subject to international legal and political tribunals, and the state's effective control of its own destiny is diminished by external economic agencies and the hegemony of the world market. Large corporations have only the slightest affiliation with particular countries, and even small ones are players in a much larger arena than that constituted by any nation state. And the world market has spawned, not the single world culture aspired to or feared in the 19th century, but a multiplicity of different cultural activities and forms, few of which are contained within the borders of particular nations.

The movement is an uneven and contradictory one. The diminished significance of the state has provided encouragement for the political ambitions of many petty nationalisms. One response to cultural fragmentation has been a renewed cleavage to what are imagined to be more traditional identities. While new forms of communication and transport are generating new identities, they have also provided means of sustaining old national identities, not merely in the home country but over half the world. States are still able to mobilize considerable resources, and nationalism remains one of the most important props of state power. There is no doubt that these and other circumstances will keep nationalism in the news for many generations yet. Indeed, they have the potential to cause major disruptions and disorder, as well as vast human misery, in the new world order. Despite this, however, it is hard not to see these developments as marginal to the main thrust of contemporary world history. They are more symptoms of a past which has yet to be exorcized than pointers to the future. As Eric Hobsbawm (1990, p. 163) pointed out, nationalism 'is no longer a major vector of historical development'. But if the age of nationalism is over there is no clear view of what will take its place. (For more on this theme, see Poole, 1996b.)

If the argument of this paper is correct, then it would be superficial (as well as premature) for liberals – or socialists for that matter – to celebrate the end of nationalism. Liberalism does not on its own represent a principle with sufficient power to stand against the contradictory tendencies towards political fragmentation, the transnational centralization of economic power and the cultural diversity characteristic of late modernity. The very forces which will erode the force of national identity are also destroying the conditions which enabled the liberal project. Liberalism, like nationalism, is a creature of a period in which the state could claim effective power within a specific geographical area. If the main item on the liberal agenda was to place limits on this power (and that of its sometime partner, democracy, to bring it under popular control), then the liberal panoply of rights needed state protection. The identification of citizenship with national identity served both to legitimize the kind of state power liberalism needed and also to provide the cultural climate in which liberal rights might be exercised.

If the new era of global capital, political fragmentation and cultural diversity spells the end of nationalism and the forms of identity which it has created and reflected, it is hard to see how liberalism can survive that demise.

References

Gauthier, D. (1986), *Morals by Agreement*, Clarendon Press, Oxford.

Goodin, R. and Pettit, P. (eds) (1993), *A Companion to Contemporary Political Philosophy*, Blackwell, Oxford.

Hegel, G.W.F. (1977), *The Phenomenology of Spirit* (trans. A.V. Miller), Clarendon, Oxford.

Hegel, G W F (1991), *Elements of the Philosophy of Right* (trans. H.B. Nisbet), Cambridge University Press, Cambridge.

Hobsbawm E.J. (1990), *Nations and Nationalism since 1780: Programme, Myth, Reality*, Cambridge University Press, Cambridge.

Kant, I. (1956), *Critique of Practical Reason* (trans. L.W. Beck), Bobbs-Merrill, Indianapolis and New York.

Locke, J. (1975), *An Essay Concerning Human Understanding*, Nidditch, P.H. (ed.), Clarendon Press, Oxford.

Margalit, A. and Raz, J. (1995), 'National Self-Determination' in Kymlicka, W. (ed.), *The Rights of Minority Cultures*, Clarendon Press, Oxford.

Miller, D. (1995), *On Nationality*, Clarendon Press, Oxford.

Nietzsche, F. (1967), 'On the Genealogy of Morals' in *On the Genealogy of Morals* and *Ecce Homo* (trans. W. Kaufmann), Vintage Books, New York.

Poole, R. (1996a), 'On Being a Person', *Australasian Journal of Philosophy*, Vol. 74, No. 1, pp. 38–56.

Poole, R. (1996b), 'Nationalism: The Last Rites?' in Pavkovic, A. et al. (eds), *Nationalism and Postcommunism*, Dartmouth, Aldershot.

Poole, R. (1996/97), 'Freedom, Citizenship and National identity' *The Philosophical Forum*, Vol. 27, Nos 1–2 , pp. 125–48.

Poole, R. (forthcoming 1998), 'National Identity, Multiculturalism and Aboriginal Rights: An Australian Perspective' in Couture, J. et al. (eds), *Rethinking Nationalism, Canadian Journal of Philosophy*, Supp. Vol.

Skinner, Q. (1990), 'The Republican Ideal of Political Liberty' in Bock, G. et al. (eds), *Machiavelli and Republicanism*, Cambridge University Press, Cambridge.

Tamir, Y. (1993), *Liberal Nationalism*, Princeton University Press, Princeton.

Taylor, C. (1985), *Human Agency and Language: Philosophical Papers I*, Cambridge University Press, Cambridge.

Walzer, M. (1989), 'Citizenship' in Ball, T. et al. (eds), *Political Innovation and Conceptual Change*, Cambridge University Press, Cambridge.

5   The Discourse of Liberalism in Post-Socialist Europe

LUBICA UČNÍK

> A spectre is haunting Europe – the spectre of nationalism. All the Powers of old Europe have entered into a holy alliance to exorcise this spectre ... (*Manifesto of the Communist Party*, 1848).

The focus of this article is contemporary debate about nationalism versus individualism, using as an example issues raised following the splitting up of Czechoslovakia into two separate nation states. In particular, I shall concentrate on problems concerning the relation between the concept of the individual and the concept of a nation, with the aim of interpreting nationalism from a more fruitful perspective than that of a singular opposition between these. My central claim is that everything depends on what exactly it is that is being asked; and I conclude that the value of many questions currently being asked is far from clear.

I

Central to the debates about post-1989 developments in Central and Eastern Europe are the analyses of the sociopolitical changes undertaken by Slavoj Žižek (1990, 1992, 1994a, 1994b and 1996)[1] and Renata Salecl (1992 and 1994). Žižek, in particular, engages with issues of nationalism and the way in which these arose in the context of Central and Eastern Europe after 1989 in a systematic manner. His Lacanialism Hegelianism, however, requires to be countered, for, as I shall argue, it ultimately disables political *dialogue*. Far from offering a new approach to the perennial problem of nationalism, Žižek's Lacanian understanding of nationalism offers little improvement on standard analyses. Take for example the typical characterization of nationalism as the resentment – usually economically based – of a particular community against some minority, such as to result in the latter's being treated as a scapegoat: a classic example of this kind of hostility is the recurring pogroms against a

Jewish population blamed for the economic and social ills of the society concerned. Žižek's account of such bigotry is much more elaborate than the typical account outlined. Whether or not such scapegoating may be clarified by describing it as a 'theft of enjoyment', his claim that liberalism actually requires its opposite, nationalism, to retain, or even to create, its own identity as 'good' – so that, no less than racist societies, liberalism depends upon an excluded 'other' – his account does not move beyond the framework of our binary way of thinking, beyond the language of *Aufklärung*. It does not, therefore, offer a way forward, whether or not its account of nationalism is rendered 'deeper' courtesy of Lacan.

Žižek suggests that nationalism arose in post-1989 Central and Eastern Europe as something to fill the void left by the end of 'actually existing socialism'. Using Lacanian psychoanalytic concepts to make his point, Žižek claims that the notions of nation and individual, far from being there, ready made and awaiting use, are examples of a 'Thing': the notion of a retrospectively posited origin, which is perceived as original only *after* its loss or its noticed absence. A 'Thing' is always posited *in the second instance* through specific rituals: for example, the celebration of national emblems or folk music; or, in the case of liberalism, the free press, elections or the idea of a limited government. Rather like the 'Victorian Christmas' of English Christmas cards, it is only then, according to Žižek, that *the effect* of these rituals produces the rediscovery or reproduction of the 'original' belief in nationalism, liberalism, democracy, equality or freedom of choice. Žižek argues that this process of the rediscovery of origins is a case of 'inverted causality' (or, as I would argue, circularity): the specific belief is generated or constructed through the nostalgic rituals of a particular community, supposedly celebrating those origins *as* origins, even though invented retrospectively.

Žižek amplifies his argument by moving on to the idea of an imagined community, building to some extent on Benedict Anderson's (1991) claim that the community is held together by a common language and the common cultural artefacts which its members share and that what is now seen as the historical roots of national identity was in fact invented by the intelligentsia in the 19th century. Žižek argues, however, *pace* Anderson, that the idea of nation is not *only* an imagined community, not only the constructed narrative of its members which defines a nation's way of life.[2] There must be something more to account for the way a community imagines itself as a nation, Žižek argues (1990, p. 51):

[T]he element that holds together a given community cannot be reduced to the point of symbolic identification: the bond linking its members always implies a shared relationship toward a Thing, toward Enjoyment incarnate.

Typically, members of other ethnic groups within the nation – their different way of life, habits and customs – are understood as a surplus of enjoyment and perceived as a threat to the very existence of the nation, to the nation's *particular* enjoyment. Žižek suggests that what is at stake in the development of an idea of a nation is the idea of the hatred of the Other as essentially the hatred of our own enjoyment which we cannot handle and do not want to acknowledge. But this perception of the Other's enjoyment as an impediment to one's own fulfilment is, in actual fact, a fantasy to mask the impossibility of our own full enjoyment. More generally, the problems inherent in society are articulated in the belief in the inferiority of the Other. On Žižek's view, the Other is seen as the only impediment to the happiness attendant upon our chosen way of life. In Czechoslovakia, for instance, the Czechs were unwilling to understand the Slovaks' desire for their own state. So the Slovaks accused the Czechs of centralism and of 'Czechoslovakism': that in Czechoslovakia, there was only one political identity, Czechoslovak. So, for instance, a common Slovak grievance was the fact that the term 'Czechoslovak' tended to be contracted to 'Czech', leaving Slovaks out of any linguistic, and hence political, description.

When the Slovak state was finally established in 1993, the Czechs were characterized by the Slovaks as thieves who had stolen Slovak assets by not returning to Slovakia what had rightfully belonged to it. At the same time, the Czechs, before the splitting up of Czechoslovakia, had accused the Slovaks of draining Czech money from the budget, since they were supposedly having to support the backward Slovak economy. After the establishment of the Czech Republic in 1993, the Slovaks were perceived as irrational nationalists who would rather have their own state, rather than enjoy the benefits of a free market economy and higher living standards. As a result, the common Czech perception of Slovakia was that the Slovak economy was going 'down the tube' (Tucker, 1993–94).

Žižek calls this kind of thinking the 'theft of enjoyment'. He suggests that:

[W]hat sets in motion this logic of the 'theft of enjoyment' is of course not immediate social reality – the reality of different ethnic communities living closely together – but the *inner antagonism inherent to these communities* (1990, p. 56: emphasis in original).

According to Žižek, then, the problem does not lie in the differences in the national enjoyments of these separate national communities, in this case Czechs and Slovaks, and in their different cultural heritages and languages, but rather in the internal problems of these communities which the former masks – namely the inherent problems generated by the capitalist system whose basic feature is its inherent structural imbalance, with its resultant antagonisms and constant crises, which incessantly revolutionize the conditions of its existence.

Thus, according to Žižek, the idea of a different approach to the economic management of Czechoslovakia – the need to 'revolutionize', to establish a market economy, versus the fact that closing down (largely Slovak) heavy industry would create far more unemployment for Slovaks than for Czechs – is translated into a nationalist framework. Žižek argues that the antagonism inherent in capitalist society is transposed to the conceptual framework of nationalist antagonism, which then becomes a fantasy of enjoyment: and this fantasy is projected onto the Other, excluding those designated thereby from, and seeing them as a threat to, the nation's way of life. It follows, then, that the following belief becomes widespread: 'if only we can exclude *them* from our midst, everything will be all right'. Therefore, a common argument in Slovakia was that, with the establishment of the Slovak State, the Czechs could not take away what was rightfully Slovak; and in the Czech Republic, the argument was that they could go forward alone, and that the Czech economy would boom because they would not have to support 'backward' Slovakia. These positions, however, Žižek would argue, were themselves perceived as nationalistic, rather than as fundamentally economic, ones – whereas the 'Other' of both Czechs and Slovaks actually arose out of socioeconomic states of affairs, and not out of any deep-seated nationalism already present in the then Czechoslovakia.

So far, so good. But what does Žižek's analysis leave us with which the standard notion of scapegoating – without benefit of Lacan – does not provide? What is gained by adding Lacanian psychoanalytic conceptions to economics? I shall return to this issue presently. First, however, it will be useful briefly to look at Salecl's approach to nationalism. Building on an analysis broadly similar to that of Žižek, she goes on to argue that nationalism is always likely to defeat liberalism, since, as a defence of 'us against them', it is both a starting point of a political practice *and* its final achievement. However it is in the final analysis constituted, nationalism – in its creating/expressing identity – exerts a power which neither economic nor political ideology can command. Thus the losers in the kind of political climate prevalent in Slovenia after 1989 were liberals, since they did not use the idea of nation as a final explanatory horizon for their policies. Maybe so. But can the Slovenian experience be generalized? How would this kind of analysis explain the development of political thought in the Czech Republic? In the Czech Republic after 1989, the idea of nation was used by the Czechs only to describe the alleged irrationality of the Slovaks' desire for an independent political formation. Tucker argues, in fact, that the Czechs were 'thoroughly non-nationalistic' (1993–94, p. 179). The idea of nation was not a final explanatory horizon for the Czechs. Yet there was such a final explanatory horizon in the Czech political discourse of the time – the idea of a free market, articulated in particular in the rhetoric of the prime minister, Klaus. He postulated a flourishing Western economy based on the concept of 'the hidden hand' of the market and used it against the ostensibly discredited notion of a planned economy. It was certainly a matter of 'us against them': but neither 'we' nor 'they' were nationalities, but rather economic models. It seems, then that the binary logic of 'us against them' is pertinent not only to the debate about *nationalism* but is embedded more generally in the way we understand the world around us. If so, then, it may be that it is logic, rather than (a particular understanding of) the Other and of identity which is fundamental. And it is that idea that I wish to explore.

II

I suggest that there are two possible approaches. One approach to the question of the relevance of Žižek's and Salecl's arguments to the political development of the Czech and Slovak Republics would be to question the applicability of their analyses to specific developments in the Czech Republic and therefore to call into question the theoretical significance of their respective analyses of nationalism as such. Another approach, however, would be to suggest that Žižek and Salecl's accounts are more radically flawed because they are trapped in the very language of *Aufklärung* which they criticise.

Žižek asserts that the origins of every society are connected with a violence that every subsequent history tries to smooth over. He claims to show (1992, pp. 26–7) how in 1989, in Slovenia, Slovenian communists, punks and students, as he describes them, who were genuinely working towards the democratization of society, were, in the end, disposed of: after the free elections, they were simply obliterated from the 'historical picture'. Consequently, the subsequent winners in the political struggles of the time closed off precisely those open political practices which were supposed to be specific to the origins of a new political formation. According to Žižek, those origins were dismissed from history just as soon as they had finished the task of helping to actually undermine 'actually existing socialism'. After their electoral victory, the new, nationalist, rulers of Slovenia strangled the very democratizing process which had helped them to power. Maybe so. But the Czech experience prohibits any generalization of this sort of account of 'origins': for Havel's becoming the President of Czechoslovakia in 1989, *and then again of the Czech Republic after 1993*, defies this kind of explanation. Havel was among those who were actively working towards a dismissal of an 'actually existing socialism'. Thus, he was part of the formation designated by Žižek as 'communists, punks and students'. So, his current presidency, it would seem, defies the Žižekian logic of origins. Let me try to indicate why this is so, and to justify my critique of Žižek's – and Salecl's – approach as suffering from reliance on the very dualism to which it objects.

Žižek (1992) describes the shift in political ethics from 'open' politics to nationalist 'closure' by means of Fredric Jameson's concept of the 'vanishing mediator'.[3] Žižek's claim is that political elections ended the short burst of freedom of speech and thought, closing off any open-ended possibilities of debate or action – possibilities raised by the openness of political conditions before the elections as a result of political uncertainty about the future development of society after the disintegration of 'actually existing socialism'. Multiple discursive practices were therefore possible. Once the election of 1989 was over, however, the victorious party allowed discussions pertaining only to its own political programme. There was no open public space for 'democratic dreamers' or propagators of the Third Way:[4]

> [T]hose who triggered the process of democratisation and fought the greatest battles are not those who enjoy its fruits, not because of a simple usurpation and deception on the part of the present winners, but because of a deeper structural logic. Once the process of democratisation reached its peak, it buried its detonators (ibid., p. 27).

Therefore, according to Žižek, the winners, whoever they might be, were not active participants in the struggle which precipitated their victory. The 'deeper structural logic' of history did all the work. But Žižek's 'deeper structural logic' of history is nothing less than Hegel's idea of the cunning of reason which works secretly behind the backs of historical actors to overcome the initial diremption of *Geist* and guides the way towards freedom.

However, I would argue that there is a different way to explain this putative historical logic of the Hegelian Absolute Spirit or the Žižekian deep structural logic of history. An alternative approach is to point out the possibility of different narratives and different interpretations of origins. For such causal and historical explanations, I claim, are always written backwards from the already constituted present. Thus the alleged obliteration of 'communists, punks and students' from the picture of the origins of a newly constituted society might be explained by the practice that establishes the past historical narratives as always written from the present point of view. And such an explanation does not rely on the dualism of *any* 'us/them' analysis, Hegelian, Lacanian or whatever: in asking a different question of the explanandum, it shows that opposition, whether between 'us' and 'them' or between nationalism and liberalism themselves, need not be the key to understanding such developments.

Against the background of his claim that the post-1989 politics of Slovenia were a victory for nationalism, Žižek posits a crucial question: is liberal democracy possible, and if it is, what are its limits? Žižek defines democracy on the basis of its inherent logic of constitutional checks on state powers. Therefore, as Žižek puts the matter (1992, p. 32), '[t]he elementary operation of democracy is ... the evacuation of the locus of power'. According to Žižek, this empty space cannot be filled: anyone who tries to occupy this imaginary empty locus of power is considered to be a tyrant. It may, therefore, be 'the nation', or the national 'Thing' which, according to this logic, comes to fill this empty space of power. Similarly, Salecl describes democracy as a paradox of desire, a paradox inherent in the concept of democratic power. According to Salecl (1992, p. 63), democracy 'has a desire not to desire absolute power – therefore it limits itself': '[T]he self-binding of democracy is not violence of another kind or the enforcement of power ... precisely because democratic power is in an antagonistic relation to itself: democratic power is a power that refuses to be absolute' (Žižek, 1992, p. 39).

Salecl further suggests that it is precisely this antagonistic relation inherent within the democratic concept of power that contrasts democracy and totalitarianism. According to Salecl, the totalitarian concept of power uses the future retrospectively as a device to legitimate the totalitarian state's present excessive use of power, arguing that the future becomes a reference point of legitimacy for a totalitarian government. It is the very idea of a nation as such which is used to justify a nationalistic government's use of such power as it feels necessary.

The problem with Žižek's account is, once more, his reliance on the explanatory horizon of *Aufklärung*, so that he presents a picture of some sort of *Geist* silently working to evacuate the locus of power. The problem with

Salecl's account is similar but twofold. Firstly, her understanding of the liberal concept of government is limited: she does not take into account the possibility of an articulation of a liberal concept of power as a power *limited by constitutional means*. Secondly, Salecl understands power as a unitary force that can be controlled from above. According to this way of thinking, in the case of totalitarian government a solitary leader exercises power; in the case of nationalism, a national leader controls a population using the idea of nation; and finally, in the case of democracy, a paradox of desire is thought to be inherent in the very concept of democratic power. Thus, the language of Enlightenment circumscribes both Žižek's and Salecl's understanding of the concept of power as a *unitary* notion to the extent that it precludes them from considering different possibilities, and asking quite different questions.

III

However, there is a valuable insight in Žižek's account, and one which I wish to stress here; and that is his claim that we should not understand liberalism simply as the opposite of nationalism. We should instead look at those two discursive formations, he argues, in a dialectical fashion. After 1989, most of the countries of Central and Eastern Europe did not embrace the liberal model – as had been expected by observers from the West. The reason is, as Žižek suggests, that nationalism helps to heal the anxiety of people in post-socialist countries, people who had 'lost the ground from under their feet' when the social order in which they lived disintegrated. What are, then, the answers to Žižek's question of whether liberalism is our final horizon of living?

Žižek argues that the way nationalism is perceived in the liberal West can best be described by Kant's concept of radical evil. He claims that the West sees nationalism as the 'stain that disturbs the idyllic image of pluralistic democracy' (1992, p. 31) and which allows for an eruption of 'enjoyment in its entire "irrationality"' (ibid.). Žižek presents us with an indeterminate picture of nationalism and the idea of nation, however. On the one hand, he argues that the very idea of nation is an inheritance from the past. Yet, on the other hand, in its present transformed form, the idea of nation is also a condition of the possibility of modernity, an 'inherent impetus to [modernity's] progress' (ibid., p. 39). That problem apart, however, what Žižek emphasizes is that liberalism needs its opposite – that is, nationalism – to stress its own virtuousness, so that it is the conception of nation that replaces a 'vanishing mediator' and fills the empty space of power created by the dismissal of an 'actually existing socialism' and not yet filled by liberal democracy. Furthermore, the way to understand nationalism and its ethical underpinnings is not by this simple opposition of Good and Evil, of nationalism and liberalism. For Good and Evil do not necessarily have to be understood as opposites. As he puts it (ibid., p. 33):

> [I]t is not sufficient to conceive of radical Evil as something that pertains to the very notion of subjectivity on a par with disposition toward Good; one is compelled to go a step further and to conceive of radical Evil as something that ontologically precedes Good by way of opening up the space for it·

Thus Good and Evil cannot be simply separated and posited against each other. We should understand Good as *being*, so that Evil is then Good in a mode of becoming. Therefore, given the earlier equation of nationalism with Evil and liberalism with Good, it would follow that nationalism is not an *opposite* of liberalism: there is not, as Karl Popper (see 1963) would have it, an *opposition* between open liberal societies and closed nationalistic ones. Rather, Žižek claims that one type of society *depends upon* the other. The perception of closed nationalism *as Evil* underpins the 'Good' of open liberalism: Western liberalism relies upon the supposedly evil threat to its own enjoyment from its nationalist 'Other'. And Žižek reminds us in this context of Hegel's dictum that 'the true source of Evil is the very neutral gaze that perceives Evil all around' (1992, p. 46). But he suggests no way out of this Enlightenment state of affairs, no way of remedying Western liberalism's interdependence with nationalism and its consequent misunderstanding of nationalism and of its power.

Some examples will be useful here. The lesson of Czechoslovakia in 1968 is worth recalling. During the Prague Spring, there was an attempt to put a different economic model into practice, one which tried to combine a planned economy with something of free market practices and economic competition. When the Czechoslovak Communist Party implemented this new economic model it was crushed by the military occupation led by the Soviet Union. Similarly, in East Germany after the fall of the Berlin wall in 1989, the so-called round table debates between intellectuals, workers and students tried to articulate the possibility of a third way – that is, of a different way of economic management of the state, neither free market nor state planned. These debates were cut short by German unification. One could perhaps suggest a similarity in the way in which these debates were terminated, the ending of economic experiment by Soviet invasion in the case of

Czechoslovakia and the silencing of economic debate by the economic intervention of West German capital in the case of the East Germany. The final result, however, is the same – the silencing of debate. The possibility of an articulation of a different way of thinking was cut short in both cases.

Nevertheless, I would argue that any supposed 'vanishing mediator' that tries to articulate a different way, a so-called Third Way, is already an instrumental way of thinking which is embedded in the same discursive universe as what it is directed against – the universe of Enlightenment. The idea of a 'vanishing mediator' is just another example of the metaphysical idea of the Enlightenment's language, that always tries to find the hidden determinant, which works secretly behind the veil of presence. And yet, the way this hidden reason is represented never transgresses the boundaries of the language of Enlightenment where the only rational way of thinking is thinking marked by an *economic paradigm*. The point is, as someone once remarked, that 'It's the economy, stupid.' A plangent remark by Jürgen Habermas (1990, p. 17) bears witness to this:

> [U]nless something totally unexpected happens in the Soviet Union, we will never discover whether the relations of production under state socialism could have adapted themselves to this condition [market economy] by following the Middle Way [Žižek's Third Way] of democratization.

It would seem, then, that we are back with an economic explanation of nationalism as evil and liberalism as good. Some might argue, of course, that this is sheer economism, and, as such, instrumental. The difficulty is that our present inquiry has not challenged the very instrumentality of our thinking, but only announced an alternative way. Hegel's dictum, reincarnated by Žižek, does not take us out of this impasse. The understanding of the world in terms of Good and Evil remains a way of thinking that sees the world in a binary fashion. It does not matter if Good and Evil are conceived as opposites or as sited along a continuum, forever moving from Becoming to Being: they remain symbiotically related, and as such serve to prevent us from thinking in ways antithetical to the binary structure on which that relationship depends.

IV

Žižek's dualism, however – his 'liberalism versus nationalism' model – is not the sole alternative to those other dualisms he – rightly – finds inadequate or misleading. Nor is Salecl's. It is more productive, I think, to look at nationalism in Central and Eastern Europe in terms of *the extension of individualism* rather than in terms of an opposition between liberalism and nationalism. Rather, just because discussions of 'individualism' and 'nationalism' are both embedded in a particular discourse – that of the Enlightenment or the liberal tradition – the seeming contradictions between them can be resolved. For both rely on the same concepts and use the same 'modern vocabulary of freedom [which] is largely European', to use John Plamenatz's expression (1963, p. 45).

Plamenatz points out that 'freedom', as such, is not a modern European phenomenon, but that the notion that human beings as by nature *free because rational* is a modern European concept. The European understanding is that it is only self-consciously rational people, however, who put a value on freedom. In this way, then, any discussion of freedom as a rational judgment made by an individual or a nation 'wears European dress' (ibid.). Plamenatz outlines three notions of freedom: liberty of conscience, political freedom and freedom from arbitrary inferences (ibid., p. 47) and I shall focus on the latter – freedom from encroachment by outside forces – as the common ground for understanding *both* liberalism *and* nationalism, rather than seeing the one as against the other. Both nationalism and liberalism are premised, in my view, on the idea of negative freedom: in the case of individualism, there is a call for the rights of the individual and freedom from the state; while in the case of nationalism, there is a call for the right of a nation to autonomy, self-determination and freedom from other nations' subjugation of it. *Both* liberalism and nationalism, then, may be seen as being made possible by the very language of the Enlightenment. But because these ideas have the *potential* to conflict with, or even contradict, each other, one who wishes to engage with these notions must find either some means of resolution of the potential tension, or a method of describing the relations between these ideas. For to do otherwise – as Žižek and Salecl do – is to insist from the outset that the potential for conflict *must* be realized, since such conflict is a *necessary* condition of the viability of liberalism. I shall advocate here the second approach and attempt to describe these relations as embedded in the same discourse, rather than nationalism's arising *ex post facto* and retrospectively creating its own conceptual structure.

My starting point for elucidating the relations between liberalism and nationalism in this way is to consider Aviezer Tucker's observations (1993–94) about (and predictions for) the respective republics. Tucker concludes (ibid., p. 182: emphasis added):

[F]or now it seems that the Czech Republic is going to the Right, while *Slovakia is going down the tube*. It is even harder to guess what an anthology of Czech and Slovak political thought will look like three years from now.

What does Tucker understand by the claim, '*Slovakia is going down the tube*'? Is this judgment based on economic indicators? If so, and it seems to be the case that it is, the very phrase being in the language of (pop) economics, the answer is interesting, since the Slovak Republic, according to Western experts,[5] is actually now performing rather well. Given this Western economic evaluation – and in today's free market, discursive universe there is no other calculation possible – perhaps we should regard Tucker's remark as sociopolitical.

Perhaps another of his observations can help (ibid., p. 178):

Havel has a deeper understanding of nationalism than many Western analysts who attempt to reduce to or rationalize it in economic interests. ... Havel understands that Marxist rationalizing reduction of nationalism to economics does not work. Nationalism is an attempt to resolve a modern identity crisis. Accordingly, Havel attempted to accommodate a nationalist and a civil identity as not necessarily identical or mutually exclusive. Unfortunately for Havel, the nationalist approach to the problem of personal identity excludes all others, everywhere.

Here is not the place to analyse this magisterial judgment in any detail: but there are two particular points of interest for my case, two presuppositions at work here. First, Tucker claims that the rationalized subsumption of nationalism to economics is only possible within a Marxian framework. Secondly, he opposes without question liberalism (represented here by Czech civil identity) to nationalism (represented by Slovak nationalist identity). He sees this binary opposition as given, as unproblematic. But this opposition rests on the unquestioned assumption of the independent existence of such a thing as nationalist identity, an existence not already embedded in the same historical and conceptual framework as liberalism (rather than, as Žižek would have it, being its necessary *alter ego*).

The shortcomings of Tucker's approach can be seen by the following experiment. Suppose we consider the situation before and after the splitting up of Czechoslovakia. Take the prime minister of the Czech Republic, Klaus, to be a representative of civil identity, and the prime minister of the Slovak Republic, Mečiar, to be a representative of nationalistic identity. If we present this political characterization as a depiction of the actual political situation in the post-Czechoslovak republics, however, then something goes wrong. For it was Klaus, speaking as a representative of liberalism, who – no less than Mečiar – did not want to compromise his 'economic' approach and who agreed to the split. If we accepted that nationalism is an attempt to solve a modern identity crisis (as Tucker claims), it would follow that such an identity crisis was endemic *only* in those countries where nationalism was a prevalent mode of political thinking. It would follow from that, moreover, that every country with a liberal democratic government was immune to this modern malaise. Indeed, this is precisely the gist of Tucker's idea, which leads him further to equate nationalism with irrationality:

> [I]n reality, nationalism is more desperate than rational. Attempts to deal with nationalists on a rational level are doomed to fail. ... Right now, the nationalist Slovaks and the thoroughly non-nationalist Czechs (even in West European terms) can hardly communicate, let alone reason with each other (ibid., p. 179).

But if Tucker were right, then, given that the then Czechoslovakia enjoyed liberal democracy, how *could* Slovak nationalism have existed within it and how *could* such an identity crisis have occurred? In common with others, Tucker assumes that it was *only* Mečiar who wanted Slovak independence: the truth is that Klaus wanted it just as much – but for *economic* and not *nationalistic* reasons. No wonder there was no referendum on the issue.

What follows from all this is that, since nationalism is understood as more desperate than rational, any attempt to *debate* it must be doomed to failure, for rationality is a necessary condition of debate. But the attempt need not be doomed (as it also must be on Žižek's analysis – liberalism, remember, *requires* nationalism, so that debate would be a threat to it no less than to nationalism itself). Fukuyama (1992) might be right: there may indeed be no space to think otherwise than in the terms of liberalism, a kind of hegemony of the language of the Enlightenment. Yet that need not lead us to despair. On the contrary: the oppositions concerned – liberalism versus totalitarianism; liberalism versus socialism or communism; liberalism versus nationalism— *are already liberal-democratic categories*. Liberalism is not a neutral, stable, given category against which all other categories are positioned in opposition, its own understanding of itself notwithstanding.[6] What is perhaps surprising – or not? – is that critics of liberalism's pretensions to 'neutrality', such as Žižek and Salecl, should have accepted its own self-evaluation as such, when the terms of their critique are predicated on its radical inaccuracy. Is the postmodern turn, one might ask, just another variant of the liberalism it criticizes?

The common terms of liberalism and nationalism, embedded in the discourse of the Enlightenment, are freedom from, self-determination, autonomy and identity. If we look more closely at the language that this discourse takes for granted, it will perhaps be possible to reformulate some of that discourse and to articulate a different understanding of both liberalism and nationalism. Only then may it be possible to see nationalism and liberalism, not as opposing discourses, but as twin components of the modern European discourse of individualism. That final claim is of course no more than programmatic and its exposition demands further work. Nonetheless, it is, I think, sufficient to have made the suggestion. For such an analysis, however embryonic, offers a means of approaching the phenomenon of nationalism – and particularly in post-socialist Europe – which avoids the dead end of regarding it as an inevitable concomitant and opponent of liberalism. While an articulation of nationalism as no less an instantiation than liberalism of the notion of negative freedom will not of itself solve the political problems it raises, it might at least enable us to understand it better. It might even encourage us to think about the possibility of abandoning the language of metaphysical freedom and try instead to rethink the Aristotelian idea of freedom as a 'dialogical' freedom within the polis. Here, freedom would be defined in relation to others, through recognition of and dialogue with others – and not as absolutely opposed to the Other who constitutes a limit to my autonomy. For we need to escape the liberal framework of negative freedom, with both its 'free floating' individuals and its 'irrational' nations.[7]

Notes

1   It is interesting to note that Žižek uses 'liberalism', 'liberal democracy' and 'democracy' interchangeably in his discussions.
2   Žižek remarks (1990, p. 53): '[I]t would, however, be erroneous to reduce the national Thing to the features composing a specific "way of life". The Thing is not a collection of these features; there is something that is present in these features, that appears through them. Members of a community who partake in a given "way of life" believe in their Thing, where this belief has a reflexive structure proper to the intersubjective space: "I believe in the (national) Thing" is equal to "I believe that others (members of my community) believe in the Thing".' And: '[T]he national Thing exists as long as members of the community believe in it; it is literally an effect of this belief in itself' (1994b, p. 202).
3   The idea of the 'vanishing mediator' is a type of not-yet-institutionalized discursive practice.
4   The idea of a 'Third Way' is that of a method of economic management of the state that is different from both a free market approach and from a planned economy.
5   Any weekly 'European Business' section of *The European* offers details economic analysis of all the European countries on a weekly and yearly basis. Two categories are used: the

countries of the EU plus the USA, Japan and Canada, where economic indicators are those of 'growth' (gross domestic product year-on-year per cent); 'inflation' (annual per cent); and 'unemployment' (per cent of workforce); and the Central and East European countries where the economic indicators to be compared are 'industrial output' (change over same month of previous year in per cent); 'inflation' (month-to-month change); and 'unemployment' (as above).

6   See, for example, the articles in this volume by Edward Garrett and Fernne Brennan.

7   This paper was first read at the 'Nationalism and Racism in the Liberal Order' conference at J.E. Purkyně University, Ustí nad Labem, Czech Republic, 1–6 July 1997; I thank participants for their contributions and advice. I also thank Sue Ashford, Bob Brecher and Claire Colebrook for their helpful criticism of earlier versions of this work.

References

Anderson, B. (1991), *Imagined Communities*, revised edn, Verso, London.

Arendt, H. (1958), *The Human Condition*, University of Chicago Press, Chicago and London.

Arendt, H. (1968), *Between Past and Future: Eight Exercises in Political Thought*, Viking Press, New York.

Arendt, H. (1970), *On Violence*, Harcourt and Brace, New York.

Arendt, H. (1973a), *Crises of the Republic*, Penguin Books, Harmondsworth.

Arendt, H. (1973b), *Men in Dark Times*, Penguin Books, Harmondsworth.

Arendt, H. (1973c), *On Revolution*, Penguin Books, Harmondsworth.

Arendt, H. (1986), *The Origins of Totalitarianism*, André Deutsch, London.

Copjec, J. (1996), *Read my Desire. Lacan Against Historicist*, MIT Press, Boston.

Fukuyama, F. (1992), *The End of History and the Last Man*, Avon Books, New York.

Habermas, J. (1990), 'What Does Socialism Mean Today? The Rectifying Revolution and the Need for New Thinking on the Left', *New Left Review*, No. 183, Sept./Oct., pp. 3–21.

Plamenatz, J. (1963), *Man and Society*, Vol. 1, Longman, London.

Popper, K.R. (1963), *The Open Society and its Enemies*, Vol. 2, *Hegel & Marx*, Routledge and Kegan Paul, London.

Salecl, R. (1992), 'Nationalism, Anti-Semitism, and Anti-Feminism in Eastern Europe', *New German Critique: An Interdisciplinary Journal of German Studies*, No. 57, pp. 51–67.

Salecl, R. (1994), *The Spoils of Freedom. Psychoanalysis and Feminism after the Fall of Socialism*, Routledge, London and New York.

Taylor, C. (1995), *Philosophical Argument*, Harvard University Press, Cambridge, Mass. and London.

Tucker, A. (1993–94), 'Waiting for Mečiar', *Telos: A Quarterly Journal of Critical Thought*, No. 94, Winter, pp. 167–82.

Žižek, S. (1990), 'Easter Europe's Republics of Gilead', *New Left Review*, No. 183, Sept./Oct., pp. 50–62.

Žižek, S. (1992), 'Eastern European Liberalism and its Discontents', *New German Critique: An Interdisciplinary Journal of German Studies*, No. 57, pp. 25–49.

Žižek, S. (1994a), 'Introduction: The Spectre of Ideology' in Žižek, S. (ed.), *Mapping Ideology*, Verso, London and New York.

Žižek, S. (1994b), *Tarrying with the Negative: Kant, Hegel, and the Critique of Ideology*, Duke University Press, Durham.

Žižek, S. (1996), 'The Fetish of the Party' in Apollon, W. and Feldstein, R. (eds), *Lacan, Politics, Aesthetic*, State University of New York Press, Albany, NY.

6 The Republican Alternative to Nationalism: Citizenship as Public Office in America

DAVID RICCI

A strong commitment to republican citizenship – partly in principle and partly in practice – is central in helping Americans to maintain political stability and public order. Although this commitment is probably not reproducible in many countries today, it can nevertheless serve scholars as a standard of comparison. As such, it shows how far most other countries are from enjoying a similar sense of citizenship, one which is particularly beneficial in forestalling ethnic antagonisms and national conflicts. Some elements of nationalism do of course exist in America: but they are tempered by the republican vision which is the main theme of this essay.

I

For academics, it was the British sociologist T.H. Marshall who most famously described citizenship as a social status consisting of three parts: civil rights, political rights and social rights. In this typology, the first kind of right conveyed to designated categories of people the status of formal membership in the state; the second permitted some of those members to help make the state's laws and public policies; and the third confirmed that various members of the state were entitled to certain kinds of state support, such as old-age pensions, in times of need. On Marshall's analysis, and especially in the case of the United Kingdom, European governments established these three kinds of right somewhat chronologically, from the 18th to the 20th centuries, as Europe's *ancien régimes* modernized (Marshall, 1964, esp. 71–83). Marshall's typology may be shown as follows:

Marshall's view of citizenship

Elements	Era
civil rights	18th century
political rights	19th century
social rights	20th century

For Americans, citizenship also has three elements. But when Americans think about this subject, they have in mind a set of three civic realities which are not adequately described by Marshall's terms. In the following diagram, these three realities appear as Citizenship I, II and III.

The American view of citizenship

Citizenship	Resources	Ends
I	legal status	obey laws
II	political rights	participate
III	legal status and political rights	exercise virtue

On this view, Citizenship I appears as a *legal status*, consisting of various rights and duties, which is conferred on citizens – in contrast to whatever status is granted to alien residents and tourists. Under ordinary circumstances, good citizenship in this mode is devoted mainly to obeying the laws of one's country so as to help maintain public order and domestic tranquillity. Citizenship II is a *political status*, consisting of rights of which people can take advantage to participate in public life and thereby help create and develop their country's laws. Only some Americans enjoyed Citizenship II in the late 18th century, but government gradually conferred it on an increasingly wider constituency, eventually including women and the country's minorities. Citizenship III is a *public office*, the holding of which in principle obliges everyone enjoying Citizenship II not just to exercise their political rights but to do so virtuously.

On these American terms of reference, the rights that Marshall described may be regarded as attached to Citizenship I and II. However locally defined, they exist in greater or less degree in various countries around the world, as well as America. In many countries, most people acquire these rights either by being born in their state's territory (*jus soli*), or by being born into a family which already enjoys those rights (*jus sanguinis*).[1] In America, however, many people acquired such rights in the past, and some people continue to acquire them today, by coming to the country from abroad and *committing* themselves to uphold America's political ideals. And therein lies a tale of republican citizenship which Marshall's terms do not tell.

II

Americans take their cue from a civic dilemma noted by Aristotle: everyone who is fortunate enough to be a citizen should obey their country's laws and therefore help to maintain public order and the benefits of community; yet the same person, acting as a good person, may undermine public order and endanger the benefits of community by disobeying those laws if they believe that they encourage immorality (Barker, 1958, pp. 101–5). According to Plato, after a duly constituted jury decided that Socrates had corrupted young Athenians and then sentenced him to death, Socrates considered the civic dilemma and chose to commit suicide rather than disparage the jury's legal standing by fleeing from Athens into exile (Plato, 1910, pp. 350–64).

One solution to this dilemma later appeared in republican thinking. A republic, as one kind of commonwealth, was defined by Cicero as a state ruled by citizens *who are united by a sense of justice.*[2] Accordingly, a republic maintains Citizenship I and II but also insists on Citizenship III, which will lead its citizens to propose and uphold mainly *good* laws. In this scheme of things, where Citizenship III is deemed necessary, political participation in a republic takes on the properties of a political *office*, unpretentious but vital, whereby just as elected officials are required to serve the public interest, so citizens are expected to act virtuously in politics – when they vote, for example.[3]

III

America's founding generation made a revolution and wrote a constitution. In the process, they transformed themselves from being British subjects into being American citizens, and they adopted a republican understanding of the new polity they subsequently created.[4] At first, it was mainly property owners who exercised political rights in member states of the federal Union. Republican theory maintained that only such men were economically independent of other men; were able to think for themselves; and therefore were most likely to take into account the community's interests when they voted or held elected office.[5] Here was the ideal of Citizenship III, of disinterested and therefore virtuous political participation. George Washington, a man of substantial property who served his country during the revolution as military commander-in-chief without pay, epitomized this ideal.

One shortcoming of the original republican concept was that it suggested that only a limited number of citizens were likely to behave virtuously and therefore deserved to exercise the rights of Citizenship II.[6] In real life, however, a much larger number of Americans demanded what modern states call political inclusion. Consequently, by 1830, the great majority of white citizens, or at least the men among them, workers as well as farmers, were entitled to vote and hold office in America.[7] Apparently, most Americans eventually decided that widening the franchise to what were then considered to be democratic proportions would not necessarily dilute the stock of public virtue. Instead, they argued that it was not just owing property but also work that builds good character, by sharpening men's perceptions and bringing them into fruitful contact with other people. Therefore it could be work and not just the property that work earned which creates a capacity for political virtue.[8]

IV

Here, then, is the core of a distinctively American concept of citizenship, taking firm shape somewhat before and into the 1820s and 1830s. In technical terms, it is as if Americans had decided that Citizenship II should be *democratic in quantity* even while Citizenship III was *republican in quality*.[9] There was, however, a further American consideration on this subject, which linked citizenship as theory with immigration as fact. On this score, the republican ideal says almost nothing about national origin as a criterion of acquiring citizenship: and therein lies another part of our tale.

V

Some measure of racial and ethnic prejudice has always infected American life. Thus it is true that African-Americans struggled for generations to acquire Citizenship I and II.[10] It is also true that, from time to time, federal legislators enacted various ethnic quotas for immigration. For example, the Johnson Act of 1921 and the Native Origins (Immigration) Act of 1924 restricted the influx of Eastern and Southern Europeans.[11] And there can be no denying that, inspired by open racism, a massive violation of civil rights occurred from 1942 to 1945. At that time, 120,000 Japanese Americans, more than 60 per cent of them born in America, were forcibly relocated away from their homes, mainly in California, to holding camps in states like Montana where, one surmises, they were deprived of any opportunity to practice bad citizenship by collaborating with agents of the Japanese Empire (see Daniels, 1971 and Irons, 1983).

On the whole, however, American political thought does not much resemble exclusionary nationalist reasoning, which can lead routinely and repeatedly to barring certain people from the political community because they are regarded as inherently unqualified to participate. Instead, even when immigration quotas for some countries were reduced, as in 1921 and 1924, most of them were not eliminated entirely; furthermore, the Immigration and Nationality Act of 1965 eventually cancelled national origin as an immigration criterion.[12] In a sense, then, exclusionary nationalism is almost exactly the opposite of what Americans usually think of when they think of citizenship.[13] For it assumes that most or all people outside of the national group are insufficiently committed to virtue as defined by those who belong, in which case they should not be permitted to share in making the nation's laws because they will do so badly.[14]

Of course, in actual everyday life Americans are often suspicious and intolerant of strangers and newcomers, no less than are other people. Neighbourhood segregation proves that point. But as far as immigrants are concerned, Americans have generally assumed, in theory at least, and with some backsliding here and there, that they are capable of behaving virtuously. And thus American immigration laws stipulate that full membership in the community – Citizenship I and Citizenship II – will be granted to those newcomers who swear to uphold America's political ideals.[15] In effect, this is as much as to say that, if someone makes the right sort of personal *commitment*, other people should not consider his or her particular social background to be an *intrinsic* impediment to Citizenship III and therefore a reason for denying him or her Citizenship I and II.[16] In reality, then, while people living in America have over time acquired some national characteristics of language, dress, eating habits and so forth, when immigrants sign on, it is as if, in principle, they were joining an American republic rather than an American nation.[17]

VI

In short, immigration to America has been justified by a republican rather than a national presumption underlying the concept of Citizenship III. But why has that republican presumption been so persuasive for so long? It is important to note that America's view of Citizenship III in fact emerged from religious and philosophical ideas that still inform the country's thinking.

On the one hand, a Protestant notion of *calling*, which eventually developed secular implications, helped to define America's concept of citizenship as a public office. Among its many connotations, the term 'calling' expresses the Protestant view that many different kinds of work are necessary to sustain a community, wherefore God calls upon men and women to serve their neighbours by doing every sort of work well (Morgan, 1965, pp. xv–xx). When the practice of Citizenship II became a fact of political life after the revolution, therefore, one had only to regard it as a special sort of work activity to conclude that it should be done well, i.e., as defined by Citizenship III.

The notion of calling and other Biblical concepts, such as that of covenant, encouraged generations of Americans to regard virtuous behaviour, both private and public, as a *sine qua non* of civilized life in the New World.[18] Even now, on various formal occasions, such as during Fourth of July celebrations, public officials and citizens remind each other of their responsibilities to the community. Here, speakers return repeatedly to what scholars call a jeremiad, a form of exhortation insisting on moral renewal (see Bercovitch, 1978).[19] Or, as John Winthrop long ago admonished his fellow Puritan colonists in Massachusetts, they must never forget that they had covenanted with God to build a new Jerusalem, to live together 'as a city on a hill' (Winthrop, 1987, p. 26).

On the other hand, some concepts which were more secular, and which arose during the Enlightenment, also informed the notion of citizenship as public office. Here, American thinking about the state of nature and its implications was especially important. Most early immigrants to America, no matter how economically deprived or politically marginal in Europe, came to the New World possessed of cultural baggage that facilitated their becoming citizens of a new state attuned to the aspirations of that continent. Political theorists did not at first pay much attention to this sociological reality, though, and, as a result, Americans commonly posited a 'natural man' who was capable of reason and understanding without reference to any ethnic background or special training that would qualify him to achieve either.[20] It followed that, when such men espoused republican principles, they were able successfully to discharge the duties of all public offices, including that of citizenship.

American leaders have frequently and even memorably expressed these Enlightenment ideas.[21] Thus Thomas Jefferson held that American farmers were more sensible than philosophers;[22] Andrew Jackson insisted that ordinary men are capable of holding public office;[23] and Abraham Lincoln had in mind a polity of 'natural men' when he praised America's Union as 'government of the people, by the people, and for the people'.[24] More recently, Henry Kissinger, Zbigniew Brzezinski and Madeline Albright have all demonstrated the apparent validity of such sentiments, showing that it is a commitment to American ideals, and not some particular ethnic background, which qualifies the 'natural man or woman' to join and serve the American political community.

VII

Let us put all of this into larger perspective. Over the last two centuries, European political thought and practice have been more nationalistic than republican. Certainly few European governments welcomed large-scale immigration.[25] In such circumstances, it seems reasonable to regard citizenship almost as a prized possession, a status that confers valuable rights on those who enjoy it, so that Marshall's evocation was of a specifically European reality when he described citizenship mainly in terms of the rights it entailed and the evolution they had undergone.

In America, by contrast, the controlling reality has long been republican thinking, something that facilitated large-scale immigration. As time passed, of course, immigrants came to constitute a diminishing fraction of the total American population, and thus most Americans now acquire citizenship like people in many European countries, by *jus soli* or *jus sanguinis*. Nevertheless, the immigrant story is vitally important to public life, for it shows how Citizenship I, II and III combine in America to help avoid ethnic frictions and national antagonisms.

VIII

This last point can be illustrated by means of scholarly terms first used more than 10 years ago by the political scientist Michael Sandel. According to Sandel (1984) at that time, the philosopher John Rawls was misguided in his reasons for suggesting that a democratic polity should distribute political rights and economic benefits almost entirely equally. Rawls, said Sandel, had argued as if, in theory, people could be regarded as socially 'unencumbered', as if men and women could think without preconceptions and were therefore likely simply to agree that justice demanded such a fairly egalitarian distribution.

The problem here, to paraphrase Sandel, is that real-world politics has to deal with people whose outlooks are shaped by living together, and who are therefore encumbered, for better or for worse, in many ways, by birth, gender, race, ethnic origin, religious inclination, economic circumstances and more. Such people cannot easily divest themselves, even momentarily, of preconceptions. Accordingly, democratic policies should not flow from a philosophical abstraction which assumes that people are in some crucial and abstract sense the same. Governments must, instead, maintain a spirit of compromise among various members of the community, even if that requires recognizing their differences rather than enacting laws which would ignore what sets them apart.

IX

In a way that Sandel did not foresee, his terms 'encumbered' and 'unencumbered' can be redeployed to provide insight into how America's concept of citizenship helps the country to avoid the more extreme group conflicts. In this regard, it is a great but useful paradox in American political thought that, although people in America know that they are socially encumbered – what human being could be otherwise? – there is a persistent sense in which the country believes they are *not*.

The paradox is ubiquitous. On the one hand, scholars, pollsters and even talk show hosts tell everyone that they and other voters are encumbered with various hopes and fears, aspirations and expectations, preferences and prejudices. Accordingly, politicians carefully assess such attitudes and run for office at least partly by appealing to them. On the other hand, politicians often refrain from addressing those attitudes openly. Instead, they usually speak to voters inspirationally, in terms taken from the republican story, as if citizens should lay aside their private ends and decide how to vote in line with some generous estimate of the public interest.[26] That was what John F. Kennedy did, for instance, when he urged Americans to ask themselves not what their country could do for them, but rather what they could do for their country ('Inaugural Address' (1961) in Kennedy, 1962, pp. 6–11).

What does this mixture of realism and idealism suggest? For one thing, American politicians use republican language because it works, and it works because it resonates with what voters want to hear. We must conclude, then, that Americans are somewhat inconsistent when they think about citizenship: at one level of consciousness they know that they and their neighbours are encumbered; even while, at another level of consciousness, they believe that they and their neighbours are capable of pursuing the public interest.[27]

Yet this is a sort of doublethink, to use George Orwell's term, that in fact contributes a great deal to maintaining public order and domestic tranquillity. After all, by maintaining faith in the republican conception of an effective community of unencumbered 'natural persons', Americans are given no cause for regarding other Americans as *a priori* unfit for Citizenship I and II. Of course, there are a great many ethnic, regional, racial and gender groups in America. But apart from normal and routine manifestations of social competition and discrimination, nothing in the republican canon encourages Americans to regard any of these groups as burdened by preconceptions which, strictly speaking, make them unworthy of exercising the office of citizen.[28]

X

To sum up, it is republican thinking which explains why, in most public forums and for many years, Americans have assumed that they should not heighten inter-group tensions by labelling any group of voters as dangerous to the rest. Here, then, is a major reason why, to a far greater extent than in Europe, *serious* group frictions in America have either not arisen or have been handled *relatively* peacefully within the everyday processes of democratic bargaining and compromise. It can be argued that slavery caused the Civil War and that serious racial friction, including lynchings and rioting, have appeared from time to time since that war. But by many standards, great progress has been made in this area. For example, African-Americans now possess full citizenship in the sense of equal political rights, and there are no indications that they will in the future be deprived on that score.

XI

A word to the future. In the cognitive world of two-level thinking about American citizenship, one may somewhat believe in certain ideals even while one does not quite believe they can be entirely fulfilled. Thus today, some American proponents of multiculturalism hope that the country will create what they would define as good laws inspired by, in effect, Citizenship III. However, the same multiculturalists may also argue, sometimes elliptically, that those laws have not yet been enacted because not all people have a capacity for sufficiently disregarding their encumberances and serving the public interest.[29]

How should we regard this recent strand of political speculation in America? On the one hand, it emerged in recent decades together with a tendency of some Americans to express, in public opinion polls, growing dissatisfaction with government and politics.[30] On the other hand, why some Americans today have less regard than they once did for major institutions of public life is not always clear and may have as much to do with their changing perceptions of those institutions as with a discovery of new facts relating to their operation.[31] However that may be, the multiculturalists probably do not speak for a majority of their compatriots on the issue of whether or not, in principle, most people can or cannot be relied upon to fulfil the duties of citizenship as a public office.[32] Furthermore, it is to be hoped that their sharp criticism of various kinds of voters, for allegedly infusing public policies with specific biases, does not lead to embitterment and Balkanization in American politics.[33]

Notes

1   For a discussion of these legal principles and how they are related to acquiring citizenship in two European countries, see Brubaker (1992).

2   In a republic – that is, in a state called *res publica* ('the public's affair') – citizens were to pursue their collective wellbeing by enacting and maintaining laws that confirm the natural law of justice. See Cicero (1929).

3   See Tussman (1960), who speaks of the democratic citizen as a 'guardian agent' (pp. 99ff) fulfilling an 'office' (pp. 108ff) which requires him or her to act in the public interest.

4   See Pangle (1988, p. 278): 'To a perhaps unparalleled degree ... [America] is founded on the contention that patriotism must express more than simply loyalty to what is one's own, that it must also express loyalty to what is good, and some truly self-conscious awareness of the possible tension between what is one's own and the good.' For an example of what Pangle had in mind, see Jefferson (1995, pp. 42–3): '... every difference of opinion is not a difference of principle. We are all Republicans, we are all Federalists. If there be any among us who would wish to dissolve this Union or to change its republican form [emphasis supplied], let them stand undisturbed as monuments of the safety with which error of opinion may be tolerated where reason is left free to combat it.'

5   On republican ideas mainly before they reached the New World, see Pocock (1975). On

republicanism in early American life, see Wood (1991, pp. 95–225).

6   More than half of America's adult white males were originally enfranchised. See Bailyn (1967, p. 87).

7   The evolution of voting rights in this era is traced in Williamson (1960).

8   On Andrew Jackson praising work for engendering virtue in the lives of planters and farmers, mechanics and labourers, see Meyers (1957, pp. 21–3). Making the same connection between work and virtue, Abraham Lincoln described America as a land of opportunity, where any man can work with natural energy and talents, can save part of his earnings to buy tools or land, can go into farming, industry or commerce, and can eventually oversee his capital, prudently and profitably, to employ other men on their way up. Thus by force of character any American, according to Lincoln, can become a man of independent means who *continues* to work and thereby *continues* to enjoy good character based on property *and* enterprise. See Lincoln (1953, Vol. III, pp. 477–80).

9   Enthusiasm for a democratic franchise complemented by republican behaviour is expressed, for example, in O'Sullivan (1954, p. 22): 'We believe ... in the principle of *democratic republicanism* ... [emphasis in the original]. We have an abiding confidence in the virtue, intelligence, and full capacity for self-government, of the great mass of our people, our industrious, honest, manly, intelligent millions of freemen.'

10 Under varying local circumstances, free Negroes obtained what amounted to Citizenship I and II in some Northern and Western states before the Civil War (1861–65). Nevertheless, the Supreme Court ruled, in *Dred Scott v. Sanford* (1857), that such persons were not entitled to the privileges and immunities of citizens of the United States. This decision was overridden in 1870 by the Fourteenth Amendment to the Constitution, which declared that 'All persons born or naturalized in the United States and subject to the jurisdiction thereof, are citizens of the United States and of the State wherein they reside. No state shall make or enforce any law which shall abridge the privileges or immunities of citizens of the United States ....' However, after Congress enacted the Fourteenth Amendment, vigilante violence and laws enforcing segregation in Southern and Border states until well after World War II prevented many former slaves and their descendents in those states from voting and exercising other political rights embodied in the concept of Citizenship II.

11 The legislative history of immigrant restrictions in 1917, 1921 and 1924 is complex. Beyond racism, it includes considerations relating to fear of newcomers undercutting old timers' wages and disdain for some kinds of immigrant family behaviour. These considerations and various racist impulses are described in Higham (1963).

12 On the 1965 Act, see Jones (1992, pp. 266–9). For excerpts from the text of the Act, see 'The Immigration and Nationality Act' in Rischin (1976, pp. 439–48).

13 The tendency of nationalist ideas to evolve towards advocacy of ethnic superiority and political exclusion is explored by Hobsbawm (1992).

14 America's non-exclusionary character is cited by Walzer (1992, p. 42): 'What is distinctive about the nationality of ... Americans is not its insubstantial character – substance is quickly acquired – but its nonexclusive character. Remembering the God of the Hebrew Bible, I want to argue that America is not a jealous nation. In this sense, at least, it is different from most of the others.'

15 See the 'Oath of Allegiance' in Hennessey (1993, p. 7). This oath is administered to naturalization applicants of good moral character who, by taking the oath, thereby swear to uphold the Constitution and perform national service if required by law.

16 See Roosevelt (1925), 'The Duties of Citizenship', address before the Liberal Club, Buffalo, New York, 26 January 1893, p. 15: 'A man [immigrant] has got to be an American and

nothing else... If, however, he does become honestly and in good faith an American, then he is entitled to stand precisely as all other Americans stand, and it is the height of unAmericanism to discriminate against him in any way because of creed or birthplace...'

17 The primary importance of republicanism is expressed in the Pledge of Allegiance, recited by American schoolchildren every day and by immigrants when acquiring citizenship: 'I pledge allegiance to the flag of the United States of America, and to the republic for which it stands, one nation under God, indivisible, with liberty and justice for all.' The Pledge is reprinted in Ravitch (1991, p. 182).

18 According to a recent research report, biblical concepts constitute one of three moral traditions, along with republicanism and individualism, that are woven into the general thrust of American political thought. See Bellah et al. (1986).

19 A recent example of such moral exhortation was President Jimmy Carter's calling upon voters to join him in asking Congress to enact a strict federal energy policy and thereby sacrifice private gains on behalf of the common good: see Carter (1980, Vol. 2, pp. 1235–41). Part of Carter's argument rested upon the following assertion (p. 1237): 'In a nation that was proud of hard work, strong families, close-knit communities and our faith in God, too many of us now tend to worship self-indulgence and consumption. Human identity is no longer defined by what one does, but by what one owns. But we have discovered that owning things and consuming things does not satisfy our longing for meaning. We have learned that piling up material goods cannot fill the emptiness of lives which have no confidence or purpose.'

20 The classic American statement of this view appeared in the Declaration of Independence, which speaks of 'self-evident' truths that include the right of 'natural men' to create a government founded on their continuing consent. The Declaration was preceded by Thomas Paine's *Common Sense*, which argued that ordinary men have enough sense to understand political principles, their historical circumstances and what must be done to create governments responsive to their will. *Common Sense* is reprinted in Fast (1943, 1945, pp. 6–39).

21 Enlightenment thinkers did not all admire men's natural abilities. Burke, for example, did not. See Burke (1955), who speaks (p. 39) of 'the fallible and feeble contrivances of our reason' and who asserts (p. 99) that '[W]e are afraid to put men to live and trade each on his own private stock of reason, because we suspect that this stock in each man is small ....' But many Americans believed that ordinary men were more competent than Burke surmised, and they borrowed from European political thought mainly its optimistic theme. See Hartz (1955). See also Commager (1977).

22 As he put it, 'State a moral case to a ploughman and a professor. The former will decide it as well, and often better than the latter, because he has not been led astray by artificial rules.' Cited in Hofstadter (1963, p. 155).

23 Jackson (1985, p. 386): 'The duties of all public officers are, or at least admit of being made, so plain and simple that men of intelligence may readily qualify themselves for their performance.'

24 This phrase is from his 'Gettysburg Address' (1863), which is closely analysed in Wills (1992).

25 Foreigners in Germany – mainly refugees, guest workers, and their children – numbered over 7,000,000 by 1997. But local immigration laws, based mainly on nationalist criteria, make it impossible for more than 1 or 2 per cent of these foreigners to obtain German citizenship each year. See 'The German Melting Pot', *Newsweek International*, 21 April 1997, pp. 16–19.

26 See Edsall and Edsall (1992), who argue that, even while race was the key issue underlying American national politics from the mid-1960s into the 1980s, most politicians were careful not to appeal openly and directly to racial prejudice. See esp. ch. 10, 'Coded Language: "Groups", "Taxes", "Big Government", and "Special Interests"', pp. 198–214.

27 The ideal can show up unexpectedly. For example, see Thurow (1981, p. 16): 'To be workable, a democracy assumes that public decisions are made in a framework where there is a substantial majority of concerned but disinterested citizens who will prevent policies from being shaped by those with direct economic interests. Decisions in the interests of the general welfare are supposed to be produced by those concerned but disinterested citizens. They are to arbitrate and judge the disputes of the interested parties.'

28 Thus the Supreme Court decision in *Plessy v. Ferguson* (1896), which expressed judicial sanction for practices that excluded most African-Americans from public life in America, was eventually overridden when the Court ruled against segregation in *Brown v. Board of Education* (1954). At that point, the country became formally committed to gradually overcoming, with considerable agonizing and many delays, much of the racial discrimination that remained.

29 The literature here is enormous. Concerning gender, for example, some multiculturalists argue that there is a sense in which men are almost congenitally unable to understand the world as women do and therefore are highly unlikely to act politically on behalf of various public interests that women tend to perceive. This is a general theme of the feminism which runs through works such as Gilligan (1982) and Elshtain (1981). For differences between men and women with regard to various political issues and candidates, see Baxter and Lansing (1981). Somewhat analogously, with regard to racial difference, Lani Guinier (1994), recommends a system of multiple-voting in local elections so that African-Americans will be able to protect themselves from what she regards as a relentless tendency of white Americans to elect government officials hostile to black interests.

30 For indications of waning political faith in recent years, see Goldfarb (1991), Dionne (1991) and Tolchin (1996).

31 Television may be the chief culprit for changing perceptions and thereby denying expectations. See Meyrowitz (1985) and Postman (1986).

32 Some Americans may oppose large-scale immigration into states like California because they are convinced that newcomers bring down wages and strain welfare budgets. But when it comes to the principle of who is capable or incapable of becoming a good citizen, multiculturalists still seem marginal in America. Thus the old, mainstream concepts of natural equality and the efficacy of individual commitment are still expressed in inspirational American best-sellers like William J. Bennett's (1993) anthology about traditional values. For a wide-ranging argument to the effect that most Americans still believe in their old-time political principles, see Lindholm and Hall (1997).

33 Fear of such possible outcomes is expressed, for example, by Arthur Schlesinger Jr (1992).

References

Bailyn, B. (1967), *The Origins of American Politics*, Vintage, New York.

Barker, E. (ed.) (1958), *The Politics of Aristotle*, Oxford, New York.

Baxter, S. and Lansing, M. (1981), *Women and Politics: The Visible Majority*, University of Michigan, Ann Arbor.

Bellah, R.N. et al. (1986), *Habits of the Heart: Individualism and Commitment in American Life*, Harper Perennial, New York.

Bennett, W.J. (1993), *The Book of Virtues: A Treasury of Great Moral Stories*, Simon and Schuster, New York.

Bercovitch, S. (1978), *The American Jeremiad*, University of Wisconsin, Madison.

Brubaker, R. (1992), Citizenship and Nationhood in France and Germany, Harvard University Press, Cambridge, Mass.

Burke, E. (1955), *Reflections on the Revolution in France* (1790), Liberal Arts, New York.

Carter, J. (1980), 'Address to the Nation on Energy and National Goals', 15 July, in *Public Papers of the Presidents of the United States, Jimmy Carter, 1979*, Vol. 2, Government Printing Office, Washington, DC, pp. 1235–41.

Cicero, Marcus Tullius (1929), *On the Commonwealth*, Book III, trans. and intr. G.H. Sabine and S.B. Smith, Bobbs-Merrill, Indianapolis, pp. 195–228.

Commager, H.S. (1977), *The Empire of Reason: How Europe Imagined and America Realized the Enlightenment*, Doubleday Anchor, Garden City, New York.

Daniels, R. (1971), *Concentration Camps USA: Japanese Americans and World War II*, Holt, Rinehart and Winston, New York.

Dionne Jr, E.J. (1991), *Why Americans Hate Politics*, Simon and Schuster, New York.

Edsall, T.B. and Edsall, M.D. (1992), *Chain Reaction: The Impact of Race, Rights, and Taxes on American Politics*, Norton, New York.

Elshtain, J.B. (1981), *Public Man, Private Women: Women in Social and Political Thought*, Princeton University Press, Princeton.

Fast, H. (ed.) (1943, 1945), *The Selected Work of Tom Paine and Citizen Tom Paine*, Modern Library, New York.

Gilligan, C. (1982), *In a Different Voice: Psychological Theory and Women's Development*, Harvard University Press, Cambridge, Mass.

Goldfarb, J.C. (1991), *The Cynical Society: The Culture of Politics and the Politics of Culture in American Life*, University of Chicago Press, Chicago.

Guinier, L. (1994), *The Tyranny of the Majority: Fundamental Fairness in Representative Democracy*, Free Press, New York.

Hartz, L. (1955), *The Liberal Tradition in America*, Harcourt and Brace, New York.

Hennessey, D.L. (1993), *Twenty-Five Lessons in Citizenship*, 97th edn, Berkeley, Ca.

Higham, J. (1963), *Strangers in the Land: Patterns of Nativism, 1860–1925*, Rutgers University Press, Rutgers, NJ.

Hobsbawm, E.J. (1992), *Nations and Nationalism Since 1780: Programme, Myth, and Reality*, 2nd edn, Cambridge University Press, New York.

Hofstadter, R. (1963), *Anti-Intellectualism in American Life*, Knopf, New York.

Irons, P. (1983), *Justice at War*, Oxford University Press, New York.

Jackson, A. (1985), 'First Annual Message (1829)' in Mason, A.T. and Baker, G.E. (eds), *Free Government in the Making: Readings on American Political Thought*, 4th edn, Oxford University Press, New York.

Jefferson, T. (1995), 'First Inaugural Address (1804)' in Dumbauld, E. (ed.) *The Political Writings of Thomas Jefferson: Representative Selections*, Bobbs-Merrill, New York.

Jones, M.A. (1992), *American Immigration*, 2nd edn, University of Chicago Press, Chicago.

Kennedy, J.F. (1962), *To Turn the Tide*, Gardner, J.W. (ed.), Harper, New York.

Lincoln, A. (1953), 'Address before the Wisconsin State Agricultural Society, Milwaukee, Wisconsin', 30 September 1859, in Basler, R.P. (ed.), *The Collected Works of Abraham Lincoln*, Vol. III, Rutgers University Press, New Brunswick, pp. 477–80.

The Republican Alternative to Nationalism   91

Lindholm, C. and Hall, J.A. (1997), 'Is the United States Falling Apart?', *Daedalus*, Spring, pp. 183–209.

Marshall, T.H. (1964), 'Citizenship and Social Class' in Marshall, T.H. (ed.), *Class, Citizenship, and Social Development*, Greenwood, Westport, Conn.

Meyers, M. (1957), *The Jacksonian Persuasion: Politics and Belief*, Stanford University Press, Stanford.

Meyrowitz, J. (1985), *No Sense of Place: The Impact of Electronic Media on Social Behavior*, Oxford University Press, New York.

Morgan, E.S. (ed.) (1965), *Puritan Political Ideas*, Bobbs-Merrill, Indianapolis.

O'Sullivan, J.L. (1954), 'Democratic Review: An Introductory Statement of the Democratic Principle' (1837) in Blau, J.L. (ed.), *Social Theories of Jacksonian Democracy*, Liberal Arts Press, New York.

Pangle, T.L. (1988), *The Spirit of Modern Republicanism: The Moral Vision of the American Founders and the Philosophy of Locke*, University of Chicago Press, Chicago.

Plato (1910), 'Crito' in Lindsay, A.D. (ed.), *Socratic Discourses*, Dutton and Co., New York.

Pocock, G.A. (1975), *The Machiavellian Moment: Florentine Political Thought and the Atlantic Republican Tradition*, Princeton University Press, Princeton.

Postman, N. (1986), *Amusing Ourselves to Death: Public Discourse in the Age of Show Business*, Penguin, New York.

Ravitch, D. (ed.) (1991), *The American Reader: Words That Moved A Nation*, Harper Perennial, New York.

Rischin, M. (ed.) (1976), *Immigration and the American Tradition*, Bobbs-Merrill, Indianapolis.

Roosevelt, T. (1925), *The Works of Theodore Roosevelt*, Vol. XV, Scribner's Sons, New York.

Sandel, M. (1984), 'The Procedural Republic and the Unencumbered Self', *Political Theory*, Vol. 12, no. 1, pp. 81–96.

Schlesinger Jr, A. (1992), *The Disuniting of America: Reflections on a Multicultural Society*, Whittle Direct Books, Knoxville, Tenn.

Thurow, L.C. (1981), *The Zero-Sum Society: Distribution and the Possibilities for Economic Change*, Penguin, New York.

Tolchin, S.J. (1996), *The Angry American: How Voter Rage is Changing the Nation*, Westview, Boulder, Co.

Tussman, J. (1960), *Obligation and the Body Politic*, Oxford University Press, New York.

Walzer, M. (1992), *What It Means to be An American: Essays on the American Experience*, Marsilio, New York.

Williamson, C. (1960), *American Suffrage: From Property to Democracy, 1760–1860*, Princeton University Press, Princeton, NJ.

Wills, G. (1992), *Lincoln at Gettysburg: the Words that Remade America*, Simon and Schuster, New York.

Winthrop, J. (1987), 'A Modell of Christian Charity' (1630) in Bellah, R.N. et al., *Individualism and Commitment in American Life*, Harper and Row, New York, p. 26.

Wood, G.S. (1991), *The Radicalism of the American Revolution*, Random House, New York.

7 National Institutions and Sub-national Separatism: Crimea and Chechnia

IRINA KHMELKO

Introduction

In 1991 the Soviet Union ceased as a legal entity. The fall of the communist regime was followed by a number of conflicts between the national states of the ex-Soviet Union and their sub-national territories, namely clearly defined territories which are generally populated by ethnic groups which constitute a minority within a national state. Conflicts between national states and their sub-national territories arose in most cases as a result of the latter's irredentist claims. In some cases, such conflicts assumed violent forms, such as that in Chechnia: in others, such as Crimea, they have not become violent. What is puzzling, however, is that the political, economic, and ethnic factors in Crimea were not very different from those in Chechnia. The populations of both sub-national territories differed ethnically from the majority in the national state; separatist movements were well-organized and active; and both territories shared a communist past. Yet Ukraine, unlike Russia, has managed the Crimean separatist movement nonviolently. The questions, then, are what factors contributed to the nonviolent solution in Crimea and what made it impossible, by contrast, for the Russian government to escape a military confrontation in Chechnia?

I shall focus in this paper on the characteristics of the post-communist democratic transition in Ukraine and Russia. In particular, I shall analyse the Crimean crisis in Ukraine and the Chechnian crisis in Russia in 1991–95. Through an analysis of the relationships between the governments of national and sub-national territories – in this case Ukraine and Crimea, and Russia and Chechnia respectively – I hope to demonstrate that the form of such conflicts depends in large part on the national institutions' actions toward the separatist movements of the sub-national territories, rather than on the particular character of those movements. Using the 'legacies of the past' and 'imperatives of the liberalization' framework described by Crawford and Lijphart (1995), and successfully employed by Wise and Brown (1997), I shall argue that the differences between the conflicts in Chechnia and Crimea are largely the result of two factors: (1) key historical legacies of the past regime which had established the framework within which crises had arisen; and (2) the structure of institutions throughout the post-communist transition. While it is the legacies of the past which prepare the ground for post-communist conflict, that conflict arises as a result of institutional actions on the part of the national state concerned.

First, I shall discuss the different arguments presented in the literature on the role of institutions in dealing with ethnic problems. Second, I shall give a short description of the communist legacies which influenced ethnic tensions in sub-national territories in the former Soviet republics. Third, I shall analyse the Crimean and Chechnian cases, with particular reference to the role played by past legacies and modern institutions. Finally, I shall summarize what this comparison suggests with regard to the separatist conflicts analysed.

The Role of Political Institutions

Political institutions play a primary role in defining forms of conflict in the sub-national territories. However, conflict itself is usually a result of interaction between legacies of the past and present institutional activities. Some authors argue that the more immature the political institutions, the more violent the conflicts that arise.

Horowitz (1993, p. 28), for example, argues that 'political institutions and decision rules can make a major difference in ethnic outcomes'. The exclusive character of immature political institutions can result in ethnic confrontation, because they do not allow all groups to pursue their particular interests within the existing political institutions. In the case of such groups in sub-national territories, they are likely to demand separation from the national state in order to build their own political institutions so as to allow their own interests to be represented in the political process. Horowitz advocates changing the rules of the institutional game in order to make institutions function more inclusively. Inclusive institutions, then, will provide conflicting parties with the means of resolving conflicts peacefully. Wise and Brown (1997, p. 2) develop this line of argument, explaining that 'political institutions play such an important role because they structure the political process, determining what political groups get to participate, what actions they can take, who gets to use what resources, and what the rewards and punishments are for each action'. This role, furthermore, is a historically structured phenomenon, so that whether conflicts between nation and sub-nation are resolved violently or nonviolently depends on the capacity of new institutions to deal with old legacies. An important contributory factor which influences the outcome of ethnic conflict is the behaviour of neighbouring states (Pikhovshek, 1995, p. 39): these may either support the sub-national territory in its separatist claims or remain neutral and regard relations between national and sub-national territories' governments as internal ones.

Fukuyama (1996, p. 320) identifies four factors which influence political outcomes: ideology, institutions, civil society and culture. He argues that the 'third wave' of democratic transition was driven by ideology precipitating a massive change at the institutional level; and that this proceeds much faster than changes at the level of civil society and culture. It is likely, therefore, that changing institutions based on emergent values will be in tension with a culture still based on older values. This tension – even contradiction – can all too easily result in conflict. In the cases under consideration, for example, religion plays a major role: religious sentiments provide a foundation for self-identity and political orientation. More specifically, the notion of Ukrainian independence from Russia runs contrary within Orthodoxy to deep-rooted religious symbolism, because of the Orthodox emphasis on the unity of Slavic people under an Orthodox Church, a picture accepted by a considerable proportion of the Russian population. The Crimean wish to separate from Ukraine and unify with Russia seems to be a logical outcome of this. On the other hand, Uniate Catholicism regards union with Russia as unnatural (Hersli, Miller, Mueller and Reisinger, 1996, p. 4). The Catholic population of Crimea (however small it is), therefore, is likely to oppose the idea of separation from Ukraine. National identities, being hardly less deep-rooted, are of course likely to prove a further counterweight to newer ideological and institutional developments.

To sum up, while solutions to conflicts in sub-national territories will depend on a variety of factors, the role of institutions is central because, as Lipset (1996, p. 153) concludes, it is comparatively difficult to manipulate cultural factors, whereas institutions are more readily changed. And indeed, this is exactly what is happening throughout the ex-Soviet Union. Where this engenders a clash with older values and identities, the character of such a clash is likely to depend on that process simply because it is, so to speak, the 'active' factor in the situation. With regard to the Russian-Chechnian and the

Ukrainian-Crimean situations, therefore, it is likely to be the nature of the political institutions at the national level – Russia and Ukraine respectively – which will determine the sub-national – Chechnian and Crimean – responses. That, at any rate, is the hypothesis I wish to explore.

Legacies of the Past

When the Bolsheviks came to power in Russia in 1917, they had to deal with numerous ethnic conflicts. In Lenin's words (1951, p. 73), 'victorious socialism must achieve complete democracy and, consequently, not only bring about the complete equality of nations, but also give effect to the right of oppressed nations to self-determination, i.e. the right to free political secession'. Defining the aim of socialism, furthermore, Lenin wrote that 'the aim of socialism is not only to abolish the present division of mankind into small states and all national isolation; not only to bring the nations closer to each other, but also to merge them'. By the 1960s and 1970s, communist ideologies claimed that the USSR had built a developed socialism; that national problems had been resolved; and that therefore ethnic conflicts had disappeared from the map of the USSR.

The actual history of the Soviet Union's ways of dealing with ethnic groups was among its most contradictory, however. According to socialist theory, ethnic tensions disappear as a result of the dissolution of class differences: that 'dissolution', however, was in practice either partial or nonexistent, and the disappearance of ethnic tensions had to be 'encouraged'. Thus, many ethnic groups were simply – and violently – removed from their territories: the Crimean Tartars and the Chechens, for example. The Soviet strategy for managing a multinational state thus involved, as one element at least, a strategy of 'pre-emptive solutions': in other words, when ethnic tensions seemed unlikely simply to disappear, the Soviet government applied military force, and it was this, together with the threat of it, which kept conflicting ethnic groups from open confrontation. However, each group opposed Russian intervention in what they considered to be their internal affairs. In many cases, therefore, conflicts between national and local sub-national groups turned into opposition to Russian intervention in internal regional affairs. Although the Soviet constitution defined the Russian Federation as a 'free union of free nations, a federation of Soviet National republics', the system was extremely centralized. In Lapidus and Walker's formulation (1995, p. 79):

Russia's 'federalism' was essentially administrative and formal, with its constituent parts lacking constitutionally protected autonomous powers. It also had some peculiar features. Although it was formally a federation, it lacked even the window dressing of a federation treaty, unlike the USSR. And in contrast with the other union republics, Russia also lacked its own separate communist Party organization, Academy of Sciences, television and radio station.

Thus, because all Union institutions were situated in Moscow, there was no perceived need for specifically Russian institutions. When the Soviet Union disappeared, therefore, while most former soviet republics transformed their existing republican institutions into national ones, Russia had to start from scratch and build entirely new institutions. As Lapidus and Walker (1995, p. 79) argue, the void created by the disintegration of the party as a nationwide institution led to a rapid and uncontrolled fragmentation of power and the de facto autonomy of local economic, political, and military actors. And very often those actors acted on behalf of particular ethnic groups.

To summarize, Gorbachev's reforms – *Glasnost* and *Perestroyka* – uncovered, on the one hand, existing ethnic tensions in the various regions of the USSR, while, on the other hand, democratization created the opportunity for ethnic groups to express their demands openly. The rapid disappearance of a major controlling institution – the Communist Party of the USSR – created a power vacuum which led to a 'fragmentation of power'. That vacuum was rapidly filled by local elites, often operating on a nationalistic basis. The way was opened for underlying ethnic tensions to rise to the surface. What is important to emphasize, however, is that the breakdown of the Soviet Union had very different implications for Russia and Ukraine. For Ukraine, it brought independence from Russia and, generally, was perceived by the Ukrainian population as a national victory. For Russia, however, it was perceived and understood as an end of empire and of Russia's domination of the former republics. And that was to affect the nature of their respective institutional developments – which would in turn create very different conditions in respect of sub-national groups in Ukraine and Russia respectively.

The Crimean Case

Crimean Separatism

As historical records indicate, Crimea has belonged to different powerful nations and states: ancient Greece, Turkey, Kievan Rus, Russia, and modern

Ukraine. The current debate over this territory has appeared in the form of a question as to whether it should have the status of an independent state or that of a sub-national territory within Russia or Ukraine. Current debate over Crimea was initiated by Russian government authorities and by political leaders in Russia and Crimea: thus only two days after Ukraine's declaration of independence was recognized, Russian president Boris Yeltsin's press secretary released a statement that, in effect, reserved to the Russian Republic the right to raise border questions with Ukraine – Moscow's mayor Gavriil Popov having declared Ukrainian independence to be 'illegal' (Solchanyk, 1992, p. 37). Anatolii Sobchak, the mayor of St Petersburg, advanced the argument that, if left to themselves, Ukrainians would soon be embarking on a programme of 'forced Ukrainianization' throughout the republic (Solchanyk, 1992, p. 38) and that Russia had therefore to safeguard the rights of the Russian minorities residing on Ukrainian soil. And these are located mainly in Crimea.

The beginning of a separatist movement in Crimea itself can be given as 25 April 1992, when the Constituent Assembly of the Russian-Speaking Population of Crimea met in Simferopol, and Anatolii Los, chair of the Russian Society of Crimea claimed that '[A]ll of us, Russians, Ukrainians, Tatars, Jews are Russians' (*Holos Ukrainy*, 1992). In an interview with the Ukrainian Press Agency on 1 May 1992, Los stated: 'The goal – frankly – is the recreation of the USSR .... Crimea will play its historic role, just as it did two thousand years ago, giving the people of Russian – that is, the people of Rus' and among them the people of Ukraine – spirit, culture, and religion' (Los, 1992, p. 64). On 15 June 1993, a group of deputies form the Sevastopol Council of National Deputies, including representatives of 'Russian Sevastopol and Crimea', the Republican Party of Crimea, the All-Crimea Movement of Voters and the Union of Russians in Crimea, appealed to the chair of the Russian parliament, Ruslan Hasbulatov, and to Boris Yeltsin to include in the text of Russia's draft Constitutional Statute a claim regarding the status of the Crimean port of Sevastopol (Pikhovshek, 1995, p. 43).

Governmental institutions in Crimea had also contributed to a separatist movement. On 5 May 1992, the Crimean parliament adopted the Act of State Independence of the Republic of Crimea. On 14 March 1994, the Crimean parliamentary deputy Alexander Kruglov started a new party to promote the peninsula's unification with Russia. The Crimean Supreme Council adopted a budget that called for Crimean tax and tariff funds to be appropriated in Simferopol instead of in the Ukrainian capital, Kiev. On 24 March 1994, the Crimean president, Meshkov, signed a decree requiring Crimean citizens to perform military service only on Crimean territory. And finally, on 20 April

1995, Crimean parliamentary deputies passed a resolution appealing to Moscow to protect the rights of Russians living in Crimea.

Solving the Problem

A number of factors have contributed to the problem-solving process in Crimea. First, Crimea is populated by many different ethnic groups, including Russians, Ukrainians and Tatars. Second, Ukrainians do not constitute a majority there: the majority of Crimeans speak Russian. Third, the ethnic groups of Crimea differ in their religious beliefs: the Slavic population is largely Orthodox or nonbeliever, while the Tatar population is largely Islamic. Fourth, there have been two major institutional crises in Crimea since the proclamation of Ukrainian independence in 1991. Fifth, international factors are of considerable importance for Crimean development: the United States has repeatedly reaffirmed its support for Ukraine's territorial integrity, which has acted as a brake on Russian claims to Crimea, claims made by certain Russian nationalists despite the Russian-Ukrainian Treaty, which commits both parties to respect each other's territorial integrity. Let us look a little more closely at the first four of these factors.

Crimean history displays constant changes in the quantitative correlation among the different ethnic groups of Crimea. Tatars were the largest ethnic group until the end of the 18th century. By 1987, however, Russians and Ukrainians, who were not distinguished in the Russian census, constituted 45.3 per cent of the population and the Crimean Tatars constituted 32.1 per cent. According to Heinrich Lanz (1919, p. 10), in 1918 Ukrainians constituted 42 per cent of the Crimean population. However, ethnic Russians have dominated the population of the peninsula during the second half of this century: according to the 1989 census, Russians constituted 76 per cent of the population; Ukrainians 25.8 per cent; Crimean Tartars 1.6 per cent – the latter having been deported by Stalin in 1944 and having gained the right to return only in the late 1980s. Different ethnic groups in Crimea thus have very different histories. Russian and Ukrainian groups migrated to Crimea in search of a better life and most settled successfully in the new territory. Tatars, by contrast, have a memory of deportation and when they returned they were made unwelcome, largely on account of their being Islamic. These diverse ethnic groups bring different legacies to the current situation. Russians, who are mostly nonbelievers or Orthodox, consider Ukrainian independence as 'unnatural'. They tend either to identify themselves either as an independent nation of (*Krumchan*) Crimeans, or as part of the Russian nation. Tatars, however, feel safer within a Ukrainian state, as does of course the Ukrainian population of Crimea.[1]

To summarize, there are different legacies at play in the Crimean case. Some are at odds with each other, such as the desire of Crimean Russians for separation from Ukraine and the Tartars' support for the Ukrainian Crimea. It is significant, however, that there is no data on what proportion of the Crimean population supports the idea of separation from Ukraine or to what degree. The best one can say, therefore, is that while legacies of the past are bound to have influenced the Crimean crisis, their importance is impossible to assess accurately.

Ukrainian Institutions

The role of Ukrainian institutions is much easier to identify than the role of Crimean legacies. Most significantly, the Ukrainian government has taken several major steps which have contributed – whether by direct intention or not – to the peaceful resolution of conflict situations in Crimea. On 12 February 1991, the Ukrainian Supreme Soviet had adopted a law restoring the autonomy of Crimea within Ukraine's borders, giving Crimea much greater local authority than it had had before – without, however, making clear its precise extent. On 29 April 1992, therefore, the Ukrainian parliament removed Article 7 of the law 'On the Demarcation of the Powers of Ukraine and the Republic of Crimea', which contained a clause that the National Guard in Crimea had to consist largely of residents of Crimea. Whereas the previous formulation had implied equality between Ukraine and Crimea, the law now clearly defined Crimea's status as an autonomous but constituent part of a unified Ukrainian state. The Crimean government, however, ignored most Ukrainian legal acts. As a result, on 22 September 1994, the Ukrainian Parliament passed a resolution 'On the Political and Legal Situation in the Autonomous Republic of Crimea', pursuant to which the Crimean Supreme Council was given until 1 November 1994 to bring the constitution and laws of Crimea into line with the constitution and laws of Ukraine. On 17 March 1995, the Ukrainian parliament passed legislation to abolish Crimea's constitution and presidency: since, however, only nine per cent of Crimeans supported their popularly elected president (*Uriadovuy Kurier*, 1995), this did not have political impact one might have expected. On 31 March, the Ukrainian president went a step further and issued a decree temporarily subordinating the Crimean government directly to the cabinet of ministers in Kiev and reserving for himself the right to appoint Crimea's prime minister.

At the same time, however, the Ukrainian government tried to gain the support of the Crimean population by pointing out that Ukraine produced nearly 75 per cent of the industrial output that Crimea used, and 85 per cent of its electricity; and that four billion karbovantsi (the Ukrainian currency) had already been spent in order to put public policy programmes in Crimea into effect. At the same time, the president emphasized the fact that Ukraine had been recognized by the international community as an independent country, and that its territory, according to the constitution, included Crimea. More significantly, the Ukrainian government instigated a peaceful resolution of the internal Crimean political crisis in 1994, a conflict between the branches of its government. The Ukrainian government engaged both conflicting parties – the Crimean parliament and the Crimean president – in the process of consultations. The Ukrainian president also stated that he would simply not allow the use of force to settle the conflict between the branches of government in Crimea and emphasized their personal responsibility for the possible consequences of their actions. Thus, the national polity, far from pursuing a classical 'divide and rule' policy, attempted to impose unity.

This was all the more notable in light of the fact that the Ukrainian national government had been acting under constant pressure from Russian authorities. For example, a declaration was adopted in 1994 stating that, although the Russian legislature recognized 'the reality of Crimea being part of Ukraine' (*Gosudarstvennaia Duma*, 1994, pp. 31–2), it was concerned at Kiev's actions and suggested that these could jeopardize negotiations over the Black Sea fleet[2] and the signing and ratification of the Russian-Ukrainian Friendship treaty. A number of Russian politicians argued that if Ukraine were to deploy its military forces in Crimea, Russia would have to intervene to protect the Russian population of Crimea. The Russian president, nevertheless, expressed his respect for Ukrainian territorial integrity and Russia assured Ukraine that it would respect Ukrainian territorial integrity, as guaranteed by the Moscow Trilateral Statement (January 1994). This was further anchored at the conference on Security and Cooperation in Europe (December 1994), with the United States also guaranteeing Ukrainian territorial integrity. These agreements counteracted the threats made by certain Russian politicians, so that it remained clear that the Crimean situation was a matter for Ukraine alone. It was therefore Ukrainian policy which remained the central factor.

To conclude, the Ukrainian national government employed a number of different instruments to stabilize the crisis in Crimea: legislative politics; the development of economic ties with Crimea; consultations; and the development of Ukrainian-Russian relations. Most importantly, as Ukraine had no experience of democratic forms of multi-level government, it experimented with different forms, from almost *de facto* Crimean independence in 1992 to the direct subordination of the Crimean government to the national one in 1995. The result was that the Crimean parliament cancelled regional laws that contradicted the Ukrainian constitution, laws which, although offering 'little economic benefit to Crimea's leadership' (Pohorilova, 1997, p. 19) stood as a provocation, so that their cancellation removed the question of dissolving the legislature.

To summarize, the Ukrainian national authorities have consistently affirmed the pre-eminence of Ukraine's national constitution and legislation over Crimea: but the Ukraine's newly-developing democratic institutions have so far proved to be effective in resolving the Crimean crisis nonviolently. It remains to be seen how the Crimean problem is finally resolved, however.

The Chechnian Case

Chechnian Separatism

When Dudaev was elected as Chechnian president on 27 October 1991, the Congress of Peoples' Deputies of the Russian Federation did not recognize the result of the election. Dudaev's response to that and to the later Decree of the Supreme Soviet of the Chechen Republic on Chechnian Independence was to issue a decree on 1 November 1991, 'On the State Independence of the Chechen Republic'. The Fifth Congress of the Russian Deputies, in turn, claimed the Chechnian decree (as well as other acts) illegal and unconstitutional, and on 1 November 1991, the Russian president announced a state of emergency in the Chechen-Ingush Republic. On 1 June 1992, Dudaev announced an ultimatum to Russia, demanding that the Russian army leave Chechnian territory. In addition, armed groups of Chechnians attacked Russian military bases: and what was at first Russian defence of these bases turned into offensive Russian action.

Commentators on Chechnia largely disagree about what factors contributed to the escalation of the conflict in Chechnia. For some it represents another step in the descent of the whole post-Soviet society towards capitalist barbarism. Others, such as Igor Bunich, argue that it was a struggle between Russian and Chechnian political elites for power which resulted in the Chechnian war (Bunich, 1995). Hasbulatov (1995, p. 24), in contrast, argues that Yeltsin's personal dislike of him led him to ignore his proposals for solving the Chechnian crisis. A common explanatory factor, however, is the extent of the Russian president's personal involvement.

Another critical factor was the modern military equipment and armaments left behind by Russian troops when they had left Chechnia – and explanations of this extraordinary 'gift' also abound. Some argue that it was simply a mistake (Nikolaev, 1995, p. 20). Others claim that it was a deliberate policy, the Russian government planning to use Chechnian military forces to protect Russian national interests in the Caucasus region (Bunich, 1995). At any event, the minister of defence, Pavel Grachev, signed a treaty with Chechnia leaving half of the Russian military equipment remaining in Chechnia to Dudaev's army. (He argued that he did not have any choice, since most of it was already in Dudaev's possession.)

Dudaev, then, supported by a well-equipped army, actively pursued a course of separation from Russia. He refused to sign the Federation Treaty, despite eleven offers of negotiation between the end of 1991 and the end of 1993. On 13 November 1992, the head of administration in North Ocetia – Shahray – agreed with the representatives of the Chechen republic – Mamodaev and Ibragimov – to separate Federal and Chechen troops and to prevent further confrontation, and two days later the Deputy Head of the temporary administration signed a treaty governing the conditions for troop separation. However, all this was to no avail: negotiations failed and military confrontation continued. By the beginning of 1994, the internal opposition to Dudaev's rule had formed a well-armed military force. Again, some argue that the population was very dissatisfied with Dudaev; others (Bunich, 1995) that the Russian national government financed the opposition to end Dudaev's rule in Chechnia. However all that may be, the armed conflict between Chechnia and Russia continued until, after Dudaev's death, gradually dying down: and a Peace Treaty was eventually signed not long thereafter.

Legacies of the Past

Lapidus and Walker (1995, p. 102) suggest that it is useful to distinguish three types of challenge which contributed to centre-periphery problems in Russia: inter-ethnic 'horizontal' conflict between particular ethnic groups; ethnically driven, 'vertical' challenges to Moscow; and non-ethnically driven political and economic opposition to central authority. The first two are relevant to the Chechnian case. 'Horizontal' inter-ethnic conflict in Chechnia resulted from long-standing territorial disputes with neighbouring territories and traditional hostilities to Russia, which traditionally considered the Caucasus a zone of national interest. This was exacerbated by Chechnia's having some valuable natural resources, especially oil. 'Vertical' challenges are often the result of the intimidation of sub-national feelings. For example, many Chechnians feel that Russians are disdainful of their traditions and culture. The majority of Chechens are Muslims, whereas most Russians are either Orthodox or nonbelievers; and this makes Russians 'impure'. Russia, in turn, has a centuries-long history of domination over other nations.

Not Solving the Problem

In 1991, the Russian government made an important change in the administrative structure of the Russian state: the 16 autonomous republics and four of the five autonomous *oblasts* were given the status of republics. Chechnia, which had an autonomous status, became a republic within the Russian Federation. Those changes were legally recognized in the new Russian constitution which was ratified in December 1993. However, these administrative structures were not clearly defined. As Lapidus and Walker (1995, p. 92) argue,

> [N]ot only the division of powers between the center and the territories but also the administrative borders themselves were in dispute. In particular, conflicts arose over whether the constitutive elements of the federation would be the existing or new administrative units; whether these constitutive units would be equal in local powers and representation at the center or whether distinctions should be made on the basis of size of population or ethnicity; and whether existing administrative units should be redrawn without regard to ethnic distinctiveness.

The traditional dilemma of a federal state was, then, present in the new Russian state. Generally speaking, Russia needed to find an administrative structure which would reflect and do justice to the interests of its sub-national territories. It was important, therefore, to decide precisely where power should be relocated, and how much power sub-national territories should have. But these issues were not resolved.

The new Russian constitution proved even more controversial: should the new constitution be preceded by a treaty of federation voluntarily entered into by the constituent parts of the federation; should those constituent parts be given the right to ratify or reject such a treaty; should 'sovereignty' rest with the centre of the localities (would the republics' laws have precedence over federal laws, and would republican constitutions have to be compatible with the Russian constitution); and finally, should secession be a matter for the voters in the constitutive units or had it to require approval by the federal parliament or a nationwide referendum? Nevertheless, 18 of the 20 republics signed a treaty, on 13 March 1993: Chechnia refused. The Treaty left unresolved many of the Russian centre-periphery problems, however. Among these were what the Treaty meant by the 'ownership' of land and natural resources; how profits from exports were to be distributed between the centre and the provinces; relative tax burdens; and the extent and distribution of subsidy of local budgets from the federal treasury. Even more importantly, while the Treaty described the republics as 'sovereign' units – which suggested that the republics not only had a right to refuse to join the federation but could also secede on their own initiative – it specified nothing explicit about any right of secession or secession procedures.

These unclarities were themselves to a considerable extent the result of political confusion over the nature and rule of the Russian state. Thus, for example, the military elite had actively lobbied for a military solution in Chechnia in 1991, a policy blocked by the then Soviet president Gorbachev, who argued that Chechnia was a Russian territory and he did not want any military action on Russian land (Hasbulatov, 1995, p. 21). The Russian president, Yeltsin – had he been contactable at the time – might well have taken a different view. Despite continuing military posturing, however, the Russian government continued its economic support of Chechnia regardless of even the most provocative of Dudaev's actions, arguing that it did not blame the Chechnian population for Dudaev's actions and would support Chechnians in the same way as any other Russian citizens. It seems that its policy was to keep Dudaev's regime in power in the hope that he would change his mind about secession.

Several attempts, meanwhile, had been made to bring the Federal and Chechen governments to the negotiating table. In August 1993, the Chechen minister of foreign affairs visited Moscow unofficially, but no fruitful meeting took place, despite Dudaev's apparent readiness at that stage to negotiate. Again, the reasons for this failure remain unclear – but they certainly suggest at least an element of confusion on the Russian side. The Russian parliament voted in March 1994 to recommend to the Russian president and government to consult all the political forces in Chechnia before entering debate with Dudaev. It also recommended that any Russian negotiators insist on free and democratic elections in Chechnia, Dudaev's attitude notwithstanding. In other words, if Dudaev did not comply with the conditions stated, no negotiations would be possible. President Yeltsin accordingly issued a decree on 15 April

1994, making the Russian government responsible for such consultations. But no negotiations took place: Moscow blamed Dudaev's approach as unreasonable; and Dudaev in turn blamed Moscow. The Russian government's response was to negotiate with the leaders of the Chechen opposition, arguing that Dudaev was not a legitimate leader and did not have the support of the population. Finally, on 29 November 1994, Yeltsin appealed to both sides in Chechnia – Dudaev and the opposition – and called for a ceasefire within 48 hours, threatening to use military force if they did not comply. The ministry of defence of the Russian Federation issued an order to move Russian troops into Cechnia on 11 December 1994. This was the beginning of a new escalation in hostilities between Russia and Chechnia (Bunich, 1995, p. 98). To summarize, the Russian federal government combined both political negotiation and direct military pressure in Chechnia. In the end, however, it relied on military force.

Conclusion

The problems of intergovernmental relations in Russia and Ukraine are not reducible to demands for 'self-determination' or to border disputes between ethnically defined territories. They arise as a result of interaction between the legacies of the past and new institutions: and while we wait for these legacies to change, it will be the character of the political institutions of the sovereign state which will play a crucial role in determining the form of any conflict. A comparative study of the Chechnian and Crimean cases indicates that while both sub-national territories largely shared legacies of the communist past, making conflict between levels of governments in Russia and Ukraine almost inevitable, as the latter undergo institutional transformation, the form of such conflict is greatly dependent on those institutions.

Both the Russian and the Ukrainian governments had to decide how much authority and what kind of authority should be given to the sub-national territories. Both started by granting greater authority to their sub-national territories before restricting them under secessionist pressure. In the end, however, Russia adopted a military solution while Ukraine did not.

A central explanation is that Russia, as noted earlier, had lost its imperial status, whereas Ukraine had gained independence. While a military solution would make Russian political leaders more popular because it would resurrect the image of Greater Russia, the Ukrainian situation was quite different. There was no popularity to be gained by attempting to suppress Crimea, because

Ukraine had itself been recently suppressed by Russia. The crucial difference is to be found in the relative degrees of maturity of Russia's and Ukraine's political institutions.

Russian political institutions proved still to be heavily under the influence of its past, while the Ukrainian government does not have to support an imperial image of itself. It is that which tends to determine the violent or nonviolent nature of centre-periphery conflicts, rather than the specific nature of the sub-national situation.[3]

Notes

1   A generally overlooked population is that living in the steppes: as a mixture of ethnic groups, and having been subject to constant change during the 50 years, it does not have a particularly developed self-identity.
2   At the time, the Ukrainian and Russian governments were involved in negotiations over splitting the former USSR's Black Sea fleet, which was located in the Crimean port of Sevastopol.
3   I should like to thank Bob Brecher for his comments on an earlier version of this chapter.

References

Bunich, I. (1995), *Hronika Chechnskoy Boyny: Shest' Dney v Budenovske* (*Chronicles of the Chechen War: Six Days in Budionovsk*), Oblik, Sunkt-Peterburg.
Crawford, B. and Lijphart, A. (1995), 'Explaining Political and Economic Change in Post-Communist Eastern Europe: Old Legacies, New Institutions, Hegemonic Norms, and Internal Pressures', *Comparative Political Studies*, 28, pp. 171–99.
Diamond, L. and Platter, M. (eds) (1996), *Global Resurgence of Democracy*, John Hopkins University Press, Baltimore.
Drohobycky, M. (ed.) (1995), *Crimea: Dynamics, Challenges, and Prospects*, Rowman and Littlefield Publishers, Inc., London.
Fukuyama, F. (1996), 'The Primacy of Culture' in Diamond, L. and Plattner, M. (eds), *Global Resurgence of Democracy*, John Hopkins University Press, Baltimore.
Gosudarstvennaia Duma. Postanovleniia I Drugie Dokumentu (*Russian Parliament. Decrees and Other Documents*) (1994), (11–25 noyabria 1994 goda), Vypusk 9, pp. 31–2.
Hasbulatov, R. (1995), *Mne Ne Daly Ostanovit' Voynu*, Paleya, Moskva.
Hersli, V.L.I., Miller, A.H., Mueller II, A.G. and Reisinger, W.M. (1996), 'The National Nexus: Religion, Language and Political Values in Ukraine', paper for the *92nd Annual Meeting of the American Political Science Association*, 29 August–1 September, San Francisco.
Holos Ukrainy (*Ukrainian Voice*), 30 April 1992.
Horowitz, D.L. (1993), 'The Challenge of Ethnic Conflict: Democracy in Divided Society', *Journal of Democracy,* Vol. 4, No. 4, October, pp. 18–38.
Lanz, H. (1919), *Ukraina* (*Ukraine*), Gerog Stilke, Berlin.

Lapidus, G.W. and Walker, E.W. (1995), 'Nationalism, Regionalism and Federalism: Center-Periphery Relations in Post-Communist Russia' in Lapidus. G.W. (ed.), *The New Russia: Troubled Transformation*, Westview Press, San Francisco.

Lenin, V.I. (1951), *The Right of Nations to Self-Determination: Selected Writings*, International Publishers, New York.

Lipset, S. (1996), 'The Centrality of Political Culture' in Diamond, L. and Platter, M. (eds), *Global Resurgence of Democracy*, John Hopkins University Press, Baltimore.

Los, A. (1992), interview by Viktor Tkachuk of the Ukrainian Press Agency on 1 May in M. Drohobycky (ed.), *Crimea: Dynamics, Challenges, and Prospects*, Rowman and Littlefield Publishers, Inc., London.

Nikolaev, V. (ed.) (1995), *Chechenskaya Tragedia: Kto Vinovat (Chechen Tragedy: Whose Fault Is It?)*, REA, Novosti, Moskva.

Pikhovshek, V. (1995), 'Will the Crimean Crisis Explode?' in Drohobycky, M. (ed.), *Crimea: Dynamics, Challenges, and Prospects*, Rowman and Littlefield Publishers, Inc., London.

Pohorilova, I. (1997), 'Crimea Resolved: Presidential, but Not Quite Ukrainian Yet', *Eastern Economist*, 17 February, pp. 18–19.

Solchanyk, R. (1992), 'Ukraine: From Sovereignty to Independence', *RFE/RL Research Report*, January, pp. 35–8.

Uriadovuy Kurier (Governmental Messenger), 28 February 1995.

Wise, C.R. and Brown, T.R. (1997), 'Democratization and the Separation of Powers in Ukraine: The Role of the Parliament in the Passage of the New Constitutions', paper prepared for *1997 Annual Meeting of the Western Political Science Association*, Tucson, Arizona.

8 Can the Institutions of the European Community Transcend Liberal Limitations in the Pursuit of Racial Equality?

FERNNE BRENNAN

Introduction

Racial discrimination is like a canker sore on the body politic, involving as it does the differential treatment of people on grounds of race, ethnicity, colour or nationality. Closely linked to racial discrimination are the phenomena of racism and xenophobia, which involve a fear of all things foreign and irrational but perhaps excusable sentiments, capable of being expressed as much by jokes about foreigners as by violent expressions of hatred (Spencer, 1995, p. 127). Spencer argues that such language expresses aspects of mistrust of a person whose language, culture or appearance is different from that of the majority, allied with a conviction that one's own 'race', nation or culture is superior to another's. One immediate impact of racism and xenophobia on people subject to it in the context of the European Community is that a significant number are denied equal access to the internal market. Like majority populations, they are expected to comply with the laws that uphold it and to contribute to it through indirect taxation, but are not accepted as full citizens, let alone as participants. Most worrying is the psychological and political impact that racism and xenophobia have on people in terms of their self-worth and value in the Community. This is well documented.

Less commonly noted, however, is a range of economic consequences. First, racial stereotyping can determine to a considerable extent recruitment from the labour pool. But if people are chosen on the basis of their perceived racial background where that characteristic is not a requirement of the job –

as it generally isn't – this is irrational: efficiency would surely require that the best person for the job be recruited. Second, differential recruitment on the basis of non-European sounding names, for example – of which there is considerable evidence, at least in the UK – constitutes a barrier to the free movement of such workers. Third, such practices cannot but affect the Community's competitive edge in other sectors of industry and commerce in global markets. Finally, the needs of ethnic minority customers in terms of marketing are virtually ignored and the inability to create equal purchasing opportunities for ethnic minority firms to supply goods and services is lost (see Gosing, 1995).

Given that there are sound economic, let alone moral, reasons for opening up the European Community's internal market by providing measures to deal with racism and xenophobia, it is all the more disconcerting to see that the European Community has made little headway in this field. Certainly there exists a nondiscrimination clause in the European Economic Community (EEC) Treaty 1957 in relation to nationality: 'Within the scope of this Treaty, and without prejudice to any special provisions contained therein, any discrimination on the grounds of nationality shall be prohibited' (Article 6, EC Treaty 1957 (as amended by Article G(8) TEU)). This provision was sucessfully used a few years ago by *Cowan*[1] (a British national) against the French Treasury to claim equality of treatment in respect of certain financial benefits available under national law only to French nationals. Such a claim would not be available, however, to a litigant who was a non-national and whose allegation was that the discrimination had occurred on grounds of race rather than of nationality. For there is no equivalent provision that provides that there shall be no discrimination on the grounds of race at the Community level.

There have been certain cases where the issue of race and racism have arisen, but these have remained very much in the background rather than the foreground of litigation in the European Court of Justice. One might have hoped that the European Court of Justice would have taken the lead in this area as it has done in others: its use of the European Convention on Human Rights (1950) (hereinafter ECHR) to protect traditional civil and political liberties (De Burca, 1995), for instance. However, the Court has not been active in this area. In *Prais v. Council*,[2] for example, the applicant relied specifically on Article 9 of the ECHR (1950), concerning freedom of religion, for the annulment of a decision of the Council of Ministers to fix the date of an open competition for a post for which the applicant had applied. This competition was to take place on a Jewish feast-day during which the applicant could neither travel nor write. The opportunity to discuss the issue of race was not taken up by the Court, although the fact that the applicant was Jewish may have been an issue worth exploring in terms of race no less than religion. *Oyowe and Traore v Commission*[3] was a much more obvious case than *Prais* in terms of the issue of race, in that it concerned a staff case in which a claim of race discrimination was specifically raised (amongst other claims) but though the Court found for the applicants, it did so on quite different grounds: and even though this was clearly a ground of contention between the applicants and the Commission, the Court did not fully discuss the implications of the race allegation. There is some sympathy for the Court in the sense that perhaps the ECHR is more readily available for use when there is already some provision in place at the Community level, and because the Court cannot simply invent[4] provisions in order to do justice in a particular case. Yet this is not the view that the Court took with the European Parliament when, in the *Chernobyl*[5] case, it developed a procedural remedy in relation to Article 173 (see EC Treaty 1957 (as amended by TEU)[6] in order for the European Parliament to protect its prerogative powers. Prior to this no such provision had existed. In any event, furthermore, the Court has had the opportunity to develop existing provisions such as Articles 6 and 48, which prohibit discrimination on the basis of nationality. Why is it then, that the term 'nationality' is tied to place of birth or qualifying residence and not widened to include race? The argument that the Court does not have express competence to deal with claims of racial discrimination does not square with its willingness to develop other areas of Community law where it does not have express competence to do so.

As regards traditional mechanisms in existence to tackle the phenomenon of racism and xenophobia, the United Nation's International Convention on the Elimination of All Forms of Racial Discrimination (1957) forbids any form of discrimination based on race, colour, descent or national or ethnic origins; but the Committee which monitors the Convention has no teeth (see Spencer, 1995, pp. 128–9). It can bring only moral pressure to bear on signatory states. Few Member States take the Convention sufficiently seriously, and the European Convention on Human Rights (1950) is subject to the same criticism.

It is my contention in the light of these features of the EC that Member States of the European Community are marooned in a liberal past, in spite of recent desultory moves to present a Community-wide response to racism and xenophobia. The discourse of that tradition places racism and xenophobia at the margins of political thinking as a phenomenon that can be confined and limited by the night-watchman state.[7] This distortion, an inevitable concomitant of liberal preconceptions, distorts the development of the internal market and the morality upon which that internal market is based. For those subject to racism and xenophobia there can be no level playing field: the night-watchman state as played out in Community discourse is a wholly inappropriate paradigm.

Why Should the European Community Act Against Racism?

Bindman's (1996) impassioned question 'When will Europe Act Against Racism?' reflects the convictions of many who see regulation at this level as the way to ensure equality in the marketplace in the use of services and, in individual terms, protection from racial harassment and violence. But why should it be the European Community that acts against racism and xenophobia, rather than the Member States themselves? The argument is simply that a Community approach is more likely to achieve the desired result: for removing racial barriers in the Community market place requires provision for continuous development across all Member States.

Among the objectives of the European Community are these: to provide for a common market and economic and monetary union; to provide for a harmonious and balanced development of economic activities; to ensure a high level of employment and social protection; to raise the standard of living and quality of life; and to encourage economic and social cohesion and solidarity among Member States (Article 2, EEC Treaty 1957). The EEC Treaty created four institutions to enable the objectives of the European Community to be carried out: the European Council of Ministers; the European Commission; the European Court of Justice; and the European Parliament. Each institution is obliged to act within the powers conferred on it by the Treaty, some having the power to make secondary legislation such as regulations[8] and directives,[9] and to take decisions[10] (Article 189, EEC Treaty 1957). The Court has the power to interpret both the Treaty and its secondary provisions (Article 164, EEC Treaty 1957) and Member States are bound to fulfil the obligations arising therefrom (Article 5, EEC Treaty 1957). It would appear, then, that the existence of such an institutional framework provides the ground on which a comprehensive policy could develop to deal with racism and xenophobia as it impacts in the common market.

However, the Community did not until recently give itself express competence to create the political infrastructure to deal with racism and xenophobia.[11] This might seem puzzling, given that the founding persons of the original treaties (the establishment of the European Steel and Coal Community (1951), the European Economic Community (1957) and the

European Atomic Energy Community (1957)) had sought to provide constitutional documents that would ensure peace and avoid the devastation of the second world war and the Holocaust, which had strongly influenced this process. It is also in stark contrast with Article 119, which provides for equal pay in the work-place between men and women, and Article 48, which provides that there shall be free movement of workers, who must not be discriminated against on the grounds of nationality. The lack of attention by the European Community (until very recently) to racism and xenophobia may be related in part to political complacency on the part of Member States: but more significant is the view shared by many that 'the best approach is to share information and expertise but to leave the exact legislative arrangements to Member States ...' (Bindman, 1996, p. 146): in other words, to leave the night-watchman to keep an eye on these matters and to resolve them by piecemeal measures on an individual state-by-state basis.

Most Member States have some legislative provision for racism and xenophobia and believe that these issues are best resolved at the state level. In most European countries the focus is on racist harassment and violence, and in Britain the emphasis has been in the realms of employment and service delivery (Race Relations Acts of 1965 and 1968) and subsequently on incitement to racial hatred (Public Order Act 1986) and racialist chanting at designated football matches (Football (offences) Act 1991).[12] Proponents of European Community-wide action argue, however, that states are reluctant to prosecute, convict or provide effective civil remedies in the face of rising racist attacks. Bindman locates the lack of enforcement activity, high costs of litigation, problems with meeting the burden and standard of proof in discrimination cases, unfamiliarity with the legal process and lack of support by the police and the prosecution services as some of the reasons why the individual state response is woefully inadequate – and, moreover, as indicative of a lack of political will. One needs only to look, for example, at the recent evidence of how the British state has failed properly to respond to attacks which have resulted in the death of a number of members of racial minorities: Stephen Lawrence (killed in what has been described as a racial attack by five white youths); and Shiji Lapite, Richard O'Brien and Ibrahimin Sey (all unlawfully killed whilst in police custody). In the cases of Lapite and O'Brien, the decision of the Director of Public Prosecution not to prosecute the officers involved has been subject to judicial review by the English courts. INQUEST[13] has been in consultation with the European Committee for the Prevention of Torture and Inhumane and Degrading Punishment and Treatment over these two deaths. Or consider the British Airways case (1997), where it was brought to the attention of the public that BA were operating a discreet policy of taking photocopies of the passports of Afro-Caribbean British citizens. This case was never fully litigated because BA apparently compensated the complainant: but there is no doubt that a provision in Community law for the prohibition of discrimination on the grounds of race would at least have countered the pressure of the UK immigration legislation which doubtless figured in BA's decision to adopt such a practice. These examples are replicated throughout the Community.

If one of the main reasons for the failure of Member States to provide adequate mechanisms to address the issue of racism and xenophobia is the lack of political will, how would Community-wide action make a difference? Presumably Member States are as likely to pay only lip service to a Community measure as to their own domestic measures. The point is, however, that where Member States have an obligation under Community law to deal with the problems that arise as a consequence of racism and xenophobia (Article 5, EEC Treaty 1957) they have to respond or face the possibility of enforcement action by the Commission (Article 169, EEC Treaty 1957) and of financial penalties (Article 171, EEC Treaty 1957). Individuals who face racism and xenophobia in the common market would, therefore, have a remedy that the courts at the domestic and European Community levels could protect. Member States would be likely to face claims by individual litigants to damages if their failure to comply with a Community Directive constituted a causal link between the damage to the individual and the breach (*Francovich*).[14] European Community action would provide the requisite carrot or stick.

Evidence of the ability of the Community to obtain the compliance of Member States in Community policy can be seen in the development of sex equality in work and related areas based on Article 119 of the Treaty and on secondary provisions such as the Equal Treatment Directive (76/207). Thus at the level of policy and practice it has been possible to create the conditions for the removal of some of the obstacles to the employment of women in the common market and this has in turn influenced its moral culture. In 1991, for example, the Commission adopted a Recommendation on the protection of the dignity of employees at work and there set out guidelines as to what may or may not constitute sexual harassment in the work-place. Member States were called upon to encourage employers to implement its code of practice (see Craig and De Burca, 1995, pp. 859–60). Although a recommendation is not binding,[15] nevertheless it may have legal effect in the interpretation of national law; and, more importantly, prompt changes in practice. There are clear similarities between racism and xenophobia on the one hand and sexism on the other as obstacles to obtaining access to the common market; a Community response to sexism and sex discrimination has had an impact; and so one would expect Member States to follow their own example and make equivalent provision in the Treaty regarding racism and xenophobia. But this has not happened. Why not? Before I answer that question we need to examine what the Community's response to racism and xenophobia has in fact been.

The European Community's Response to Racism and Xenophobia

1997 has been designated the 'Year Against Racism' by the European Community and it has also been the period in which there has been movement on a Community-wide level to provide mechanisms to deal with racism and xenophobia. At the recent Amsterdam Summit, the Draft Treaty of Amsterdam provided for an amendment to the European Community Treaty (1957) to add a new Article, 6a. This article provides that '[W]ithout prejudice to other provisions of this Treaty and within the limits of the powers conferred by it upon the Community, the Council, acting unanimously on a proposal from the Commission and after consulting the European Parliament, may take appropriate action to combat discrimination based on sex, racial or ethnic origin, religion or belief, disability, age or sexual orientation.' In addition – by Council Regulation (EC) No. 1035/97 – a European Monitoring Centre on Racism and Xenophobia has been established, to be based in Vienna. These represent some of the most serious attempts thus far by Member States at the level of the Community to work in unison on racism and xenophobia. This movement appears to mark an attitudinal shift in what had previously been a political void. But what does this shift amount to?

Article 6a

The Community accepts the need to take measures in '… preparing the ground for the Community to develop its own action to reduce and neutralise racism and xenophobia … necessary because that activity would be in keeping with the spirit and logic of the internal market and with the key practical components of that market, free movement of persons and particularly of migrant workers' (see Consultative Commission on Racism and Xenophobia, 1996, p. 17). The introduction by the Council of Ministers of Article 6a is one such measure. The Council comprises the ministers who represent governments of Member

States. It is this body that has agreed the new provision after proposals from the Commission, the European Parliament and other organizations. Article 6a now provides the Community with express competence to bring into place measures to deal with racism and xenophobia. The Council of Ministers may take appropriate action within the limits of its powers after it has received a proposal from the Commission; and it must, as a condition of taking action, consult with the European Parliament. It is significant that the Commission has to make a proposal to the Council and that the Council must consult the European Parliament. Both the Commission and the European Parliament are less likely to be concerned with the domestic politics of individual Member States and more likely to view pro-integration policies as the primary context within which to view the racism and xenophobia dimension. These institutions are therefore more likely to present proposals that would go some way towards removing internal barriers to the common market based on racism and xenophobia. More importantly, the members of the Commission and the European Parliament have had the benefit of involvement in numerous committees and reports which provide evidence of the negative impact of racism and xenophobia on the common market. This involvement might be expected to lead to realistic proposals from the Commission, especially as the European Parliament is more likely to look at documents that come from the Council with a critically realistic eye. The requirement of unanimity is a useful tool, for if Member States renege on a measure reached by this process there is a stronger case for bringing action against them at a later date for breach of Community Law (Article 5, EC Treaty 1957). That the Council is not tied to any particular measure may also be useful in that it may be better to ensure that an appropriate measure be tailored to the specific circumstances concerned. This, however, is where the benefits of Article 6a arguably end.

Article 6a: The No Response Model

Article 6a does not really reflect a Community-wide response to racism and xenophobia at all: rather it reflects the component parts of a political discourse marooned in the naïveté of classical liberalism. For it is committed to the assumption that the best way to deal with racism and xenophobia is to allow the night-watchman function of individual Member States to oversee it, keeping state intervention at bay and Community-wide intervention to a minimum. Given the requirement of unanimity such intervention is likely to be nonexistent. Article 6a, it might be argued, in fact represents a floor rather than a ceiling for development in this area, along the lines followed by the incorporation of the ECHR into British law: although one might argue that, since the Council has evolved across a number of areas – to the stage of voting by qualified majority precisely because of the problems with unanimity in terms of stagnation and stalemate – the floor-ceiling analogy is perhaps overly pessimistic. But it is unlikely to be. Consider, for instance, the fact that the European Parliament has a right only to be consulted on these matters. While this right has been held by the Court of Justice in *Roquette Freres v. E.C. Council*[16] as '... the fundamental principle that the peoples should take part in the exercise of power through the intermediary of a representative assembly',[17] it does not amount to an effective power. What would have been more effective would have been a power of co-decision between the Council and the European Parliament, with, ultimately, the power of assent to all Council measures in this area, following the model of provisions to facilitate rights of free movement and residence as a consequence of the Treaty of European Union (1992).

Even more striking is the fact that the Court of Justice has no power as the provision now stands. Arguably, the Court of Justice could use its inherent powers to develop certain provisions of Community law to provide for reducing the negative impact of racism and xenophobia – widening the meaning of 'nationality' in Articles 6 and 48 of the European Community Treaty to include race and ethnicity, for instance. The fact that it has not done so indicates that the Court is hesitant to act without express authority from the Community. Had the provisions been written in a similar way to Article 119, for example, the Court could have used its powers (Article 164) so to develop the law. The Court has in fact seen fit to do this in the context of equal pay between men and women (on the basis of Article 119) and in the area of free movement of workers (Article 48); and there is no doubt that the Court's role in this area has had a beneficial impact for women and workers in the context of the common market. Domestic courts have relied on the precedents created by this process to 'review' the conflict between Community law and the law of their own Member States in cases brought by individual litigants. Thus where the political arm of the state may continue to play the night-watchman role, the courts, as the judicial arm of the state, may not. In *R v. Secretary of State for Transport, ex parte Factortame Ltd* No. 2)[18] Lord Bridge said that the terms of the European Communities Act 1972 made it clear that it was the duty of a United Kingdom court, when delivering final judgment, to override any rule of national law found to be in conflict with any directly enforceable rule of Community law.[19] In other words the domestic courts would ensure that Community law took precedence over any conflicting domestic law even though parliament may have legislated with the contrary intent (although the tendency is to construe provisions to take account of Community law where such is relevant).

Lord Bridge's view raises a point about enforceability. For Community law to have an impact it must come from a provision that is in the nature of an enforceable measure, such as a provision of the Treaty (*Defrenne v. Sabena*)[20] or secondary legislation in the form of a Regulation or Directive (*Van Duyn v. Home Office*).[21] A number of bodies have therefore asked the Community to adopt a Directive as the best way forward for dealing with racism and xenophobia. An interesting example was that of 'Starting Line', a final text for a draft Directive on racial discrimination first drawn up by a retired European official after a request from a variety of bodies such as the Commission for Racial Equality (UK). The draft was further discussed and agreed by a number of legal experts from France, Germany, Italy, Belgium, the Netherlands and Britain; and supported by a number of Community-wide organizations (see Dummett, 1994, p. 13). The Community failed to grasp the nettle, however. A Directive would have been a useful way to proceed because it is binding as to the objective to be achieved but leaves to Member States the choice of form and method (Article 189). It would provide Member States with a mechanism for adapting to a Community-wide policy – but in the context of individual circumstances, thereby respecting the particular circumstances and different historical backgrounds of Member States. At the same time, individual litigants might be able to rely on the Directive in actions before domestic courts. In *Van Duyn v. Home Office* the Court said that:

> [I]t would be incompatible with the binding effect attributed to a directive by Article 189 to exclude, in principle, the possibility that the obligation which it imposes may be invoked by those concerned. In particular, where the Community authorities have, by directive, imposed on Member States the obligation to purse a particular course of conduct, the useful effect of such an act would be weakened if individuals were prevented from relying on it before their national courts and if the latter were preventing from taking it into consideration as an element of Community law.[22]

Thus some power would be placed in the hands of individuals vis-à-vis Member States. As it stands, however, Article 6a does not come anywhere near meeting the concerns of many that the Community respond effectively to racism and xenophobia. It is a paper tiger.

Article 6a: The Clinical Response

It is easy to be critical of attempts by the Community to reach agreement on how to provide for mechanisms to deal with racism and xenophobia as it impacts on the common market; and perhaps the claim that Article 6a amounts to no real response is a little harsh. However, what is more disturbing is the trend by the Community, no doubt spurred on by the preponderance of reports of racial harassment and violence, to focus on the more visible side of racism and xenophobia at the expense of, or indeed in apparent ignorance of, other ways in which racism and xenophobia impact on the common market. Article 6a, and indeed the ideas reflected in the Monitoring Centre, may be symptomatic of a more worrying tendency among liberal states to perceive racism and xenophobia as the hateful expression of extra-societal phenomena, isolated instances of extreme, disruptive, illegitimate, irrational and antisocial behaviour. Hate is perceived as abnormal – as an extreme expression that arises only in moments of cultural tension (Whillock and Slayden, 1995, p. 9) (such as high unemployment and the presence of 'visible minorities') – and thus the response that follows is clinical. This encourages an extremely narrow perception of racism and xenophobia; and one which '… ignores its role in the subtle negotiations that take place daily in complex, modern society' (ibid.) and results in their being seen primarily as the product of lower class whites or of the extreme Right, as an abnormal phenomenon that can be controlled through punishment and/or by education. This response – best understood as 'clinical', or perhaps as 'therapeutic', because it is understood as something requiring that individuals be 'cured' of their racism – is the source of some of the background reasoning for the Community's response thus far. The very language of the provision – 'action', 'combat' – smacks of such a response, as though there were a war against the extreme Right. What this perception misses, argues Dijk (1995), are those groups in the sociopolitical power structure that develop fundamental policies, make the most influential decisions and control the overall modes of their execution: governments, parliaments, directors of boards of state agencies, leading politicians, corporate owners, directors, managers and leading academics. The extreme Right may reflect the edge of the subliminal antagonism underlying this, but it is by no means the only expression of it, nor does it represent the core. It is far more subtle and difficult to locate and deal with than such a relegation would suggest.

I do not advocate that the Community ignore the extreme Right. Reports abound of the extent to which some elements go to impose fear on racial minorities through violence, including murder. But surely there are domestic laws to deal with this particular phenomenon. What requires to be tackled at a higher level is not sporadic violence, but a far more insidious tactic; for there is evidence that the extreme Right is moving away from violence and forming a more credible and respectable front. The proliferation of the extreme Right in the USA cannot be ignored in Europe. Organizations such as Christian Identity have a worldwide following. Such groups argue that they are not racist, but 'racialist', that they exist to advance the collective interest of themselves as an ethnic group. These groups have been fairly active in persuading some of the neo-fascists to turn from violence on the football terraces towards the furtherance of the cause through recourse to legal and political mechanisms. These kinds of movement have perhaps been more effective than some Community campaigns directed against racism. And the question must arise, why such groups are able comparatively easily to make use of the mainstream institutions of the European Community.

I would argue that that question itself already suggests that it is *institutionalized* racism and xenophobia that is the location of the main problem: it is the mainstream that needs to be tackled. But how? Is the Regulation establishing a Monitoring Centre a sufficient response to the problem?

The Monitoring Centre

The European Monitoring Centre on Racism and Xenophobia is mandated to supply the European Union and its Member States with objective, reliable and comparative data on racism, xenophobia and anti-Semitism. By Article 3(3) the information the Centre is to collect and process relates to the free movement of persons within the Community; information and television broadcasts and other means of communication; education; vocational training; youth; social policy, including employment; free movement of goods; and culture. The Centre is to be run by a management board comprising an appointee of each Member State, an independent person appointed by the Council of Europe and a representative of the Commission. Members of the board must be persons with appropriate experience in the field of human rights and the analysis of racist, xenophobic and anti-Semitic phenomena. Decisions will be made by two-thirds majority of votes cast, with each Member State having one vote. There will be a supervisory executive board which will consist of the chairperson of the management board – one of whom must include the person appointed by the Council of Europe – and the Community representative. The Centre's budget will include a Community subsidy and voluntary and financial contributions from Member States and various organizations. Its remit is to formulate conclusions and opinions on behalf of the Community.

There is no doubt that the establishment of a centre to monitor racism and xenophobia, funded out of the Community public purse, signals a marked shift from talking about problems to doing something about them: but there remains a set of critical problems in terms of its composition, remit and powers. The proposal for the Centre was originally presented as a feasibility study, conducted by the Consultative Commission on Racism and Xenophobia and presented to the General Affairs Council, which is made up of the foreign ministers of Member States (meeting as the Council of Ministers to discuss foreign and security policy and general institutional matters). The study proposed a number of recommendations within the context of a pan-European framework of cooperation with the Council of Europe; but some were not taken on board by the Council. Before examining these, it is noteworthy that the study was itself silent regarding the Council of Europe's and the Commission's automatic right to sit on the executive body – a right not enjoyed by the European Parliament. It is disconcerting that a democratic organization such as the European Parliament does not have representation on the executive as of right, not least since this is the body that has overall responsibility for the policy of the Centre. The focus of its work is likely to be much narrower and carry less influence with the Council than would be the case if the European Parliament had a right to input at the executive level. Were this the sole problem, however, the Centre might nevertheless serve its purpose, if imperfectly. What gives far greater grounds for pessimism is the extent to which the recommendations it did make have been ignored.

In terms of staffing, the Commission had recommended that the staff should be recruited without discrimination based on grounds of nationality (curiously – and significantly – the Commission did not move beyond the Community language of nationality to that of race). However, the Council chose to ignore the nondiscrimination clause, requiring rather that such appointments be made on the basis of appointees' 'independence' and 'appropriate experience'. But what constitutes experience? There is no provision in the statute of the Centre for interpreting such words as 'independence' and what exactly is 'appropriate': nor does there appear to be any provision for judicial or democratic intervention in the determination of these questions.

In terms of its remit and powers, the Commission was quite clear that for the Centre to be effective it was essential that its remit 'should include making recommendations, the only way of guaranteeing that it will have an impact:

without the ability to recommend practical political measures, the Centre would degenerate into a scientific talking shop'. According to the European Parliament, 'the Monitoring Centre should not be limited to reportage but should propose policies which can be pursued by local authorities, national governments and the Union' (Consultative Commission on Racism and Xenophobia, 1996). In the draft statute of the Centre, the Commission proposed that one objective of the Centre would be to formulate conclusions and set out recommendations capable of being used as a basis for policy-making in the institutions of the European Union and Member States. The Council limited the Centre's remit to the formulation of conclusions and opinions for the Community and its Member States. Further, where the Commission saw the prime objective of the Centre as maintaining vigilance as regards racism, xenophobia and anti-Semitism, the Council decided that its prime objective should be to provide the Community and its Member States with data. And those are very different objectives.

The downgrading of the potential power of the Centre reflects in part a clash of conflicting interests between the Commission, with its federal pro-integration perspective, and the more cautious, intergovernmental perspective of the Council, a perspective rooted in the liberal assumption that racism and xenophobia are phenomena that can be packaged, punished and put away, as something that only abnormal people engage in. The Council's ignoring the above recommendations of the Commission is no accident: it reflects its conviction that these problems are essentially ones of individual behaviour, rather than being structural.

Conclusion

To criticize the legislative approach of Member States in the context of Article 6a and the establishment of the Centre is not to say that both these might not have their uses. It might be the case that if the Centre does focus on the growth of extreme Right-wing groups, then Member States will take this phenomenon seriously and re-examine whether it is indeed the case, as Jipson argues (1997), that their claim to legitimacy is based, in part, on the way in which mainstream institutions operate. That, in turn, might lead to the reflection which is required on the nature of those institutions. But it is difficult to assess how likely this in fact is. Certainly past experience does not suggest that such a radical break with the European Union's liberal foundations will be so easily achieved. For such a break would demand an engagement with the issues that are fundamental to the European Union's perception of itself as a collection of individual units – on the model of its Member States' understanding of their own identities – rather than as an evolving entity whose institutional frameworks themselves are no less constitutive of the whole than its individual constituents. And unless such a shift occurs, racism and xenophobia – misperceived as individuals' failings alone – are unlikely to recede. In a word, the European Community, both as structure and concept, would appear to have incorporated racism and xenophobia as institutional components of its identity.[23]

Notes

1   Case 186/87 *Cowan v French Treasury* [1989]ECR 195.
2   Case 130/75 [1976] ECR 1589.
3   Case 100/88 [1989\ ECR 4285.
4   According to Article 164, EC Treaty 1957 (as amended by TEU), 'The Court of Justice shall ensure that in the interpretation of this Treaty the law is observed.'
5   Case 70/88 *E.C. Parliament v. E.C. Council* [1980] ECR 2041.
6   Prior to this amendment the European Parliament did not have a Treaty right to rely on this provision to protect its prerogative powers.
7   By this I refer to the conception of a state as not proactive.
8   'A regulation shall have general application. It shall be binding in its entirety and directly applicable in all Member States' (Article 189, EC Treaty 1957).
9   'A directive shall be binding, as to the result to be achieved, upon each Member State to which it is addressed, but shall leave to the national authorities the choice of form and methods' (Article 189, EC Treaty 1957).
10   'A decision shall be binding in its entirety upon those to whom it is addressed' (Article 189, EC Treaty 1957).
11   The Draft Treaty of Amsterdam (1997) has in its provision competence for the European Union to develop common action to combat racism and xenophobia (new Article K.1. in the TEU). However, this provision relies on police and judicial cooperation rather than on Community legislation.
12   The British Government proposes to introduce new offences of racial violence and racial harassment in the near future.
13   The pressure group INQUEST, founded in 1981, provides emotional support and legal expertise for families and friends where controversial deaths have occurred. See Ryan (1996, p. 1).
14   Case C-6 & 9/90 [1991] ECT I-5357.
15   'Recommendations and opinions shall have no binding force' (Article 189, EC Treaty 1957).
16   Case 138/78 [1980] ECR 3333.
17   Ibid., para 33 of judgment.
18   [1991] 1 AC 603, 658.
19   Ibid., p. 658.
20   Case 43/75 [1976] ECR 455.

21 Case 41/74 [1974] ECR 1337.
22 Case 41/74 [1974] ECR 1337, para. 12 of judgment.
23 I am grateful to my colleagues Janet Dine, Peter Stone, Bob Brecher and Anthony Brennan for reading and commenting on an earlier draft of this paper.

References

Barnard, C. (1996), *EC Employment Law*, John Wiley and Sons, London.

Bindman, G. (1996), 'When will Europe Act Against Racism?', *European Human Rights Law Review*, 2, pp. 143–9.

Commission of the European Communities (1995), *Communication From the Commission on Racism, Xenophobia and Anti-Semitism, and Proposal for a Council Decision*, (Com. (95) 653).

Consultative Commission on Racism and Xenophobia (1996), *Feasibility Study for a European Monitoring Centre for Racism and Xenophobia*, 6871/1/96, Raxen 18, 28 May.

Craig, P. and De Burca, G. (1995), *EC Law, Text Cases and Materials*, Clarendon Press, Oxford.

De Burca, G. (1995), 'The Language of Rights and European Integration' in Shaw, J. and Moore, G. (eds), *New Legal Dynamics of the European Union*, Clarendon Press, Oxford and London.

Dijk, T. van (1995), 'Elite Discourse and the Reproduction of Racism' in R.K. Whillock and D. Slayden (eds), *Hate Speech*, Sage Publications, London.

Dummett, A. (1994), *Citizens, Minorities and Foreigners*, Commission for Racial Equality, UK.

Ellis, E. and Tridimas, T. (1995), *Public Law of the European Community: Text, Materials and Commentary*, Sweet and Maxwell, London.

European Parliament (1995a), *Committee of Inquiry into the Rise of Fascism and Racism in Europe*.

European Parliament (1995b), *Committee on Civil and Political Liberties and Internal Affairs*.

Foster, N. (1997), *Blackstone's EC Legislation 1996–97,* Blackstone Press, London.

Gilroy, P. (1994), 'Stepping out of Babylon – Race, Class and Autonomy' in Centre for Contemporary Cultural Studies (ed.), *The Empire Strikes Back: Race and Racism in 70s Britain*, Routledge, London.

Gosing, P. (1995), 'A work force waiting to be tapped', *Independent*, 26 October.

Jipson, A. (1997), 'Challenging the Conceptualisation of the Law: White Supremacists and the Critical Legal Movement', unpublished paper presented at the *Critical Legal Conference 1997*, University College Dublin.

Mill, J.S. (1984) 'On Liberty' in M. Warnock (ed.), *Utilitarianism*, Fontana, London.

Read, J. (1997), 'One Day Soon our Own Bill of Rights?', *London University Law Journal*, 9, Spring/Summer, pp. 18–21.

Ryan, M. (1996), *Lobbying From Below: INQUEST in Defence of Civil Liberties*, UCL Press, London.

Shaw, J. and Moore, G. (1995), *New Legal Dynamics of the European Union*, Clarendon Press, Oxford and London.

Spencer, M. (1995), *State of Injustice*, Pluto Press, London.

Stockdale, E. and Casale S. (1992), *Criminal Justice Under Stress*, Blackstone Press, London.

Vincenzi, C. (1996), *Law of the European Community*, Pitman, London.

Whillock, R.K. and Slayden, D. (eds) (1995), *Hate Speech*, Sage Publications, London.

9   Rawls: A Racist Theory of Justice?

EDWARD GARRETT

For Rawls racism is ruled out by his principles of justice. Here I wish to question in one particular way the extent to which, nevertheless, Rawlsian theory is as a matter of fact non-racist. There may be other arguments. In particular it might be suggested that the early Rawls is racist in proposing a comprehensive political morality with a universal reach when it is only the product of a particular political culture.[1] More generally, it might be argued that Rawls is implicated in liberalism's commitment to the imperial project and its creation of 'natives' as savages as part of the substantiation of liberal law (see for example Fitzpatrick, 1990). The approach taken here differs from these possible arguments, however, in that it considers how Rawlsian justice may generate racism within societies rather than between them; and it considers this generation of racism within one specific context, that of criminal justice.

Bearing these qualifications in mind, this paper argues that racism is a possible, though not a necessary, consequence of a system of Rawlsian justice. The first section considers in detail Rawls' original position; it is argued that the characterization of the parties to this contract as reasonable is a controversial assumption which demands the existence of the unreasonable, or those outside liberal justice. These are the criminals of liberal justice. Section two, with a focus on the criminal as the unreasonable, considers ways in which the unreasonable might be a racist category. Section three suggests, very briefly, how the conclusions reached in the previous section might be substantiated in political practice.

The paper's contribution to a concern about liberalism's relations to questions of racism and nationalism lies, therefore, in its questioning liberalism's theoretical capacity to provide the basis for a genuinely inclusive society. Its exposure of the limits to liberal diversity takes a particular form, namely a focus on the liberal polity's structure and conceptualization of criminal justice: nevertheless, its analysis may still have application beyond this specific application.

The Original Position: The Beginnings of Racism

In this section I consider how Rawlsian theory may be committed to the production of criminality. Essentially, it is suggested that the conception of the individual as reasonable, which is central to the justification of the Rawlsian principles of justice, demands a conception of the unreasonable. In this sense it demands the criminal. Sections two and three explore how 'the criminal' may be a racist category.

The criminal is the enemy of the state. A criminal wrong is distinguished from a civil wrong in that it is an action that offends the public or the state rather than simply another individual. The criminal therefore stands outside the principles of justice of that state. His or her action is of the type proscribed by these principles, whatever they may be. The existence of criminality is, on the face of it, problematic for the state. By pointing to activities or ways of life which are outside the principles of justice of that state it indicates a condition of conflict within itself, a lack of support for the rules which constitute that state. It is this question of support for a public conception of justice that Rawls explicitly addresses in his later work. For Rawls, the modern state, or at least liberal democracies, is characterized by a plurality of comprehensive and incompatible religious, philosophical and moral doctrines. The challenge for political philosophy is to explore the possibility of shared understandings in the political conception, even if these are not possible on a comprehensive level. He claims that his principles of justice, as articulated in *A Theory of Justice*, would receive an overlapping consensus of support from reasonable comprehensive doctrines. Since political liberalism has its roots in how seriously it takes the possibility of conflict in pluralistic societies, criminality, on the analysis adumbrated, must constitute a problem for any claim to such consensus, even if negatively.[2]

I argue that Rawls' hopes in this regard are overstated. At points in *Political Liberalism* they seem to be rather despairing: for example, he claims that views contrary to his principles of justice 'may not be strong enough to undermine the substantive justice of the regime. That is the hope; there can be no guarantee' (Rawls, 1993, p. 65). It is concluded here that for Rawlsian liberalism to take conflict seriously in fact involves a commitment to that conflict. In particular, as suggested earlier, I argue that Rawls is committed to the production of criminality, to the production of people whose actions or ways of life are in direct conflict with the principles of justice that he proposes. I doubt that this commits me to arguing that Rawlsian liberalism is productive of all criminality: but its being productive of some is sufficient to suggest the conclusion that criminality, far from being simply problematic for the state, is in fact an essential part of its maintenance.

This argument is conducted largely through a consideration of the nature of the parties to 'the original position'. Yet though the contract struck between these parties is an important part of Rawls' argument for his two principles of justice, it is far from being a justification on its own: the links with the broader process of reflective equilibrium are essential, and towards the end of this section, my conclusions will be briefly considered in the context of this broader process.[3]

Rawls' original position is a situation of choice in which ideal individuals who do not know where they themselves will end up in the structure they are constructing will select certain principles of distributive justice. Rawls argues that, given a reasonable theory of rational motivation and the informational constraints outlined – the veil of ignorance – the parties to this contract would select, from a list of possible principles of virtue, the two Rawlsian principles of justice.

This original position is hardly, as Rawls tells us (1971, p. 139), a general assembly of all people past and present. Rather it is a representational device which models some of our basic convictions about justice. As such the parties to it are conceived of in a certain way. Essentially they are to be thought of, not as individuals with specific goals and desires, but rather as citizens who already embody some basic convictions about justice (Rawls, 1993, pp. 258–9). It is of course a peculiarity, and one the significance of which will be explored at greater length later, of Rawls' contract that it is not really a contract at all. The parties to it are characterized in such a way that, with the assumption of a certain model of rational choice, they *have* to come to the agreement that they do (Rawls, 1971, p. 138). There is no room for real contractual bargaining between them. Essentially, then, the parties to the contract already embody the principles of justice that they are to select. To be outside of these parties is to be outside of justice and, despite Rawls' claim that this contract is between all citizens, the parties as citizens are exclusive, in the sense of excluding other conceptions of the person, in at least two ways.

As a citizen, Rawls says (1993, p. 18), one can be 'a normal and fully cooperating member of society over a complete life'. The reference to the normal should put us on our guard. Only those with capacities within the normal range are admitted to the original position. Those who fall outside this range are excluded:

[S]ince the fundamental problem of justice concerns the relations among those who are full and active participants in society, and directly or indirectly associated over the course of a whole life, it is reasonable to assume that everyone has physical needs and psychological capacities within some normal range (Rawls, 1993, note at p. 272).

The exclusion of people outside this range in theory leads to an exclusion of their interests in practice, as Rawls goes on to acknowledge (ibid.): 'Thus the problem of special health care and how to treat the mentally defective are set aside. If we can work out a viable theory for the normal range, we can attempt to handle these other cases later.'

This, I suggest, is the first type of exclusion from the original position. I shall return to it later. There is a second type, however, which is perhaps more central for the issue of criminality. The parties to the original position are characterized as both rational and reasonable. Anyone pursuing their self-interest (broadly conceived) may be regarded as a rational agent. On its own, however, rationality is not going to be enough to generate or select principles of justice. As Rawls says (1993, p. 51), '[R]ational agents approach being psychopathic when their interests are solely in benefits to themselves.' Thus the agent as reasonable expresses at least the desire to engage in moral cooperation. Now, the reasonable is not derived from the rational. Rawls is quite clear about this: justice as fairness 'does not try to derive the reasonable from the rational. Indeed, the attempt to do so may suggest that the reasonable is not basic and needs a basis in a way that the rational does not. Rather, within the idea of fair cooperation the reasonable and the rational are complementary ideas' (Rawls, 1993, p. 52). Putting the reasonable and rational together, we have a conception of the individual in the original position as regulating the pursuit of their ends through a desire to justify these actions to others and to listen to others' justifications.

It is through the idea of the reasonable – a desire to justify one's actions to others – that the second exclusion from the original position takes place, the one relevant to criminality. The rational cannot be a way of discriminating between the just and the unjust. One can be unjust and still be rational, as Rawls notes by the possible psychopathy of solely rational agents. Therefore if parties to the contract are to make this discrimination it must be through the notion of the reasonable, the unjust being the unreasonable rather than the irrational. So it is the unreasonable which is excluded from the original position. Now, Rawls specifies two aspects to the reasonable: (1) it is 'the willingness to propose fair terms of cooperation and to abide by them provided others do', and (2) the acceptance of the burdens of judgment, or the causes of disagreement between reasonable individuals (Rawls, 1993, p. 54). Conversely, to be unreasonable is to lack this moral sensibility and not be willing to accept these burdens of judgment , or as a citizen to assert one's own comprehensive view as true and as such the only one appropriate for the political conception, those basic institutions of our public life which are structured according to our principles of justice.

There are two ways in which the unreasonable might be excluded from the Rawlsian state. The first is when the way of life is in direct conflict with the principles of justice. Rawls (1993, p. 196) gives racism as an example. Such ways of life could not be approved by the parties to the original position. As reasonable people they could not accept as reasons for ways of life something which denies the capacity of some other person as a free and equal source of reason. The second means of exclusion or discouragement is more confused. Here the way of life may be admissible but fail to gain sufficient adherents under a liberal regime. Rawls seems to have in mind certain forms of religion at least, though it is not entirely clear what he means by 'admissible' here. Certainly he indicates that it is reasonable since it is not in conflict with the principles of justice. Yet he does characterize such a good as able to survive only 'if it controls the machinery of state and is able to practise effective intolerance' (ibid., pp. 196–7). Such a characterization does seem to be in line with the suggestion that '[I]t is unreasonable for us to use political power, should we possess it, or share it with others, to repress comprehensive views that are not unreasonable' (ibid., p. 61). So we might say that these goods are rejected in the original position; or to put it another way, the reasonableness of the parties to this position precludes such goods and excludes therefore those who might hold to them.

On the other hand these goods might be seen as reasonable. This possibility allows for goods to be excluded from a liberal society but still be reasonable. What this possibility implies, therefore, is that the notion of reasonableness, as it appears in the original position, is not as central to exclusion as I am trying to argue that it is. This conclusion need not affect the substance of the argument, however, since there may be other ways of excluding ways of life from liberal society other than through the idea of the reasonable. The reasonable, though, is still an idea which may exclude insofar as it is part of the definition of certain ways of life as unreasonable, and therefore excluded, as indicated in the first kind of exclusion above. Nevertheless, an argument may be made for these ways of life, in the second type of exclusion, also to be excluded as unreasonable.

Galston can help us here. He argues (1991, p. 147): 'If I know that the principles adopted in the original position may impair my ability to exercise, or even require me altogether to surrender, the values that give my life its core meaning and purpose, then how could I agree in advance to accept those principles as binding?'. Wouldn't I rather retreat into a homogenous community which would respect that which is central to my life? And an acceptance of the fact of a pluralism of comprehensive religious, moral and philosophical doctrines is fundamental for Rawls' position, as he has recently emphasized: that justice should be independent of these is to 'apply the principle of toleration to philosophy itself' (Rawls, 1993, p. 10). In other words, what is important is not the possible truth or otherwise of any of these doctrines (Rawls is not a sceptic) but the fact that people hold different ones. Accepting this plurality, Galston argues (1991, p. 147), comes at a cost for some people – 'for it is a pluralism that excludes them' if they hold a comprehensive view that cannot flourish under the tolerant colours of a liberal society. Furthermore, the notion of reasonableness used by Rawls seems to be very closely linked to this acceptance of plurality. For it is only by accepting a heterogeneous society that the demands of reasonableness need to be built into the original position. Those who are excluded from the original position by the fact of plurality are also therefore excluded by the conception of the parties to this contract as embodying reasonableness as a reaction to this plurality.

To sum up. Two forms of exclusion from the original position have been isolated: (1) the explicit exclusion of groups outside the normal range of physical and mental abilities; and (2) the exclusion of those groups who hold unreasonable comprehensive views. Now, it may, on the face of it, appear clearer who is excluded by (1) than by (2). However, the exclusion of those outside the normal range of physical and mental abilities, or the disabled, can help us to understand the exclusion of the unreasonable, for it is based on a commitment to some conception of the normal, a conception which people with disabilities and mental health problems are deemed not to fall under. Exclusion on this theoretical level means that their interests and needs suffer in a practical context. We see this lack of consideration in the world around us. Yet it is not clear that this conception of the normal is actually a given. In fact, arguments today stress how disability is at least in large part a function of the relationship between the person and their social environment, and to this extent it exists in a state of mutual construction with the normal.

A similar process might be applied to the notion of the reasonable: it is in fact controversially produced out of its relationship with the unreasonable. If it is, then we find at the theoretical heart of Rawls' theory a creation of that which is opposed to just those principles of justice which the theory advocates.

To explore this possibility, the role that the reasonable plays in the original position needs to be looked at more closely.

Margaret Moore finds two problems with the concept of reasonableness postulated. She questions whether the assumption that people have a fundamental moral motive is a plausible assumption (Moore, 1996, pp. 169–70). This objection does not provide a particularly fruitful line of argument of itself, however: whether it is plausible or not would seem to be an empirical question, the answer to which would be hard to discover. But that it is an assumption is important in the light of the central role it plays in Rawls' argument. For Moore argues (ibid., p. 172) that into the idea of the parties as reasonable are built the very conclusions that the contract between them is supposed to generate. In the original position the veil of ignorance models the conviction that one's social position or particular comprehensive doctrine is not a reason to favour this position or impose this view on others. It is in this way that the original position models the reasonableness of its parties. It is suggested, of course, that the principles the parties come up with to govern their society will be those that can be endorsed by an overlapping consensus of reasonable doctrines (Rawls, 1993, p. 134). This is a point that we have already noted; the original position cannot provide a justification of the principles of justice on its own, but is rather part of the wider justificatory process of reflective equilibrium.

Rawls, of course, would probably argue that such an argument is rather missing the point, or perhaps that it is no argument at all. For the original position is a device of representation, and a part of a larger argument, into which we put what we want. For him, 'the nature of the parties is up to us' (ibid., p. 28). Furthermore, this nature is implicit in our political culture. Therefore what you get out depends on what you put in. However, and conversely, what you do not put in you do not get out. Since what you do not put in depends on what you do, and since the characterization of the parties as reasonable is strong enough to do away with the need for them to come to an agreement at all, there is cause for concern here. For the Rawlsian conception of the reasonable may be constructed in opposition to a conception of the unreasonable. If it is, then the unreasonable is essential for the reasonable and conflict is inherent even at the level of the theoretical justification of the liberal principles of justice. We must therefore be concerned about a form of argument dependent on a concept which is produced out of opposition to that which it excludes.

Rawls' account of the reasonable does not allow for the possibility, which would mean that he could escape the force of the argument being presented here, that while some people may be unreasonable, there does not need to be a category of the unreasonable. In other words it does not allow for the possibility that not only are all the parties to the original position reasonable, which they are, but that there are no others, beyond it as it were, who are not reasonable. If this were possible it would show that the reasonable is not produced out of an opposition with the unreasonable.

As we have seen, reasonableness is conceived of as a powerful moral virtue, which allows us to justify ourselves to other people through reason, whilst similarly accepting the justification of others. In this sense it works its way towards the impartial standpoint that liberal legalities attempt to embody, that in which all reasonable goods coexist peacefully because its laws are based on no good in particular. Thus the right is prior to the good. But it is not at all clear that the reasonable may not be conceived of in other ways. Moore gives as an example laws in Quebec which seek to protect the Quebecois' cultural identity. Reasons might be given justifying these laws, but these are reasons from a partial rather than an impartial point of view (Moore, 1996, p. 171). It would not be hard to think of other ways in which one might be partial but reasonable all the same. For example, my choice of a certain football team for the Cup might be partial but reasonable given my support for them. More seriously, to anticipate a later example, the demand for the legalization of cannabis may be partially motivated by certain interest groups, but reasonable nonetheless.

It might of course be objected that it is precisely this notion of reasonableness that justice as fairness rejects. However, to make this move would be in effect to concede the point that I am trying to make, for it would show that the reasonable and the unreasonable produce each other. In this dynamic process of production the unreasonable then serves as a way of defining the reasonable. Therefore from the beginning the unreasonable is as essential to the parties in the original position as the reasonable. They – the unreasonable – may be excluded from the original position but their exclusion is central to the self-definition of the parties to this contract and therefore to the principles of justice that the characterization of these parties is designed to lead to.

We come back to, or arrive eventually at, the criminal in the original position. The criminal as the unreasonable is part of the original position, not strictly as a party to this contract, as these parties are defined in a certain way, but as part of the process of this definition. This conclusion undercuts the Rawlsian commitment to the importance of stability, for he in fact seems committed to conflict through the creation of criminality. Again I am not claiming that all criminality is produced or constructed, at least not in this way, but only that some of it is, which is enough for the argument here. Rawls claims proudly that one of the great virtues of his state is that in it nothing need be hidden: 'in a free society that all recognise as just there is no need for the illusions and delusions of ideology for society to work properly and for citizens to accept it willingly' (Rawls, 1993, note at p. 68). And yet it seems that there is something hidden at the heart of Rawls – namely those opposed to a Rawlsian theory of justice, and, in particular, the criminal.

This conclusion is confirmed in the context of the larger argument for his principles of justice that Rawls gives. The original position, of course, can hardly offer a justification of these principles on its own. A hypothetical agreement between highly idealized parties cannot be sufficient reason for you and me, and it is to us that Rawls wants to justify his theory. Rather it forms part of the process of reflective equilibrium, part of the balancing of our considered judgments about justice with principles that can account for and support these judgments. The conception of justice that best reaches this balance is, Rawls claims, the one most reasonable for us to accept. The principles of justice are to be justified to us as reasonable people (ibid., pp. 25–8).

There is a dangerous circularity in this argument. Just as the conditions defining the reasonable in the original position already embody the perspective of justice that the contract reaches, so the characterization of us as the objects of justification as reasonable already presupposes the principles of justice that are to be justified to us. However, and to whatever extent this circularity affects the strength of Rawls' justification of his principles, there is something equally interesting and possibly more damaging going on here. It was suggested earlier that the circularity of the original position taken on its own as a justification of the liberal principles of justice is an indication of the controversial background out of which and against which Rawls produces his notion of the reasonable. This conclusion, of the production of the reasonable through the unreasonable, might be reached without involving discussion of the circularity of the argument. Nevertheless, what this circularity does suggest is that Rawls intends to produce principles of justice which do exclude, as we have seen and as he would admit, through a conception of the person which, characterized in the same way as these principles of justice, is similarly exclusive. Thus Rawls' notion of the person as reasonable cannot but be controversial. Nor can we turn to reflective equilibrium for a stronger argument, for this method of justification is equally circular. So in the larger argument the larger circularity indicates a similar background of controversy. The criminal is part of this background against which the reasonable is asserted. You and I are reasonable only if the criminal as the unreasonable is part of the picture.

A Racist Criminal Justice

Thus far we have a reading of Rawls as productive of criminality. It is by turning to Foucault that we may understand how this Rawlsian creation of the criminal as the unreasonable may be connected to racism. In particular we may see how the targeting of certain groups, including racial groups, may be part of the actual substantiation of liberal justice.

Crime is defined in two related ways. (1) Whilst the civil law is primarily concerned with the rights and duties of individuals among themselves, the criminal law is concerned with the duties the individual owes to society (Card, 1995, p. 1). A criminal, therefore, as suggested earlier, becomes an enemy of society. (2) This difference implies a difference in the objects that the law aims to pursue – civil law seeks redress or compensation, criminal law seeks to punish (Geldart, 1991, p. 153). It is on this connection between punishment and the relation of the individual to society that Foucault's *Discipline and Punish*[1] focuses.

The foundations of the right to punish lie in the notion of the society which the criminal is supposed to have offended. In the classical age, Foucault argues (1991, p. 47), the law was the expression of the will of the sovereign; someone who broke this law was therefore attacking the sovereign. Here it is relatively easy to see the justification for punishment. Power lies with the sovereign. To cross that power is to leave oneself open to the will of that sovereign. The matter is not quite so obvious when the law is not the expression of a single will but the result of a contract between the members of that society as rational wills. As Foucault says, this theory of the contract leaves the criminal as a 'juridically paradoxical being'. On the one hand s/he has broken the rules by which s/he agreed s/he may be punished. Yet, as a member of society, s/he participates in his or her own punishment (ibid., p. 90). It is within this transition between the law as founded in the sovereign and the law founded in the contract that Foucault considers changing methods of punishment. Of course, the approach to law chosen for consideration here, that of Rawls, is similarly based on a contract of sorts. Why, on this basis, should we tolerate being punished? Foucault answers (ibid., p. 303):

> [T]he theory of the contract can only answer this question by the fiction of a juridical subject giving to others the power to exercise over him the right that he himself possesses over them. It is highly probable that the great carceral continuum, which provides a communication between the power of discipline and the power of law, and extends without interruption from the smallest coercions to the longest penal detention, contributed the technical and real,

immediately material counterpart of that chimerical granting of the right to punish.

This answer points to two theories of the foundations of punishment. Firstly, there is the contract made between equal juridical subjects, as in Rawls' theory of justice. But, Foucault argues, on its own this contract is not enough to explain why these subjects 'subject' themselves to punishment. This subjection can be achieved only within a whole system of disciplining the individual, what Foucault refers to above as the 'carceral continuum', with the prison as its focus. Only disciplined individuals will be prepared to be punished. Thus the foundations of punishment are not the contract between equal juridical subjects but rather the system of discipline and control which operates in the school, the hospital and the work-place, creating in us the subjection necessary for prison. Or at the very least, it is not simply the fiction of a social contract. Certainly it is a useful fiction for contract theorists to have us believe that we are subjects who create and found the law rather than objects subjected to it. Anne Barron (1990, p. 109) argues that '[L]iberalism, in theorising power as sovereign power, and sovereign power as the relationship between abstract subjects – each characterised by an autonomous, responsible will – and the law, ignores those practices of government by which living individuals becomes the objects of detailed manipulation and management'.

However, there is a further aspect of Foucault's explorations of the connection between discipline and punishment that is relevant here. With the law as the expression of the sovereign's will, punishment tended to be directly inscribed onto the body of the criminal; thus the great public spectacles of torture and execution as displays of the power of the sovereign. Imprisonment, on the other hand, works on the 'soul' of the criminal. It is a deprivation of rights, an attempt to rehabilitate, to treat. Other bodies of knowledge than just the judicial become involved in this punishment (Foucault, 1991, p. 19). The criminal, rather than the crime, becomes the focus of punishment. These other bodies of knowledge define a set of norms which the criminal acts against, and it is part of the system of disciplinary punishment to make the criminal conform to these norms. In a sense this means that the prison takes over from the judiciary as the place where justice is carried out, for what is important is not the offence for which the criminal was imprisoned but the individualizing of the penalty, the means towards his or her reformation (ibid., p. 244).[5] Foucault argues that what the prison operates with is in effect not the convicted offender but the delinquent, who is 'to be distinguished from the offender by the fact that it is not so much his act as his life that is relevant in characterising him' (ibid., p. 251). What we have here are two interconnected processes. First, the prison as part of an overall system of discipline; within the carceral continuum a connection is made between a transgression of the law and deviation from a norm. The imprisoned criminal therefore becomes the abnormal, the social deviant. But, second, the prison is also productive of a certain type of abnormality, defined as delinquent. And this delinquency is important in establishing the validity of norms. So in effect criminals are needed to establish these norms. Therefore society must create criminals. And, what I want to focus on here, the creation of these criminals may be racist.

Before the late 18th century, Foucault argues, each social stratum had a margin of tolerated illegality. This toleration, in the case of each social grouping, disappeared under growing economic pressures and wealth. For example, the transition to intensive agriculture necessitated the end of the tolerated rights of commoners over land. The practice of these rights now became theft: 'The illegality of rights, which often meant the survival of the most deprived, tended, with the new status of property, to become an illegality of property. It then had to be punished' (ibid., p. 85). In particular the illegalities of the peasantry and the working class were attacked. Foucault's argument also provides an understanding of why these measures were aimed at certain groups and not others. What Foucault refers to as this 'differential administration of illegality through the mediation of penalty' (ibid., p. 272) helps us understand what might be regarded as the 'failure' of the prisons. Prison was immediately denounced as a failure on its widespread introduction 150 years ago. It was argued that prison did not reduce the crime rate, caused recidivism, produced delinquency and allowed criminals to organize together (ibid., pp. 264–9). The same criticisms have been repeated ever since. We may understand this failure of prison in tackling crime if we go back to the differential administration of tolerated illegalities: for it is in fact in the interest of those with power that prison fail to reduce crime. Criminal law, as the law of one particular class addressed to another, manages to produce 'the delinquent as pathological subject', the criminal type who offends again and again. This location of crime in certain economic and social groupings, appears to have two main consequences. (1) It is a way of controlling other popular illegalities. Differentiated from them, it can no longer rely on popular support, and it turns inwards and attacks its own popular base. Foucault (1991, p. 278) argues that illegalities are thus limited to a state of petty crime of which the powerful classes are often the main recipients. (2) It reinforces the norm of the non-delinquent. It is important to see, however, how the delinquent criminal is a creation of the disciplinary system and of prison in particular. The criminal doesn't simply commit an offence by chance: 'it is not crime that alienates an individual from society, but that crime is itself due rather to the fact that one is in society as an alien' (ibid., pp. 275–6).

We come back to the criminal as the enemy of society. We can see now that the criminal doesn't simply make him- or herself an enemy of society by transgressing its rules as the expression of a contract between rational wills. S/he is also created as a criminal. We mustn't see the definition of crimes and punitive measures as merely negative functions aimed at preventing certain types of behaviour. Rather they also function as positive measures designed to establish a certain norm of behaviour which the criminal must necessarily transgress (ibid., p. 24). It is useful perhaps to contrast the criminal's relationship with society in a disciplinary society with their relationship with societies whose power structures are different. Under the power of the sovereign, the criminal is an outcast from society, often physically extinguished by the power of the sovereign. For the reformers and their contract of abstract juridical subjects the criminal was labelled an enemy or outcast; but the intention was to integrate them back into society. For the disciplinary society, finally, the criminal is both outcast but right at the centre of society, the very status as outcast enemy being central to the operation of the law.

Racism in Practice

Foucault provides an analysis of the production of criminality which may allow us to understand how liberal justice may be a racist justice. It has been argued that Rawls' theory of justice depends on the production of the unreasonable, or the criminal. This argument was taken further through a discussion of Foucault on crime. Of particular importance here are his ideas that criminals are needed to reinforce the norm of the non-delinquent, and that this reinforcement may be targeted at certain groups in society. This targeting need not be racist; but it might be. This final section explores briefly an area of criminal justice where it certainly is racist.

There has recently been a renewed emphasis on incarceration in the US and now increasingly here in Britain, a process begun under the previous government and not obviously in abeyance under Labour.[6] This language of the war on crime is the language of the exclusion of the criminal. Physically excluded in the prisons, they also become excluded from the norms defining reasonable behaviour in the liberal polity. Unsurprisingly perhaps, the increased use of prisons has not had the effect of reducing crime. There are now over

1.5 million people incarcerated in the USA, but, as Elliot Currie argues, this has done nothing to reduce violent crime. As an example he quotes the case of New Orleans, where the prison population today is five times higher today than in the 1970s, but where one is four times more likely to be murdered today than in the 1970s (Currie, 1996, pp. 6–7). Of particular relevance here is the disparity in prison numbers along race lines. Nearly one in three young black men are under criminal justice supervision on any given day in the USA. One explanation for this disproportionately high figure might be the expanding numbers of drug offenders imprisoned, an area of criminal policy where black people have been disproportionately targeted (Mauer, 1996, p. 13). Another reason, of course, might be that it is precisely by targeting an area of previously tolerated illegalities, as in Foucault's analysis – such as drugs – that one can criminalize people from a specified 'dangerous' social grouping. The war on drugs, that is to say, may be read as a racist war.

The analysis might be taken further. However, the actual workings of the criminal justice system are not my prime concern here. What these figures (with their parallel British counterparts) do show is that there is an apparent targeting of certain racial groupings – whether or not by specific intent – in the criminal justice systems of Britain and the USA. This targeting is a possible practical confirmation, along racist lines, of the theoretical position developed on liberal justice's production of the criminal through discussion of Rawls and Foucault. What it does is to make clear how the potential for racism within a Rawlsian system of criminal justice may be instantiated.

This potential has been exposed in an argument of two parts. Firstly, we saw how the Rawlsian conception of the subject of liberal justice demands a conception of the unreasonable, or the criminal. Secondly, through using some of Foucault's arguments on punishment and the location of criminality, we came to see how the construction of criminality might be targeted at specific social groupings. These arguments reveal the limits of liberal theory's capacity properly to accommodate diversity. This non-accommodation may express itself in part through racism. The final brief comments on Anglo-American penal policy, particularly with regard to drugs, showed how this expression works in practice.

Notes

1   The early Rawls is to be most importantly distinguished from the later Rawls by his clarification, made in *Political Liberalism*, that his theory of justice is to be regarded as a political rather than as a comprehensive conception. Thus it is something that we merely

affirm as we exist in the political sphere as citizens. The principles of justice as articulated in *A Theory of Justice* are not themselves under question.

2   Rawls argues that his is a political philosophy that is not withdrawn from the world, but one that is really trying to address the practical conflicts that we all face. Its level of abstraction is 'a way of continuing public discussion when shared understandings of lesser generality have broken down' (Rawls, 1993, pp. 45–6). In the same vein, Galston (1991, p. 142) suggests that an 'ever increasing social diversity' has produced in liberal political philosophy 'a renewed emphasis on the task of forging a meaningful and usable political unity'.

3   The exact role the original position plays in reflective equilibrium is not important here, since my concern is with the conception of the individual to which the principles of justice are justified, rather than with questioning the justification itself. Dworkin (1975), for example, argues that the original position serves as an intermediate conclusion in a deep theory arguing for a right to equal concern and respect.

4   Foucault's philosophical histories have been criticized: for example, Merquior (1985, p. 97) says that Foucault prefers 'ideological drama to the wayward contingencies of actual history'. However, to focus too much on such possible problems would be to ignore how Foucault's ideas can help to give an interpretation of the present, or in his words, history as writing the 'history of the present' (Foucault, 1991, p. 31). It is important to note that Foucault's intention is not to write a history of the prison, but rather to offer a study of disciplinary technology (Dreyfus and Rabinow, 1982, p. 144).

5   For the prison to operate successfully as a reformatory it needs to have certain rights over the prisoner, in particular the right to modulate his or her sentence (Foucault, 1991, p. 244).

6   In Britain's case this recent emphasis on imprisonment as the prime tool of penal policy may be traced back to the Conservative Party conference of 1993 in which Michael Howard, the then Home Secretary, announced, '[W]e shall no longer judge the success of our system of justice by a fall in our prison population .... Prison works .... It ensures that we are protected from murderers, muggers and rapists – and it makes those who are tempted to commit crime think twice' (quoted in Rose, 1996, p. 328). It was only two years earlier that the previous Home Secretary, David Waddington, had argued that prison was simply 'an expensive way of making bad people worse' (quoted in Rose, 1996, p. 323).

References

Barron, A. (1990), 'Legal Discourse and the Colonisation of the Self in the Modern State' in Carty, A. (ed.), *Post-Modern Law*, University of Edinburgh Press, Edinburgh.

Card, R. (1995), *Criminal Law*, Butterworths, London, Dublin and Edinburgh.

Currie, E. (1996), 'Imprisoning Justice', *Criminal Justice Matters*, 25, Autumn, pp. 7–8.

Dreyfus, H. and Rabinow, P. (1982), *Michel Foucault: Beyond Structuralism and Hermeneutics*, Harvester Press, Brighton.

Dworkin, R. (1975), 'The Original Position' in Daniels, N. (ed.), *Reading Rawls*, Basil Blackwell, Oxford.

Fitzpatrick, P. (1990), '"The Desperate Vacuum": Imperialism and Law in the Experience of Enlightenment' in Carty, A. (ed.), *Post-Modern Law*, University of Edinburgh Press, Edinburgh.

Foucault, M. (1991), *Discipline and Punish*, Penguin, Harmondsworth.
Galston, W. (1991), *Liberal Purposes*, Cambridge University Press, Cambridge.
Geldart, W. (1991), *Introduction to English Law*, Yardley, D. (ed.), Oxford University Press, Oxford.
Mauer, M. (1996), 'Shocking Disparities', *Criminal Justice Matters*, 25, Autumn, pp. 13–14.
Merquior, J. (1985), *Foucault*, Fontana, London.
Moore, M. (1996), 'On reasonableness', *Journal of Applied Philosophy*, 13, pp. 167–78.
Rawls, J. (1971), *A Theory of Justice*, Oxford University Press, Oxford.
Rawls, J. (1993), *Political Liberalism*, Columbia University Press, New York.
Rose, D. (1996), *In the Name of the Law*, Vintage, London.

10 Liberalism Without Universalism?

GIDEON CALDER

This paper is partly about liberalism, partly about communitarianism and mostly about the drawbacks of both. It is also, and primarily, about univeralism. I use this term in various, not always interchangeable, senses. Two, though, are predominant: the idea that to be adequate, ethics and ideas of political progress require, at some level, a notion of universal respect for human beings *qua* human beings; and the idea that the critical norms used in ethical discourse must in some sense be independent of their immediate socio-historical context – that they are not, in other words, simply culturally relative. Now universalism in both these senses is, to put it mildly, under a fair amount of pressure – both theoretically and historically. On the one hand, there is the retreat from universalism common to the most influential among current political theories, especially those of a communitarian or postmodern hue. On the other, there is the resurgence of particularisms, exclusionary nationalisms and outright racisms witnessed across the board of 1990s politics, most especially in Europe.[1]

In the light of these developments, human universality as an idea, or as an ideal, might begin to seem like an overweening Enlightenment conceit, a legacy of modes of inquiry which were naïve enough to see no insuperable difficulty in speaking freely of a universal human nature or rationality, or of critical principles which transcend mere local circumstance. From this angle, the mere postulation of human solidarity across separate, incommensurable cultural contexts and discourses – or across divides of class, race or gender – risks both a necessarily imperialistic overriding of differences and a misreading of the genealogy of morals. We do not, it is argued, get our values straight from some metaphysical hot-line to the Great Tribunal of Right and Wrong. We get them locally, contingently, as an accident of our cultural situation and of circumstances beyond our control. Blithely to presume that there are intercultural norms (in terms either of 'good' ethical practice or of the possibility of the ethical critique of practice) worth speaking about is to miss

140

the point that difference in cultural identity resists the homogenizing gloss of traditional universal ethics-speak, and is also in some important sense *prior* to sameness as an ethical value: an end in its own right. Thus the shifting of ethical focus from universalism to the affirmation of particularity and difference (in the name of a criticism itself inevitably 'situated' and contextual) is seen as a liberatory detonation of the hubris of metaphysics and the violent generalizations it produces.

Several things strike me about this general anti-universalist impetus, brief as this caricature of it has been. One is that the way these debates tend to be presented – as a simple standoff between universalistic liberals and particularistic communitarians, for example, or between unreconstructed fans of the Enlightenment and sophisticated, reflexive, pluralistic postmoderns – skews the issues at stake in a way which closes off certain potential ways of resolving them. Another is that, though there is much to be gained from the recognition of 'concrete' cultural context (as opposed to abstract rule-formation) in the framing of our moral values, going too far down that road issues in a state of critical paralysis when we are confronted by the kind of upsurge of morally ambiguous particularisms already mentioned. A third is that there can, and should, be another, more helpful way of presenting the issues. These three threads run through this paper, as motivations and as background themes. They are joined by a fourth, which underlies and in a sense underwrites them all: that there is scope for dealing with the particular challenges thrown up by our pre-millennial political situation (nationalisms and racisms and all) only if the very idea of universality can be kept intact. This is a large claim. The rest of this paper is an attempt, if indirectly, to justify it.

In the first part, I try to show that in looking at the work of Richard Rorty, a thinker kept largely to the margins of mainstream political-philosophical debate,[2] we find in fact a kind of summation of the way in which much of that debate is going: a fusion of certain definitive themes of contemporary liberalism, communitarianism and postmodern-tinged progressive leftism (postmodernism being another 'ism' lurking in the backdrop here). I argue that Rorty draws out key implications of those themes – most notably, the drift towards cultural relativism – to an extent which other thinkers with similar motives, like John Rawls, are less ready to admit. Though I reject his own political conclusions, I argue that the negative labour of Rorty's work, in showing how the disputes between liberals and communitarians might be dissolved, helps clear the way for a reconstructive, more nuanced, approach to the relationship between individual and collective identities, or difference and sameness, which avoids the familiar dichotomy between the sovereignty of the atomized individual on the one hand and a bland cultural determinism on the other.

It is this dichotomy, I think, which is the problem. It leads those suspicious of the metaphysical presuppositions of classical liberal thought (centring on its positing of an isolated, monadic, lifestyle-choosing self) to an overhasty jettisoning of the very idea of the universal and makes for a steady slide into a particularism which is both theoretically incoherent and politically dangerous. So in the second part of the paper I try to show how we might talk of universalism in a way which avoids the unhelpful dichotomies thrown up by the liberal/communitarian debate, and which are replicated in a great deal of postmodernist discourse and the attitudes it inspires.

Liberalism Redescribed: Rawls, Rorty and Rorty's Rawls

It is a curious thing that ever since the publication in 1971 of John Rawls' *A Theory of Justice*, a work commonly credited with having rehabilitated liberal thinking, liberals have been beating a steady retreat from many of its key contentions. Rawls himself, largely in response to the challenges of communitarian critics such as Michael Sandel and Charles Taylor, has redescribed, recontextualized and 'softened' central aspects of the theory to the extent that its complexion, and arguably its substance, have been greatly changed. The changes are perhaps best summed up by his decision to present his theory as a *political*, rather than a metaphysical, account of liberal selfhood and rationality – pertaining specifically to American public policy rather than appealing to an abstract or ahistorical model.

Rawls introduced *A Theory of Justice* as an attempt to 'generalize and carry to a higher level of abstraction the traditional theory of the social contract as represented by Locke, Rousseau, and Kant' (Rawls, 1971, p. viii). Its central, most influential conceptions – of the 'veil of ignorance', the 'original position', and 'justice as fairness' – were presented as elements of a neutral formula for the definition of a distinctively liberal distributive justice: as the algorithmic conditions and principles which rational individuals in all societies would arrive at if they stopped and thought about it. The words 'generalize' and 'abstraction', then, were key – and it was aspirations like these in Rawls' theory which did most to provoke the subsequent communitarian critique. The main allegations arising from the work of critics like Sandel and Taylor centred on liberalism's formalistic emptiness with regard to the nature of moral selfhood and community: the 'unencumbered', atomized liberal self was in fact too empty to be morally meaningful, and hardly the sort of self anyone would actually want to be; liberalism ignored our necessary embeddedness in particular cultural practices and forms of life; it pretended to have access to some strictly unattainable universality or objectivity, and so on. Moreover, Rawls, it was alleged, was claiming for his theory a transcendental applicability when all his 'rational choosers' were really embodiments of the contingent cultural preferences of modern American liberals.

To these allegations Rawls has now effectively replied, 'So what?'. He has spent much of his more recent work explaining why notions such as 'justice as fairness' figure in his theory not as 'claims to universal truth' based on 'presumptions about the essential nature and identity of persons', but rather as reasonable political suggestions with a particular set of social and economic institutions in mind. His, then, is a conception of justice which 'tries to draw solely upon basic intuitive ideas that are embedded in the political institutions of a constitutional democratic regime and the public traditions of their interpretation' (Rawls, 1985, pp. 223–5). This disclaimer follows from Rawls' assertion (1980, p. 519) that:

> [W]hat justifies a conception of justice is not its being true to an order antecedent to and given to us, but its congruence with our deeper understanding of ourselves and our aspirations, and our realization that, given our history and the traditions embedded in our public life, it is the most reasonable doctrine for us.

The details of Rawls' original presentation of his theory and its subsequent tweakings are not strictly relevant here, and I shan't go into them: what I'm more concerned with is this qualification of its nature and scope.

For it is precisely this qualification which has made it possible for a self-proclaimed liberal pragmatist like Rorty to interpret Rawls' work as heading in much the same 'post-philosophical' direction as his own. Since the early 1980s, Rorty has turned his attention from debunking the presuppositions of metaphysics and analytic philosophy as traditionally practised in the universities of the West (see Rorty, 1980, *passim*) to trying to sketch what a post-metaphysical, indeed 'post-philosophical' way of justifying and criticizing our political practices might look like. In 'The Priority of Democracy to Philosophy', he suggests that the revamped Rawls, freed from any association with the grand metaphysical project, suits these post-philosophical purposes very well. This is, broadly, because he affirms the value of liberal-democratic institutions without pretending that this value can or should 'be measured by anything more specific than the moral intuitions of the particular historical community that has created those institutions' (Rorty, 1991c, p. 190). In other words, he drops the customary liberal preoccupation with the nature of moral selfhood, and its attendant prioritizations: of individual over community, and the right over the good. As Rorty puts it (ibid., p. 189):

> [O]n the interpretation of Rawls I am offering, we do not need a categorical distinction between the self and its situation. We can dismiss the distinction between an attribute of the self and a constituent of the self, between the self's accidents and its essence, as 'merely' metaphysical. If we are inclined to philosophize, we shall want the vocabulary offered by Dewey, Heidegger, Davidson, and Derrida, with its built-in cautions against metaphysics, rather than that offered by Descartes, Hume, and Kant. For if we use the former vocabulary, we shall be able to see moral progress and a history of making rather than finding, of poetic achievement by 'radically situated' individuals and communities, rather than as the gradual unveiling, through the use of reason', of 'principles' or 'rights' or 'values'.[3]

Rorty sees Rawls' recent work as 'thoroughly historicist and antiuniversalist' (ibid., p. 180), and thus as fitting neatly with his own orientation towards the local, the particular and the contextual – rather than the universal, the ahistorical or the transcultural – as a guide to moral practice. Morality in these terms becomes, as Rorty has often put it, 'the sort of thing *we* do', and immorality the sort of thing 'we' don't (see, e.g., Rorty, 1989, pp. 59–60). Our actions are subject not to the adjudication of some abstracted tribunal of moral reason but to comparison with the existing, cemented intuitions and practices of good liberals.

Thus Rorty, as both liberal and anti-metaphysician, thoroughly endorses the changing of priorities of recent liberalism.[4] He can present Rawls as 'not attempting a transcendental deduction of American liberalism or supplying philosophical foundations for democratic institutions, but simply trying to systematize the principles and intuitions typical of American liberals' (Rorty, 1991c, p. 189). And that, as Rorty would have it, represents more or less the limit of what any political philosophy can do: seek an ever-more faithful, ever-more hopeful and constructive redescription of our own particular and historically contingent moral parameters and prospects. His point here is that there is nothing to be got Right or Wrong about philosophical concerns like justice, truth or rationality, and no way of tying up an account of any of them with an 'objective' account of social progress usable as a benchmark by which to gauge the maturity or relative acceptability of our current circumstances. As he has also put it (1994a, p. 26),

> [C]oncepts as abstract and flexible as truth, rationality, and maturity are up for socio-political grabs. They are material to be shaped, not essences to be grasped. The only thing that matters is which way of reshaping them will, in the long run, make them more useful for democratic politics.

For Rorty, liberal democracy and its status as the best framework for public institutions so far invented are to be taken as historically given, and then worked around as the raw materials for change. Our ideas about what 'good' change might be will be inevitably local and ethnocentric. What 'we' should want from our new, metaphysics-free philosophy is useful descriptions of the world, helping us to fashion a future which is better, but 'only in the sense of containing more of what we consider good and less of what we consider bad' (Rorty, 1994b, p. 9). And we should turn for these descriptions not to 'deep thinkers', but to those 'superficial dreamers':

> [W]ho dangle carrots before democratic societies by suggesting concrete ways in which things might better – become more democratic, fairer, more open, more egalitarian, more decent. They supply local hope, not universal knowledge (Rorty, 1987, p. 12).

Communitarian Liberalism

Whether or not Rorty can fairly include Rawls among such 'superficial dreamers' (and I'm not denying the mootness of this point)[5] I think there is a case to be made that the upshot of mainstream liberalism's response to its communitarian critics has been to redescribe itself along communitarian lines. Its central values – of individual choice, of toleration and equal treatment in the eyes of the law – remain nominally intact, but are presented in terms of their relation to an immediate cultural context rather than as an abstract algorithm for justice. This accommodation may at first not be apparent when comparing Rorty's explicitly pragmatist apologia for liberalism with the more standard defences of the liberal position: gone is the emphasis on individual autonomy and rationality as the basis for morality; gone too is the more recently posited liberal tenet (in, for example, the early Rawls) that the state both can and should be neutral between competing ways of life and conceptions of the good. Rorty's liberal self is nothing like a transcendental ego. It is the centreless, bundle-like product of a strictly causal, contingent accumulation of beliefs and desires: Hume's model rather than Kant's. And Rorty's ideal liberal state can hardly aspire to neutrality between conflicting versions of the good life when its very *raison d'être* is provided at core by a common assent to the idea that its own liberal ideals are 'the best hope of the species' (Rorty, 1991b, p. 208), and that 'there is nothing wrong with liberal democracy' (Rorty, 1991d, p. 34). Nonetheless, and perhaps more importantly, there is much in Rorty's liberalism that chimes with the communitarian approach. The communitarian response is that liberalism ignores our embeddedness in given cultural practices, practices which are constitutive of our ends and of our conceptions of the good rather than being simply incidental to them. So liberalism claims a distance from the particularities of lived existence in the name of some pseudo-levitation above the contingencies of our local, contextual social determination. With the thrust of these charges Rorty could hardly beg to differ. Rorty's pragmatism is heavily inflected by communitarian attitudes: and in fact we find in Rorty (and, though less forthrightly, in the later Rawls) an admission precisely that old-style liberal theorizing was founded on an untenably atomized and asocial view of the self.

This strikes me as a crucial step to take. But one effect of this concession is that it leads Rorty into a roundabout endorsement of the more problematic aspects of communitarian thinking. On the one hand, the most damaging criticism of liberalism is that it abstracts from intersubjective relations and factors such as systematic social inequality to the extent that on its return from suspension in the metaphysical ether it is singularly ill-equipped to deal with the details of everyday injustice. Hence the common enough allegation that the purported neutrality of liberalism masks an ideological attachment to the values of free market capitalism and its various exploitations: that the 'disinterested' liberal state is at best a self-delusion.[6] On the other hand, contemporary communitarianism tends to lean too far in the other direction: to overemphasize the force of cultural determination to the extent that it readily collapses into a conservative recognition that 'tradition comes first' (whatever the iniquities of a given tradition), or into cultural relativism or into both. If cognitive and moral standards are purely a matter of historical circumstance, or purely a matter of those habits of thought and action which happen to have obtained, by whatever means, a certain social dominance, then there is no room for social critique beyond the sum of those cultural parts, or the outer reach of that language-game. Reason just *is*, on this reading, the sum total, or the common denominator, of current social practice. And if context is all, then racism is all right as long as everyone's a racist.

I'll try to put this slightly differently to clarify the point. Rorty himself offers a resolution of the liberal-communitarian debate by collapsing one into the other. In doing so, he retains what I would argue are the least appealing aspects of both. In adopting a model of rationality and selfhood as *nothing but* the side-effects of convention – as *completely* dependent on the contingencies of cultural circumstance – we find that we have lost precisely that critical leverage required to transcend the limits of immediate cultural context. What follows from this is a situation in which the currency of sedimented belief, of social convention however pernicious or mendacious, provides the only horizon of what is desirable and possible, of good and bad. This means that dissenters, by dint of their being lonely voices pitted against whatever consensus may happen to predominate (be it Nazism, Islamic fundamentalism, or welfarist liberal democracy) must always and necessarily be *wrong* – or 'wrong' in the only sense in which notions of rightness and wrongness can apply under purely pragmatic conditions. This hardly chimes in sweetly with the liberal doctrine of tolerance. Nevertheless, this is just what Rorty argues, namely that the liberalism which the 'post-philosophical' liberal can advocate as a standard for our ethical and political judgments:

> [C]an only be something relatively local and ethnocentric – the tradition of a particular community, the consensus of a particular culture. According to this view, what counts as rational or as fanatical is relative to the group to which we think it necessary to justify ourselves – to the body of shared belief that determines the reference of the word 'we' (Rorty, 1991c, pp. 176–7).

It is a liberalism, in other words, made relative to precisely that set of necessarily *local* determinants which communitarians counterpose to the ahistoricity of the liberal subject as traditionally conceived. If liberals prioritize abstract, universal rights and rationality, and communitarians concrete affiliations and culture-bound practices, then – in terms of methodology and epistemology – Rorty fits much more snugly with the latter, even while retaining some of traditional liberalism's surface rhetoric. It is in this sense, then, that Rorty splits the difference between liberalism and communitarianism.

In so doing, I think that he provides a valuable, if negative, service. This is because the lessons of Rorty's political thinking are the lessons to be drawn from the dropping of the liberal concern with universality and the retreat to the confines of the local, the given and the historically contingent. My interest is not in saving either Rorty or liberalism from this fate. It is to rescue the universalism that both seem ready to leave behind. This need involve no claim that the traditional liberal account of such universality is correct. But it does require that one keep open the possibility of universality, not so much to serve as some supposedly value-neutral template or lens though which to make humanity one, but as a value in itself, as a regulative idea, and indeed as a necessary component of any workable conception of what political progress is or might be.

Universalism Revisited: Denial

Rawls, in denying that the principles advanced in *A Theory of Justice* represent any appeal to universal truth or to a 'thick' conception of moral subjectivity, reacts almost as if the very suggestion that universality may have some relevance to contemporary morality and politics were laughably unthinkable (see, e.g., Rawls, 1985, pp. 223–5). He accepts that such an account is strictly unfeasible, and anxiously protests that of course he is not, and never has been, trying to offer one. This response strikes me as mistaken. It neglects the possibility of an account of universality which, rather than relying on the sorts of substantive presumptions about human nature which are fairly easily made to look ideologically loaded (blind to distinctions of gender, race or class), presents universality in terms of its preconditional relevance to just any ethical thinking. One does not need to posit a pan-global network of floating liberal 'rational choosers' to insist that there is something important about aspects of our moral humanity which transcends the merely local and particular, or to hang on to the idea of universal respect for human beings in virtue of their humanity.

Those who seek to junk universalism altogether tend to presume that it rests on certain key claims which, it is argued, can no longer be seen as tenable. These might be one or all of the following: (i) a 'thick' account of human nature imbued with purportedly 'neutral' but effectively value-laden presumptions; (ii) a way of looking at moral actions which requires of agents a flatly improbable 'God's-eye view' of the world, such that they can literally consider the implications of their actions for humanity at large (one thinks here of certain crass cartoon accounts of Kant's categorical imperative); or (iii) a way of looking at the good for human beings such that it is always substantially the same, and the same for everybody. Universalism so presented will provoke immediate doubts: about the moral desirability (or possibility) of positing fixed human orientations across cultures and centuries; about the potential wrongs involved in making ethics solely a matter of the application of formalistic, context-insensitive rules; or about the imperialistic implications of making our political future conform to a single utopian blueprint. These doubts have tended to be voiced most recently in the writings of postmodernist theorists, critical as they are of philosophy's alleged 'metanarrative' tendency to attempt to legislate for everyone, everywhere, forever. And, put as simply as they are here, the objections have a point. Looked at this way, universalism does indeed seem a symptom of supreme philosophical hubris.

But I shan't dwell on the cogency or otherwise of these objections. Switching focus slightly, I want to suggest that there are other ways of presenting the idea of universality such that its rejection represents a much bigger, and more likely specious, claim than its (qualified) assertion. One way emerges in the work of those who, like Norman Geras, have tried to keep space for some account of human nature in the face of relativist and cultural-determinist objections. It might best be put in the form of a question: What might be involved in the claim that there is strictly *no* common, transcultural and transhistorical human nature worth talking about? Geras makes the point like this. If, when confronted by the claim (shared by Rorty-style liberal communitarianism with most species of postmodernism) 'that there is no human nature, everything is historically formed, socially determined, culturally specific, and the like':

> [Y]ou point out in response that there are certainly transhistorical human needs and capacities, you get the reply: 'Oh well, if *that's* what you mean by human nature …. But we meant that people are not (for example) intrinsically cruel or selfish or possessive; and/or that the character of individuals is significantly shaped by the specificities of their society and culture (Geras, 1995, p. 109).

So it turns out, as Geras observes, that there *is* a human nature there somewhere, only it is importantly affected by non-universal factors. But that is hardly a wildly contentious point. In other words, no one *really* denies that there is anything at all that can be said about human nature, any more than they can deny that eating food is, by and large, a good thing for human beings to do. Certainly there are many qualities that are not universal, and this fact is politically important. But the idea that certain crucial, or even the *most* crucial, aspects of our make-up as moral/political agents are derived purely from historical or cultural context hardly makes all and any talk of human universality automatically redundant. Indeed, talking as if the very idea of a common human nature is *strictly* out of bounds runs the risk of radical incoherence, or at least drastic counter-intuitiveness. If we can talk at all of human beings as an identifiable species, delimited and distinct, then this rather suggests that we know who it is we're talking about, that there is some sort of coherent whole there. It's a trivial point perhaps, and may sound wilfully naïve. But, cybernetics notwithstanding, it is worth remembering that there are some brute, unique, mundane facts about being human which any amount of cultural interference is going to have to struggle quite inordinately to negate.

What really matters, of course, is whether anything might *follow*, politically, from the features which make us human. Things get muddier here. Might there be a relation between our basic needs and capacities and the nature of practical reason? At this point I am going to proceed negatively. Consider the following crude précis of Rorty's line of thinking. (i) There is no common human nature or shared way of morally or politically confronting the world; (ii) therefore moral values are socially received (rather than derived from anything objective), and received in a specific cultural context; (iii) thus morality is a matter of 'we's and 'them's, of contrast-effects, of gauging practices by their relation to in-place social convention. So it is that Rorty (1989, p. 191) arrives at the following, much-cited, conclusion:

> Consider ... the attitude of contemporary American liberals to the unending hopelessness and misery of the lives of the young blacks in American cities. Do we say that these people must be helped because they are our fellow human beings? We may, but it is much more persuasive, morally as well as politically, to describe them as our fellow *Americans* – to insist that it is outrageous that an *American* should live without hope.

Now, Rorty presents this simply as back-up to his suggestion that 'our sense of solidarity is strongest when those with whom solidarity is expressed are thought of as "one of us", where "us" means something smaller and more local than the human race' (ibid.). In a trivial sense, this point may seem fairly uncontentious. Everyday solidarity and felt allegiance will probably be strongest among fellow workers, fellow victims of discrimination, fellow MI6 secret agents or others with a shared sense of circumstance and purpose. We know some people better than others. But nothing much follows from this in terms of moral principle. And anyway, his point goes rather deeper than that. It is more like an attempt to circumscribe the scope of morality, or transcendentally to limit the scope of practical reason, and thus to say who among humans counts as a fellow moral being and who doesn't. Or at any rate, if it *isn't* such an attempt, then it's a rather pointless sort of point to make.

So let's assume that it is. Let's assume that Rorty is saying: that the scope of morality is confined within set geographical and linguistic limits. Now, to borrow a point made by Will Kymlicka (1989, p. 68):

> [I]f this were just a *prediction* about the limits of practical reason, then it wouldn't

be objectionable. It would be just speculation, and we'd have to wait and see how far the reasons and arguments had taken us at the end of the day. We'd have to see whether there are standards of rational persuasion which can lead us to reject a particular historical tradition. Perhaps, at the end of the day, the only reason we can give for our actions is 'this is what we do around here' – an appeal to localized and particular standards, not shared by others.

Perhaps indeed. But the thing is, Rorty *isn't* just making this sort of prediction. He's not just saying, 'Here's a hypothesis. Let's see if it's confirmed.' Bear in mind his claim that standards for moral judgment 'can *only* be something relatively local and ethnocentric – the tradition of a particular community, the consensus of a particular culture' (Rorty, 1991c, p. 176 – my emphasis). This changes things entirely. For it means, as Kymlicka goes on to argue (1989, p. 69), that Rorty claims 'to *know* such limits exist – [he claims] to know this *in advance of the arguments*. [He claims] to know that reasons will only be compelling to particular historical communities, before those reasons have been advanced'. In other words, Rorty is making a transcendental claim about the very possibility and limits of moral deliberation.

To say that there can be *no* link between transcultural human attributes, or indeed values, and practical reason – that the scope of such reason is *necessarily* confined to the current values of my community – is a weighty claim indeed, and one which requires rather more than dogmatic assertion to be taken seriously. How, indeed, could one know this in advance? By appealing to the facts of historical and cultural variation? By pointing to the vast divergence in forms of life and discourses of justice across the globe? In what sense could either sort of observation *rule out* the possibility that there might be context-transcendent ethical or critical norms, or that those norms are worth seeking? I cannot see how they could. What I would contend is that Rorty is led to this specious-looking claim by his tacit presumption that there are only two alternative courts of appeal on offer: the *strictly* local and ethnocentric on the one hand, or the *strictly* acultural and ahistorical on the other. And this, too, seems a rather rash dichotomy. Those 'strictly's seem to me to need rather more argumentative support than Rorty ever seems willing to provide.

The consequences of this are rather ominous. A danger in strictly delimiting communitarian identities, be this on a national level or in terms of race or cultural difference, is that it lends muscle to exclusionary tendencies: to a politics of 'us' and 'them'. For it fixes and closes given identities in a way which creates firm boundaries between them, and makes undecidable the relative validity of their various moral or political claims. If identity is all, if the sole purpose of morality is the articulation of already-established commonalities in a way which makes for good social glue, then negotiations of future identities, and the possibility of resolving existing conflicts, are effectively constricted from the start. Such an approach will not get us very far in seeking any sort of resolution to, say, the current surge in European nationalisms: all it allows is simple, relativistic assertions of their equal right, *qua* identities, to exist.

Now Rorty, it should be said, need not necessarily presuppose a *single*, fixed identity as the be-all and end-all of moral jurisdiction. In fact, he moves freely between levels of community – from 'we fans of our local baseball team' to 'we American bourgeois liberals' to 'we inhabitants of the rich North Atlantic democracies'. Each of these is constitutive of an 'us' to which there is a relative 'them', and so provides a context in which codes and habits of moral conduct and judgment are firmed up. He cannot, as it happens, rule out the possibility that a range of presently variegated cultures might one day constitute an 'us' – indeed he recommends that we 'keep trying to expand our sense of "us" as far as we can' (Rorty, 1989, p. 196). In this sense, as has been noted, one might call him a sort of 'weak universalist', insofar as he allows for a possible pan-global moral community without suggesting that there is anything which makes us definitively human or worthy of equal respect (see, e.g., Brunkhorst, 1990, p. 188).

As I shall argue later on, though, to start from current moral convention and suggest that maybe it wouldn't be such a bad thing if the whole of humanity were persuaded to adopt Western liberal-capitalist values is not something which qualifies as 'universalist' in the sense I should like to endorse. Universalism in this sense is pitted precisely *against* the very idea that we can simply appeal to existing moral-political practice and declare that this is the way the rest of the world should be living. For Rorty, that is *all* we can do: our cultural situatedness makes certain other ways of looking at the world simply wrong and incomprehensible to us, such that they serve to reinforce our ethnocentric faith in our own ways of doing things. For his pragmatic liberalism to work as a collective acting upon shared norms, there must be relatively fixed and stable local moral conventions which are not really open to fundamental revision. And, as we have seen, though the range of one's community affiliations can expand and contract, their limits must always, for Rorty, represent the absolute limits of our moral responsibilities. For 'we are,' he claims, 'under no obligations other than the "we-intentions" of the communities with which we identify' (Rorty, 1989, p. 198).

Universalism Revisited: Affirmation

So the claim that there is *no* possible link between universal aspects of being human and the substance of morality or standards for social critique looks rather bigger and shakier once we unpack it a little. What about the claim that there *is* such a link?

Rorty and Rawls, as we have seen, reject universality primarily on epistemological (or anti-metaphysical) grounds: it is simply beyond the grasp of a theory of justice to expand its scope beyond the bounds of the particular historical community in which it is conceived. Rorty, as we have seen, is not disputing the *value* of such an expansion, just its possibility. Often though, the rejection of universalism has a specifically ethical aspect. Typical of postmodernist critiques, for example, is the objection that the mere idea of universalism – in liberal, Marxist, or whatever other form – inevitably entails the imperialistic projection of one, culturally-situated and so in no sense 'objectively' superior, conception of humanity across other, incommensurable, cultures. This makes cultural relativism more than just a product of the 'facts' of moral epistemology: on these terms, it is an ethical *requirement*. Terry Eagleton has pointed out that – real though the danger of value-imperialism is – postmodernism's mistake is in presuming that this is *all* that universalism can mean. For universality and difference are not necessarily at odds:

> [T]ake, for example, the concept of human equality. You can understand this as meaning that all people are equal in their concrete attributes, which is clearly fatuous: some people are a lot finer or shabbier than others, in particular respects. Or you can see it, along with the liberals, as meaning that everyone must have an equal opportunity of becoming unequal. This fails to capture our strong intuition that human equality goes deeper down than this, to do in some obscure way with what some socialists have called 'equality of being' .... What, then, does it mean to treat two individuals equally? ... To treat two people equally must surely mean not giving them exactly the same treatment but attending equally to their different needs. It is not that they are equal individuals, but that they are equally individuals (Eagleton, 1996, pp. 116–7).

Universalism in this sense, as Eagleton points out (ibid., p. 116), simply means that, 'when it comes to freedom, justice and happiness, everyone has to be in on the act'. It is a definite political goal rather than a presumption of existing equality or an ethical *fait accompli*. The universal is that horizon, or regulative idea, which provides a necessary benchmark for any non-exclusionary account of what progress or emancipation might mean.

In this sense, I would argue, the very framing of the problem of the overriding of cultural differences (a prime concern, of course, both for liberal toleration and for communitarian identity-politics) itself depends on a sort of universalism. Say, for example, that one wants to make a case that one cultural identity or way of life has been oppressively marginalized by another, or others. A relevant instance here might be the case of the Roma population in the Czech Republic. The suggestion is made that such an elision of cultural difference is a bad thing, that somehow or other the Roma are entitled to a voice which they have hitherto been denied. But simply in going this far we are invoking a moral epistemology that must in some sense transcend the merely local and particular. Otherwise, how might one conceive of a right *not* to have one's cultural particularities swamped by alien norms and priorities? Or an obligation on the part of dominant cultures to acknowledge the status of different ways of life? If there can be no such right or obligation, why should that swamping be a problem? On our own, specific, particular, separate, culturally-determined terms? What, then, if those terms are cheerfully approving of cultural imperialism? In that case, is no wrong committed? This would mean that the claims of the Roma to a right to political recognition would be negated simply by the fact that the dominant mode of discourse in the country in which they live happens not to endorse that right.

There is a problem of consistency here. The trouble with giving difference and anti-universality priority as ethical ends in themselves is that in the process they become installed, in effect, as a new, immutable universal: a categorical imperative to celebrate diversity. And that rather suggests that there is no necessary opposition between universality and difference at all – and indeed that they are mutually dependent. I would argue that the simple counterposing of universality to difference misses an important condition of being able to talk about difference in the first place. Just to be different, difference must be relative to something else. If differences are to be able to be compared and identified as 'differences', there must be some mutually applicable standard (however thin, or shifting) of comparison – unless, that is, everything that is not easily assimilable with a given world-view is simply unfathomably 'other' in a homogeneous, undifferentiated way. Perhaps, indeed, that's the case. But if it is then it is hard to see how we can protect differences which we can't even identify. So the very idea that difference should be protected and nurtured requires that there be some scheme for so doing: minority rights, perhaps, or rights to freedom of expression. And in even going just this far, we have already begun to talk a little too universally for those who presume that a violence is involved as soon as we apply standards of morality and progress to the world at large. What they miss is that to talk about a 'world at large' in the first place, to assume that we have some ethical responsibility *not* to impose the views of (however generous-spirited) rich white Western males upon it, or, again, to assume that it has some 'right' not to be so imposed upon – all these things require some sense of universality simply in order to be articulated. As Ernesto Laclau has argued (see 1996, pp. 48, 65), the very assertion of a particular identity requires the appeal to something transcending it, or else it hardly makes sense. To reject the very idea of the universal, one would need to appeal to some kind of fully homogenous community beyond which there is nothing else, no remainder or residue, so that there is nothing for particularity to be relative to – in which case, of course, the need for the protection of difference would never arise.

Of course, to backtrack a little, those who, like Rorty, would limit the scope of our moral responsibility to people in some substantive sense 'like us', and who account for all moral acts in terms of local affinity and sentiment rather than anything to do with principles *per se*, can (and often do) agree that universality is a goal worth having. They are at least consistent, unlike those who favour difference at all costs, in thinking that it would be a good thing if everyone agreed on which sorts of public institution and practice are best. (Rorty would, of course, say that slavery was a bad thing, and that the world would be better if everyone thought this – but that it is only a bad thing by our particular, contingent cultural lights rather than by some 'objective' standard of human decency.) But what they cannot allow themselves is the sort of critical framework which could account for, or gauge, such universality. This is precisely because if *everything* is culture-relative then any extension of moral sentiment to the whole of humanity will be exactly, and only, that – an *extension* of our own, contingent, culture-bound moral codes and practices across recalcitrant boundaries in the name of some necessarily partial conception of the common good. The emphasis in Rorty and the later Rawls on the need for political ideals to be framed fully in the context of existing institutions seems simply to mean that what is given, currently dominant or able to assert itself most strongly has some prior claim to be the starting-point for justice.

Conclusion

To my mind, the attempt to discount universality as strictly out of bounds in questions of ethical and political criticism is both flawed and undesirable. Its undesirability is borne out most starkly in the work of those like Rorty who see nothing to be wary of in honest ethnocentrism. But the same problems which his work displays *in extremis* will hamper all arguments to the effect that universality is either impossible or necessarily violent. My argument has been geared towards quite the opposite conclusion: that universality is better seen as a precondition for, and an uneliminable dimension of, any adequate conception of social progress. What exactly universality will *mean* here has been left open. This is not to say, as does Laclau for example (see 1996, pp. 34, 59), that the universal exists solely as a sort of empty signifier, a necessary but strictly formless symbol of that which is outside of current received opinion. This seems to me to reduce universality to an emptiness bordering on redundancy. I want to use 'the universal' in a more affirmative, normative sense – not simply as a floating signifier or strategic postulation, but, again, as a precondition of social progress.

The main problem as I see it with Rorty and the later Rawls is that they seek to restrict the scope of normative inquiry to the circumstances of existing Western democratic states – arguing, even, that fine-tuning those practices and institutions is *all* that normative inquiry can do. This step is taken with a cheerful affirmation that there is nothing much that theories of selfhood, rationality or social interaction can tell us which is of any direct relevance to political theory. As a way of looking at what social criticism is and what it can do this strikes me as being both counter-intuitive and potentially disastrous. I would agree with Seyla Benhabib (1992, p. 7) that:

> [I]n the final analysis, conceptions of self, reason and society and visions of ethics and politics are inseparable. One should regard such conceptions of self, reason and society not as elements of a 'comprehensive' Weltanschauung which cannot be further challenged, but as presuppositions which are themselves always open to challenge and inquiry.

The problem with the liberal-communitarian-postmodern attempt to delimit all such questions within strict historical and cultural boundaries is precisely the *limits* it places on providing an adequate forum in which differences can be negotiated, in which identities can be articulated and developed, and in which claims to particularity can be evaluated.

Communitarianism's great contribution has been to show how moral selves are not blandly generalized or neutral archetypes, but are situated beings with particular life histories and other 'encumbrances' which crucially affect the ways in which moral generalizations might be formulated. The mistake of much recent liberalism has been to assume that in order to be sensitive to such contingencies of context, moral and political theory must confine itself within particular community limits (community here presented as something definitively local, as distinct from 'humanity'). The upshot of this is a slide into communitarianism's murky downside: its conservative tendency to valorize the traditional as a good in itself and seek a reclamation of integrative, constitutive ways of life in a way which is rather blasé about the oppressions of those traditions: their racisms and sexisms and the rank economic inequalities which provided the basic structure for ostensible moral cohesion and stability. In highlighting these oppressions, postmodernism has provided a great service. But liberalism, in acknowledging the force of communitarian and postmodern objections, has largely given up on the very idea of principled, universalist ethical-political thinking.

My argument is not just that such thinking is a good thing, but that it is compatible with, and indeed a vital ingredient of, an ethics which is as context-sensitive, as respectful of cultural difference, as present circumstances patently demand. Yes, we are situated selves. But for the sake of progressive politics, we must be situated selves with the power to challenge our situatedness in the name, as Benhabib has nicely put it, 'of universalistic principles, future identities and as yet undiscovered communities' (Benhabib, 1992, p. 8).[7] Liberalism without universalism seems, on this score, a flimsy combination – and curiously unable to conceive of any real distinction between progressive and pernicious assertions of national or racial identity.

Notes

1 I'm thinking here of the militant nationalisms born out of the splintering of Yugoslavia, the wave of far-right activity in Germany, Denmark, and elsewhere in central Europe, and of the rise to electoral respectability of the Front National in France – to name but three among many instances. The fact that there are other causes more worthy or benign – like those of Basques and Catalans in Spain, or of Irish nationalism – seems to make even more urgent the need for a theoretical framework which can do justice to the ambiguities involved in claims of separate identity.

2 When Rorty *isn't* kept to the margins of that debate, he is often introduced either as a bit of a maverick whose case is relevant only to the extent that it can be shown in an instant to be made of straw and then summarily dispatched, or else, conversely, as showing that the whole history of political philosophy – its presumptions and its aims – is bunk. Neither response seems to me adequately to confront the seriousness of Rorty's challenge. If he is wrong, he must be shown to be wrong. If he is right, then the very project of social critique is in pretty deep trouble,

3   The term 'radically situated subject' is used by Michael Sandel to denote a conception of selfhood such that there is no distinction between 'I am' and 'I have', and so 'my identity would blur indistinguishably into "my" situation' and 'it becomes impossible to distinguish what is me from what is mine' (Sandel, 1982, pp. 20–1). Rorty would rather call himself a liberal than a communitarian because, in short, he thinks communitarians try to posit a theory of moral selfhood to link into a justification of certain political institutions, when actually no such theory is needed (see Rorty, 1991c, *passim*). Communitarians more commonly recognized as such do tend to differ on this. Consider this quotation from Sandel, for instance (1982, p. 20): 'Any theory of the self of the form "I *am x, y,* and *z*", rather than "I *have x, y,* and *z*" (where *x, y,* and *z* are desires, etc.) collapses the distance between subject and situation which is necessary to any coherent conception of the self.' What Rorty would object to here is the idea that there is any self at all beyond the 'radically situated subject', any 'I' in the sense of something which is distinct from its own shifting make-up: the self is not something which "has" beliefs and desires, but is simply the network of such beliefs and desires' (Rorty, 1991a, p. 123). This might, for some, disqualify Rorty as a proper communitarian. I would suggest instead that it simply means he is a communitarian who has an ultra-Humean (rather than, say, a Hegelian) view of the self.

4   I do not take Rawls, let alone Rorty, to be entirely representative of the state of play within contemporary liberal thinking. There are of course those, like Ronald Dworkin and Alan Gewirth, who hang onto and defend a strong account of human rights, of the priority of the right to the good, and other 'metaphysical' dimensions. But the sheer, unparalleled interdisciplinary influence of Rawls' work makes him an obvious candidate for present-day liberal standard-bearer.

5   For an argument against Rorty's reading of Rawls, see Mulhall and Swift (1992, pp. 232–4). Earlier in the same book, interestingly enough, they suggest that Rawls' conception of justice as fairness 'is ... communitarian both in terms of its source – it articulates the shared values of the community which it addresses – and in terms of its content – those shared values themselves involve a commitment to an understanding of politics which is distinctively communitarian' (p. 201). It seems to me that both these criteria apply just as much to Rorty's ideas, and in a similar way.

6   See, for example, Ed Garrett's piece in this volume for an account of how the framing of Rawls' original position makes for racist implications.

7   In a similar vein, Keith Graham sums up the respective key insights of liberalism and communitarianism (1998, p. 187):

> It is true, for example, that any individual person is part of a multiplicity of communities and collective agents, and that the identities, values, and loyalties that they manifest can be traced back to those communities and collectives. That is what licences communitarian talk of the individual being embedded or encumbered. But that is what is true of an individual in advance of any critical reflection. The important insight in liberalism is just that I can always distance myself from any such particular encumbrance, at least in imagination, and in that sense take up an endorsing or a critical stance towards it. Moreover I can in some cases divest myself of encumbrances not merely in imagination but in practice. I can cease to be what I am. Accordingly, it is inaccurate to say that my encumbrances, as such, *determine* my identity and my values. Some may do so, but we need to distinguish between what I am inescapably and what I am escapably.

Graham's own proposed way of making such a distinction, by appealing to human materiality as what he calls a 'constraint of precondition' behind all human deeds and aspirations, strikes me as a productive way of proceeding, and one which would seem to follow on from Geras' focus on common human needs and capacities. I had hoped to follow this through a little more; unfortunately, constraints of space have thwarted that intention.

References

Benhabib, S. (1992), *Situating the Self*, Polity Press, Cambridge.

Brunkhorst, H. (1990), 'Adorno, Heidegger and Postmodernity' in Rasmussen, D. (ed.), *Universalism vs. Communitarianism: Contemporary Debates in Ethics*, MIT Press, Cambridge, Mass.

Eagleton, T. (1996), *The Illusions of Postmodernism*, Blackwell, Oxford.

Geras, N. (1995), *Solidarity in the Conversation of Humankind*, Verso, London.

Graham, K. (1998), 'Being Some Body: Choice and Identity in a Liberal Pluralist World' in Brecher, B., Halliday, J. and Kolinská, K. (eds), *Nationalism and Racism in the Liberal Order*, Ashgate, Aldershot.

Kymlicka, W. (1989), *Liberalism, Community and Culture*, Clarendon Press, Oxford.

Laclau, E. (1996), *Emancipation(s)*, Verso, London.

Mulhall, S. and Swift, A. (1992), *Liberals and Communitarians*, Blackwell, Oxford.

Rawls, J. (1971), *A Theory of Justice*, Oxford University Press, Oxford.

Rawls, J. (1980), 'Kantian Constructivism in Moral Theory', *Journal of Philosophy*, Vol. 77, No. 9, pp. 51–72.

Rawls, J. (1985), 'Justice as Fairness: Political not Metaphysical', *Philosophy and Public Affairs*, Vol. 14, No. 3, pp. 223–51.

Rawls, J. (1993), *Political Liberalism*, Columbia University Press, New York.

Rorty, R. (1980), *Philosophy and the Mirror of Nature*, Blackwell, Oxford.

Rorty, R. (1987), 'Posties', *London Review of Books*, Vol. 9, No. 15, 3 September, pp. 11–12.

Rorty, R. (1989), *Contingency, Irony, and Solidarity*, Cambridge University Press, Cambridge.

Rorty, R. (1991a), 'Non-Reductive Physicalism' in his *Objectivity, Relativism, and Truth: Philosophical Papers Volume 1*, Cambridge University Press, Cambridge.

Rorty, R. (1991b), 'On Ethnocentrism: A Reply to Clifford Geertz' in his *Objectivity, Relativism, and Truth: Philsophical Papers Volume 1*, Cambridge University Press, Cambridge.

Rorty, R. (1991c), 'The Priority of Democracy to Philosophy' in his *Objectivity, Relativism, and Truth: Philsophical Papers Volume 1*, Cambridge University Press, Cambridge.

Rorty, R. (1991d), 'Solidarity or Objectivity?' in his *Objectivity, Relativism, and Truth: Philsophical Papers Volume 1*, Cambridge University Press, Cambridge.

Rorty, R. (1994a), 'Are Assertions Claims to Universal Validity?', unpublished.

Rorty, R. (1994b), 'Truth without Correspondence to Reality', unpublished English version of ch. 1 of his *Hoffnung statt Erkentniss: Eine Einfürung in die Pragmatische Philosophie*, Passagen Verlag, Vienna.

Sandel, M. (1982), *Liberalism and the Limits of Justice*, Cambridge University Press, Cambridge.

11 Communitarianism and Obedience

ALISON ASSITER

Obedience

In his book *Obedience to Authority*, Stanley Milgram presents the results of some psychological experiments that suggest the extent to which people from a wide range of walks of life are prepared to act in a way that is contrary to their conscience, simply because they are obeying authority. In chapter 2, he makes the following point (1974, p. 13): 'of all moral principles, the one that comes closest to being universally accepted is this: one should not inflict suffering on a helpless person who is neither harmful nor threatening to oneself'. Yet the cases he describes are instances where many people, none of them particularly sadistic or violent by nature, are prepared to inflict pain on others.

The experiment consists in two psychological subjects, one of whom plays the role of 'learner' and the other that of 'teacher'. The experimenter explains that the study is concerned with the effects of punishment on learning. The 'learner' is conducted into a room, seated in a chair, his arms strapped to prevent excessive movement, and an electrode attached to his wrist. He is told that he is to learn a list of word pairs; whenever he makes an error, he will receive an electric shock of increasing intensity. The 'teacher' sits in front of a horizontal row of 30 switches, ranging from 15–450 volts. There are verbal descriptions ranging from 'slight shock' to 'danger – severe shock'. S/he is told to start at the lowest level and to increase the level each time the 'learner' makes an error. (The 'learner' actually receives no shock at all, but the 'teacher' does not know that.) A range of people was asked, before the experiment was carried out, whether they thought that the experimental subjects playing the role of 'teachers' would administer the shocks. The vast majority said that they thought they would not. They thought that people would not go beyond 150 volts, because people are basically decent, empathetic. In fact some subjects in one experiment carried on to the maximum shock level of 450

160

volts. Four experiments were carried out, and the subjects were more likely to defy the experimenter and cease operating the voltage machine when the 'learner' was brought into close proximity to the 'teacher'.

I'd just like to describe two of those playing the role of teacher. This is the first.

> Jack Washington is a black subject, age thirty-five, who was born in South Carolina. He works as a drill press operator and stresses the fact that although he did not complete high school, he was not a dropout but was drafted into the army before he could get his diploma. He is a soft man, a bit heavy and balding, older-looking than his years .... When the victim's first protests are heard, he turns toward the experimenter, looks sadly at him, then continues reading the word pairs. The experimenter does not have to tell him to continue. Throughout the experiment he shows almost no emotion or bodily movement. He does what the experimenter tells him in a slow, steady pace that is set off sharply against the strident cries of the victim. Throughout, a sad, dejected expression shows on his face. He continues to the 450 volt level, asks the experimenter what he's to do at that point, administers two additional shocks on command, and is relieved of his task. ... He explains in an interview that although he feels the shocks were extremely painful, he accepted the experimenters' word that they would cause no permanent damage. He reaffirms his belief in a questionnaire answered almost a year after his participation. ... Of the learner, he says, 'He agreed to it, and therefore must accept responsibility.' ... 'I merely went on. Because I was following orders .... I was told to go on ...' (Milgram, 1974, pp. 49–50).

The second reads as follows:

> Mr. Batta is a thirty-seven year old welder. He was born in New Haven, his parents in Italy. He has a rough hewn face that conveys a conspicuous lack of alertness. His overall appearance is somewhat brutish. An observer described him as a 'crude mesomorph of obviously limited intelligence'. But this is not fully adequate, for he relates to the experimenter with a submissive and deferential sweetness.
>
>   He has some difficulty in mastering the experimental procedure and needs to be corrected by the experimenter several times. He shows appreciation for the help and willingness to do what is required. ...When the learner first complains, Mr. Batta pays no attention to him. His face remains impassive, as if to dissociate himself from the learner's disruptive behaviour. When the experimenter instructs him to force the learner's hand down, he adopts a rigid mechanical procedure. He tests the generator switch. When it fails to function, he immediately forces the learner's hand onto the shock plate. All the while he maintains the same rigid mask. The learner, seated alongside him, begs him to stop, but with robotic

impassivity, he continues the procedure. What is extraordinary is his apparent total indifference to the learner; he hardly takes cognizance of him as a human being. Meanwhile, he relates to the experimenter in a submissive and courteous fashion.

...When he administers 450 volts, he turns to the experimenter and asks, 'Where do we go from here, Professor?' His tone is deferential and expresses his willingness to be a cooperative subject, in contrast to the learner's obstinacy. ... The experimenter has great difficulty in questioning the subject on the issue of responsibility. He does not seem to grasp the concept (Milgram, 1974, p. 46).

In the experiment, there is no coercion of the 'teacher' involved in the experimental process. It is almost as though the teacher becomes 'constitutively attached' to the experiment; she immerses herself in it; he submerges his identity and his values to the norms of the experiment. Sabini and Silver (1980, p. 342) have offered the following account of what is going on:

Subjects enter the experiment, recognizing some commitment to cooperate with the experimenter; after all they have agreed to participate, taken his money, and probably to some degree endorse the aims of the advancement of science ... every shock is only slightly more powerful than the last. The quality of the subject's action changes from something entirely blameless to something unconscionable, but by degrees. Where exactly should the subject stop? At what point is the divide between these two kinds of action crossed? How is the subject to know? ... If the subject decides that giving the next shock is not permissible then, since it is (in every case) only slightly more intense than the last one, what is the justification for administering the last shock he just gave? ...

The Holocaust is the most often quoted (in Europe) example of a series of abhorrent immoral acts being carried out by thousands of people in the name of obedience; in the name of their simply going about their daily lives. Hannah Arendt has argued that one of the most extreme perpetrators of the violence was not a monster. Rather, he was simply a bureaucrat sitting at his desk and doing his job. She says (1963, p. 287):

Eichmann was not an Iago or Macbeth .... Except for an extraordinary diligence in looking out for his personal advancement, he had no motives at all. And this diligence in itself was in no way criminal; he certainly would never have murdered his superior in order to inherit his post. He merely ... never realised what he was doing .... He ... had a lack of imagination.

As Milgram says (1974, p. 6), 'ordinary people, simply doing their jobs, can become agents in a terrible, destructive process. Even when they are asked to carry out actions incompatible with the fundamental standards of morality, relatively few people have the resources needed to resist authority.' Milgram offers a few explanations: he suggests that people can become preoccupied with the technical aspects of a task. Edward Bond has written a play that compares a supermarket today with the Holocaust, in this respect – that people can become preoccupied with the technical aspects of a task, and lose sight of the overall picture. I remember something analogous happening when I was a student at Oxford in the early 1970s. Gareth Evans – an incredibly bright young Fellow of one of the colleges – was giving one of his hugely well attended seminars on names. After an hour of detailed technical discussion, someone said, 'Why are we talking about names?' This incredibly talented person had forgotten. He had becomes lost in the technical detail. In that context it didn't matter. In others, though, it does. The film *Dr Strangelove* satirized the absorption of a bomber crew in the exacting technical procedure of dropping nuclear weapons on human beings. People might alternatively be drawn by a crowd, as are the gang members in the film *The Accused*. They might just not see themselves as responsible for their own actions. 'I was just doing what I was told.' 'I was doing my duty.' This is the story that was heard over and over again at Nuremberg. The moral concerns of the individual shift to how well they are performing for the authority. If they do continue to see some moral responsibility, it is not theirs. They blame 'the system' or in the above case 'the experiment'. They might alternatively look for a nobler cause, such as – in the case of the experiment – the pursuit of scientific truth; or the defence of the nation. As Baumann has put it (1991, p. 160), inside a system of authority, the language of morality acquires a new vocabulary: 'It is filled with concepts like loyalty, duty, discipline – all pointing to superiors as the supreme objects of moral concern.'

Some time ago I, as the Head of a university department, had to make someone compulsorily redundant. That was what I was required to do if I was to do my job. I believed that, even if it were acceptable to engage in a compulsory redundancy process, the wrong person had been selected, and according to criteria I did not devise. I considered all sorts of courses of action, from refusing to do it to resigning. I believed that if I resigned, I would be represented as mentally ill – as a woman who was not tough enough to do the task that needed to be done. Thus, to turn around a point that Mary Midgley makes in her book *Wickedness* (1996, p. 49), private following of conscience turns in to mental illness. At the time, I heard reasons precisely analogous to the reasons given in the Milgram experiments and given by individual Nazis: 'I was just doing my job'; 'I'm doing it to save the institution'; 'I have no choice.'

No-one was physically hurt, let alone killed. There were no death camps; no pogroms; no Nuremberg. If we think in terms of rights, we all have a right to life but not rights to permanent secure employment. Increasing numbers of people, worldwide, do not have the latter. Does the end of saving the institution, saving the rest of our jobs, justify the means: making someone – and the wrong person – redundant? What is the institution, if not the students and the lecturers? Of course it is more than this particular group of students and lecturers and this is what makes it an entity in its own right – a social structure with its own causal properties and powers. But does that justify the means?

The similarity between the Holocaust, the recent situation in Bosnia and Rwanda, to take just a few examples, and the situation in many universities and in many walks of life today lies not in the consequences of the behaviour, which are radically different in each case. Making large numbers of people redundant bears no resemblance to the act of systematically torturing and killing people. What is similar, though, is the process of thinking and of the rationalization of behaviour which leads those who carry out the act of torturing or making the wrong person redundant to that point. The similarity lies in the complicity of each person in a sequence of behaviour which he or she cannot rationalize in any other way than through following the norms of the 'constitutive community'. Many will rationalize the behaviour as not wrong; they will argue that X or Y deserved what they had coming to them anyway. More commonly they will pass the buck; they will say that it was not them, but someone else who is directly responsible for the act. Thus someone in my position will say that he or she had no choice; if they had not done it, then someone else would have done. Universities are constructed as entities, like nations were for the Nazis, in opposition to one another.

I would like to argue that the communitarian philosophy endorsed by Tony Blair and the British 'New Labour' Party encourages forms of thinking like the above and is therefore particularly unhelpful in the present climate. Specifically, I will argue that the concept of community is insufficiently clear in the literature and that it allows the above examples to function as communities. I shall conclude by suggesting an alternative.

Communitarianism

Communitarians attempt to recover a lost sense of community, nation and family, and to record the integral connection between the values inherent in membership of these collectivities and self identity. In an article in the journal

Prospect, Tony Blair says (1996, p. 11): 'we need to fashion a new social order to meet the anxiety and insecurity people feel about the breakdown of traditional norms and institutions, and the fragmentation of families and communities'. Communitarianism, as Beatrix Campbell has put it (1995, p. 48), 'has prospered handsomely in Britain under the patronage of the new boys in the Labour leadership'. Communitarianism is seen by Blair and New Labour in the UK, and by several similarly placed individuals in the USA, as the solution to the moral disintegration that they see to be manifest in the contemporary world.

Communitarians argue that we are social beings; that we are embodied agents deriving our self understandings from the social world. We cannot, *contra* liberals, detach ourselves from our ends and values. They argue that political thinking involves interpreting shared understandings bearing upon the political life of a community, in contrast to the liberal view that there are universal principles based upon an abstract consideration of an individual's needs and wants. Communities, for the communitarian, can be communities of place; of memory; or can be grounded in 'psychological sharings' like, for example, friendship. They are claimed to provide a narrative through which we live our lives: our identities are formed through them, and we find our value systems embedded in them. The liberal individual – the abstract person – is, it is argued, too thin a notion on which to pin any real conception of an individual life; it is too fragile to provide a conception of a real person making real choices in real situations.

Communitarians, then, attach very considerable importance to the concept of community. However, I do not find a clear definition of 'community' in the literature. What constitutes a community? One of the thinkers often referred to, MacIntyre (1981, p. 175), deploys the notion of 'practice' and characterizes it in the following terms: it is '... any coherent and complex form of socially established co-operative human activity through which goods internal to that form of activity are realised in the course of trying to achieve those standards of excellence which are appropriate to, and partly definitive of, that form of activity ...'. Internal goods are ones that cannot be realized in any other way than by engaging in the activity itself. He also suggests, in common with many others, that a community should provide a 'narrative' through which individuals' lives are lived.

What, then, is a community? Could, for example, the category 'human beings' count as a community? It might be argued that such a community is too broad or too thin to do the work required of it. The 'community of human beings' appears not to be able to provide a narrative through which individuals' lives could be lived. It does not differentiate one group of people from another. But is this not too strong a condition of 'community'? There is, for example, one form of activity that, according to Marx, is distinctively human: namely productive activity, which is certainly complex, cooperative and coherent. It is also difficult to think of other ways in which the results of productive activity might be realized. There are, therefore, internal goods realized by human beings as a group. On whichever definition of humanity one takes, a broad history can be offered that is distinctive of human beings. Were we to provide a rich and inclusive concept of what it is to be a human being, by outlining the qualities shared by all humans, why should the community of humans not constitute a community in the communitarian sense?

At another extreme one might ask: can the community of the psychological experiment count? The latter is, of course, absolutely unlike the examples of community usually discussed in the literature. Yet it provided, for the two individuals concerned, and for the duration of the experiment, a 'narrative' through which they lived their lives. Indeed, it might be argued that it is precisely because it did this that the actions of the 'teacher' can be explained and rationalized. In some respects, the experiment constitutes a 'practice' precisely in MacIntyre's sense (1981, p. 175). It is a coherent and complex socially organized activity. What it lacks, though, is one of the features that MacIntyre and other communitarians certainly emphasize, and that is that it is not 'socially established'; it does not form part of what he calls a 'tradition'. This condition, however, could be met if we imagined a series of Milgram experiments, taking place with the same subjects over days or weeks. The type of activity could be varied – the questions asked might alter, and the kind of punishment administered changed, but the essential point could remain the same.

However, the usual examples of communities mentioned or discussed in the literature are: the family, the nation, the work-place (the university?) and communities based upon a common ethnicity. Communitarians have argued that each of these communities shares a set of meanings that constitute it as a community, and that forms its central values. For example, Waltzer (1983) defends the view that one of the shared meanings for contemporary Americans is a consensus about health care and its proper distribution. Or, to take another example, Daniel Bell (1993), in his book *Communitarianism and its Critics*, argues that Jewish people have a special bond of solidarity with other Jews, and that this bond gives meaning to their lives. Perhaps so. But then we can ask: what are the commonalities between family, nation, work-place, university and a collectivity based upon a common ethnicity? What are the similarities between these disparate entities? Each entity has some features in common with all the others; each consists in a group of people, but the 'group' exists over and above the collection of individuals. Individuals claim allegiance to the group as a group. There are some similarities in respect of some of the entities insofar as there are some things about a person's membership of some of the groups which they have no choice but to accept. For example, I cannot choose my parents; my birthplace; the nation into which I was born. In these senses, some aspects of my family and my nationality are 'givens' – facts about me that are unamenable to alteration. The significance of country and place of origin, however, is radically different for someone who is uprooted from their place of residence because of political upheaval, or, indeed, for someone who moves their main place of residence halfway through their life. It is different again for someone who identifies as belonging to a particular nation, but for whom that nation has no place of residence – as was the case for Jews before the existence of the state of Israel and is the case now for Kurdish people. It is difficult, therefore, to see how even the facts about membership of the constitutive communities favoured by the communitarian that appear to be immune from alteration can provide a clear set of values that flow automatically from the 'community fact' about the person. And as soon as we move to weaker constitutive values, like facts about a tightly knit family where arranged marriage is the norm versus the family of the late financier Goldsmith that includes 'mistresses' as well as wives, or the extended gay and lesbian family, the differences between families are greater than the similarities. Given, therefore, the lack of common features of 'constitutive communities', cannot any community we propose – such as that of the experiment – count?

A further question that arises is this: what sense of shared meaning do the members of any one of these collectivities have? And even if there is some sense of shared meaning, why should what is shared be constitutive of a person's value system? What sense, for example, of shared meaning do two Jewish people have who have neither upbringing in a common country, nor a political and moral outlook in common? What do two Jewish people share, who are both born and raised in Israel, and both share a common distaste for the policy of the present Israeli government, but one of whom 'critically' celebrates the Passover whilst the other resolutely refuses to do so, on the grounds of its association with the policies of the Israeli state? They have some shared meanings, and these derive from their shared language, their shared history and their ability to interpret the bible in terms of those shared meanings. However, to describe their Jewishness as being formative of their value systems on a par with, for example, a 20 year attachment to a non-Jewish, secular system, or a person brought up traditionally as a Jew in the religious sense, seems arbitrary and even pernicious.

I'd like to quote from Anne, in Daniel Bell's philosophical play (1993, p. 100), to elaborate the sense in which it may be pernicious to do this sort of thing.

> [A] constitutive community provides a largely background way of meaningful thinking, acting, and judging, but I want to emphasise that applying effort to 'escape from its grip', trying to flee this setting which gives meaning to your life, is not merely self defeating in the sense that one has adopted a project which cannot be significantly realised. It's much more serious than that – those who seek to cast aside a constitutive community will suffer from an acute form of disorientation, their world will come to be seen as deprived of sense, as emptied of meaningful possibilities. This painful and frightening state will take different forms in different places – excessive brooding in trendy cafes for the French, the Swedes will toy with suicidal thoughts ....

Think what this sentence means for the many migrants from the Caribbean to Britain; for those from South Asia to this country; or for the Turks in Germany. Put that sentence next to this one, from Edward Said, in *The Politics of Dispossession* (1995, p. xiii):

> Until the June 1967 war I was completely caught up in the life of a young professor of English and comparative literature at Columbia University. I was born in Jerusalem in late 1935, and I grew up there and in Egypt and Lebanon; most of my family – dispossessed and displaced from Palestine in 1947 and 1948 – had ended up mostly in Jordan and Lebanon. Sent to America as a school boy .... In 1967 (as a result of the war) I was emotionally reclaimed by the Arab world generally and by Palestine in particular.

Said is Palestinian, but between 1951 and 1967, that part of his history and his identity was completely submerged into the community of the American professor of literature. Which of these communities forms the ultimate ends or purposes of Said? Which is the more deep-seated? And what possible connection can there be, here, between the deep-seatedness of the values and their justice or rightness? It may be pernicious to talk about individuals suffering 'an acute sense of disorientation' when this sort of uprooting is precisely the experience of many people today. Some refugees indeed have suffered in the way that Anne imagines. But this has more to do with the way they have been treated than with the experience of dislocation.

Some individuals, indeed, have flourished as a result of their dislocation. Think of Salman Rushdie, formed partly by the British public school system (one of his communities), partly by the racism he experienced there and partly by his earlier immersion in colonial and (just) ex-colonial India. It was certainly not his dislocation *per se* that caused his present parlous state. But think also what it means for the individual in the Further Education college, or the university, who refuses to go along with what is happening there. In his column in the *Guardian* on 16 June 1997, Paul Foot describes the case of a lecturer in an FE college, who was known to be a good teacher, and who had been in post for some 20 years. He was asked if he would like, voluntarily, to sign a new management contract. He refused. He then received, along with several others, a letter of redundancy, but saying that the redundancy would be revoked if he signed the new contract. The others in his position duly signed. This man refused and was made redundant. No doubt he is feeling dislocated, but many would see as perverse the diagnosis that this is because of the dislocation of his value system. These examples are simply the tips of the iceberg

Ironically, in fact, communitarianism provides a very good explanation for why the 'teachers' in Milgram's experiments did what they did. They would have felt 'dislocated', 'disorientated', if they had *not* done as they were asked. They would have been functioning outside the norms of the experiment. However, it is also arguable that they functioned as they did precisely because they suspended consideration of any real values. In other words, the constitutive values of the experiment were actually contrary to any real values. This is also the case, surely, in the case of others who go along with the norms of certain communities rather than doing what may be seen to be the right thing to do.

It may be argued at this point that I have overstated the communitarian thesis. No communitarian, it could be argued, is saying that actual existing present-day communities provide the sorts of value system that are constitutive of self-identity. Indeed, it is precisely the communitarian argument that present day communities do not do this any longer and that communities need to be recreated or reconstituted in such a way that they are able to do so. However, it is not only the actual experience of contemporary communities that fails to provide the sorts of value that MacIntyre or Sandel, to take two examples, aspire to: it is also theoretical writing about constitutive communities. One example of this is Gellner's work on nationalism.

In 1983, Gellner defined nationalism thus (p. 36): 'a theory of political legitimacy which requires that ethnic boundaries should not cut across political ones, and in particular that ethnic boundaries within a given state ... should not separate the power holders from the rest ... and therefore state and culture must now be linked'. But it is highly unlikely that such a 'pure' national state has ever existed anywhere in the world. There are always settled residents of nations who are not members of the dominant national collectivity. Minorities become defined as deviant from the 'normal'. Gellner's argument has a dubious normalizing effect. It is an effect, moreover, that arguably is actually required by communitarianism – because without it there are no constitutive values. In order to be consistent, therefore, the communitarian requires some such normalizing assumption about the entities that go to make up the constitutive community. Isn't there therefore something deeply contradictory about MacIntyre's view that the existence of values that help constitute the self is compatible with individual autonomy and self reflection? Of course it will depend what these constitutive values are. But it is difficult to see how, within a specific community, values can be both constitutive and subject to individual choice and reflection. The Milgram experiment puts this point starkly. The individual 'teacher' had the choice to leave the experiment. Similarly, individuals can choose to reject the norms of family or nation. Someone brought up in a culture where arranged marriage is the norm can choose to reject this option. But if identity is formed through the constitutive values of these entities, then the individuals can choose to reject the constitutive values only by dislocating their identity. Communitarianism is akin to identity politics in this respect: those committed to the latter argue that being a woman, or a black woman, or a member of the South Asian diaspora in the UK, for example, gives you a certain outlook on the world; a certain set of values. There is an intrinsic connection, within the perspective of the believer in identity politics, between being a woman, for example, and having a certain outlook on the world. For the communitarian, one's identity is formed in the 'constitutive' communities of family, nation and so on. A version of identity politics provides a plausible explanation for what went on in the case of the experiment. The experiment gave Mr Batta and the others a certain identity and therefore a certain outlook on the world. Mr Batta's identity and his values became internally connected. He would have suffered a dislocation of his 'experimental identity' if he had rejected its constitutive values.

Recently Waltzer has argued, in *Thick and Thin* (1994), that real criticism of the norms of a particular community depends upon being embedded in that community itself. He provides examples of successful and 'just' dissenters – Luther, the Czech dissidents in 1989 – who, he argues, were marginally successful in improving the basic 'justice' of the communities in which they were embedded. He suggests that success in challenging unjust community practices depends upon operating within the constitutive norms of the community. No doubt this may be largely true. Yet his argument presumes that there is room, within existing communities, for the critical dissenting voice to be heard and acted upon without dislocating either the individual or the community. However, sometimes communities are to be criticized precisely because they do not provide room for this critical voice. What would Waltzer say, one wonders, about Mill's examples: about Socrates – executed for impiety and immorality; about Jesus – killed for blasphemy. The Milgram experiments did not allow, within their 'constitutive community' for this critical voice. Nor did the Nazi Party. There are sometimes, indeed, acts of extreme violence which form part of the constituent values of a community – women have been desecrated or killed if, representing the spirit of the community, as they do in the case of 'mother Russia', for instance – they violate the boundaries of the collectivity.

The argument that communitarianism encourages forms of thinking like the Milgram experiments, then, runs as follows: (i) communitarians do not specify exactly what constitutes a community, therefore almost any hypothetical 'constitutive community' including that of the experiment, might legitimately count; (ii) the communitarian notion of a community with its constitutive values provides a very good explanation for the behaviour of the individuals in the experiment. I would suggest that the most frequently discussed alternatives to communitarianism, by contrast, not only fail to provide a 'justifying' explanation for what went on in the experiment, but they would actually rule out such behaviour. A liberal political philosophy, for example, would surely rule it out as failing to conform to the norms of justice, or as failing to treat the 'subject' in the way that any human being should be treated.

The central problem appears to be that when communitarians emphasize the notion of a community, they don't spell out what they mean. They tend to rely on examples: the family, the nation. Alternatively, in some communitarian writers, the emphasis moves to something more generic such as 'liberal-democratic societies'. But with such a broad array of entities as examples, many more might reasonably be though to fit the bill.

Some Reflections

The communitarian is right, surely, in his or her argument that the self is encumbered; that it is tied in a network of relationships of dependency with others. The nature of these encumbrances, however, requires careful spelling out. There are different types of encumbrance, and more or less extreme options for action. At one extreme there is nothing that constitutes a constraint on my action. Not even constraints of basic materiality influence behaviour. Antigone opted to do what she did knowing that death would be the consequence. The same is true of those black slaves in the USA who chose death in preference to the continuation of slavery. However, in many cases, there is the basic constraint that we need to eat in order to survive. Some other kinds of constraint have been spelled out by Keith Graham (1996). The communitarians, however, have attempted to build-in collectivities to which the individual is supposed to be attached which may, in the end, be fictional – the family, the work-place, the nation. No one is necessarily attached to any of these in either a logical or a causal sense. Nira Yuval-Davis (1997) has argued that the fashionable search amongst adoptive children for their 'natural' mother is a peculiarly Western mode of identity construction. Thus even the link with a biological parent, which is something that cannot be altered, she is arguing, has a very different significance depending on how it is viewed socially and culturally. As far as the family is concerned, again, it is not possible, in adulthood, to alter the events of one's childhood. However, it is possible, through psychoanalysis, to change their significance in one's memory and attitudes, and therefore to alter their place in identity construction.

The connection to a work-place or to a nation is of a different order altogether, and in many cases it will never have been forged. Thus, despite appearances to the contrary, communitarianism, with its emphasis on communities that supposedly give meaning to a person's life, actually fosters the creation of entities like nations and work-places, and gives them a spurious justification. Communitarianism provides a rationale for Nazism, and for the behaviour of individuals in the types of bureaucratic Fordist entities that now constitute many work-places, where individuals are afraid to speak out, and where fear appears as 'loyalty' to the institution.

In fact the enterprise culture which preceded New Labour is, in this respect, less deeply conservative than Communitarianism. It fostered an unencumbered liberal self. The liberal self is unencumbered; it has no attributes or aims other than those it has voluntarily chosen. MacIntyre sees Sartre as the epitome of this liberal individualism, as his 'self' is distinct from any particular social role that it may happen to assume. One possible response to the communitarian is to endorse this Sartrean self. If individuals want to be authentic, to be what they want to be rather than what society or the family or the work-place or the nation expects them to be, then they must choose themselves – they must make themselves into the free and creative beings that they could become. Sartre's project assumes that individuals are autonomous; that they can deliberate on their goals and their projects. A Sartrean could give an entirely opposing reading of Antigone from that of Hegel: rather than Antigone's being immersed in a tradition and being unable to exercise any choice, a Sartrean reading would suggest that she, alone of the characters in the play, assumed responsibility for herself: she did not remain, as her sister Ismene did, in her role of following her uncle's dictat. My own situation, too, could be resolved along similar lines: I am free to follow my conscience and I do not have to be enslaved to the dictats of an artificial entity: my place of work.

Yet there are limitations to this approach. Antigone chose a course of action knowing that death would be the consequence. Perhaps this is the ultimate vindication of the Sartrean self: we can all choose to die. If that is the chosen option then the self is genuinely and literally unencumbered. But in most situations, the self is not unencumbered. Eichmann needed to eat. No doubt he needed a lot more. I have a family. One option – the Sartrean one – is to stand for what you believe to be right, and to take the consequences. Antigone stood fast by what she believed to be right. So did the lecturer in Paul Foot's column who refused to sign the new contract and was therefore dismissed from his job. However, the lecturer is now powerless to influence what goes on in the further education sector. Antigone became powerless. I would have become powerless too. Sartre argues (1956, p. 549) that any situation can be transcended by an individual: '[T]here is no privileged situation. We mean by this that there is no situation in which the given would crush beneath its weight the freedom which constitutes it as such – and that conversely there is no situation in which the for-itself would be more free than others.' Sartre's is the sort of liberalism against which the communitarians and others set their faces. Others, for Sartre, are seen as potential threats to individual autonomy and freedom. The self, essentially, is constituted in the absence of any of the social roles and situations that give it meaning. We have come full circle. Such a self, as the communitarians argue, stripped of any special features, is ultimately incoherent.

What, then, is the alternative? I would say that there are three parts to such an alternative. One part is to outline what kinds of attachment the individual has, to what degree, and which ones are significant in identity construction. The nation will be more significant in the latter regard for some people than it will be for others. For contemporary Kurds, who have no location as Kurdish people, it is symbolically vital that they identify with their symbolic nation. But whether any significant values flow from that attachment is a separate matter. Whether, for example, all Kurdish people accept or should accept that it is important to go to war in the defence of a particular territory or state is an entirely separate issue. Therefore, secondly, there is the project of determining which values are significant. I would argue, and have done so elsewhere (Assiter, 1996), that encumbrances and values should be disconnected from one another. We are indeed encumbered selves. But many of these encumbrances have nothing to do with values that are significant. We can form new communities or collectivities that are based on the acceptance of common values, as for example is the community of socialist feminists worldwide. We can also judge the values that are implicit in a given community and value some communities and some of our attachments more highly than others. I would argue, thirdly, that in order for a community to be capable of furnishing certain moral values, it would need itself to be founded upon certain moral principles. The problem with the sorts of community frequently taken as examples in the communitarian literature – the family, the nation – is that each of them embodies some value that is antithetical to liberty, justice and equality, to take three values that have been much referred to in the liberal and indeed in the Marxist literature on morality. Taking the first of these, many liberals would see the absence of coercion as necessary and sufficient for liberty. If we take it as a necessary condition for something's being a community that is capable of furnishing moral values that there be no coercion within it, then, ironically, the Milgram experiment provides a better example of such a community than the family. Women inside families have frequently been coerced into sexual relations they have not wanted. If we were to uphold a stronger definition of liberty and characterize it in something like the following way – 'the availability of, and capacity to exercise, meaningful and effective choice' (Norman, 1982, p. 90) – then fewer existing communities would satisfy it. Indeed, it is arguable that no existing community does so, since all of them contain fundamental power differentials that constrain the ability of some individuals from making and carrying out their choices. I would argue, finally, that articulating what constitutes the kind of community that can furnish moral values is something that cannot itself be left to tradition.

References

Arendt, H. (1963), *Eichmann in Jerusalem*, rev. edn, Penguin, Harmondsworth.
Assiter, A. (1996), *Enlightened Women*, Routledge, London.
Baumann, Z. (1991), *Modernity and the Holocaust*, Polity Press, Cambridge.
Bell, D. (1993), *Communitarianism and its Critics,* Oxford University Press, Oxford.

Blair, A. (1996), 'Ideological Blurring, *Prospect*, 9, pp. 10–11.

Campbell, B. (1995), 'Old Fogeys and Angry Young Men, a critique of communitarianism', *Soundings*, 1, Autumn, pp. 47–65.

Foot, P. (1997), *The Guardian*, 16 June.

Gellner, E. (1983), *Nations and Nationalism*, Blackwell, Oxford.

Graham, K. (1996), 'Coping with the many-coloured dome: Pluralism and Practical Reason', in Archard, D. (ed.), *Philosophy and Pluralism*, Cambridge University Press, Cambridge.

Hegel, G.W.F. (1952), *The Philosophy of Right,* trans. T.M. Knox, Oxford University Press, Oxford.

MacIntyre, A. (1981), *After Virtue*, University of Notre Dame Press, Indiana.

Midgley, M. (1996), *Wickedness, A Philosophical Essay*, Routledge, London.

Milgram S. (1974), *Obedience to Authority, an Experimental View*, Tavistock, London.

Norman, R. (1982), 'Does Equality destroy Liberty?' in Graham, K. (ed.) *Contemporary Political Philosophy*, Cambridge University Press, Cambridge.

Sabini, J. and Silver, M. (1980), 'Destroying the Innocent with a Clear Conscience: a Sociopsychology of the Holocaust' in Dinsdale, J.E. (ed.), *Survivors, Victims and Perpetrators: Essays on the Nazi Holocaust*, Hemisphere Publishing Corp., New York.

Said, E. (1995), *The Politics of Dispossession: the Struggle for Palestinian Self-determination 1969–1994*, Vintage, London.

Sandel, M. (1981), *Liberalism and the limits of Justice*, Cambridge University Press, Cambridge.

Sartre, J.P. (1956), *Being and Nothingness* , trans. H. Barnes, Washington Square Press, New York.

Waltzer, M. (1983), *Spheres of Justice,* Blackwell, Oxford.

Waltzer, M. (1994), *Thick and Thin: Moral Argument at Home and Abroad,* University of Notre Dame Press, Indiana.

Yuval-Davis, N. (1997), *Gender and Nation*, Sage, London.

12 Being Some Body: Choice and Identity in a Liberal Pluralist World

KEITH GRAHAM

Introduction

The concentration camp at Auschwitz kept stunningly and chillingly meticulous records on its inmates. One particularly striking aspect of this was the wide range of badges which had to be worn to indicate one's categorization: Jew, gypsy, homosexual, political offender and so on, and all the cross-categorizations they gave rise to. This paper is about badges of identity and the conditions which give rise to them. No one can say in advance what features of your identity will assume greatest salience in particular historical circumstances. For millions of people it has been their race or their nationality, with tragic results. For some individuals, in some situations, it has been something as contingent and fortuitous as the football scarf they happened to be wearing, with similarly tragic results for them. In this discussion I try to make sense of the interplay between contingent and necessary features of human beings in the formation of social identity. Any such discussion is bound to be coloured by recent debates between liberals and communitarians, but my paper is not strictly *about* that debate. Rather, it attempts to dig down to deeper presuppositions about what human beings are like and to subject them to greater scrutiny than they are able to receive within the terms of that debate.

In the second section, I discuss the place of autonomy in the context of a *de facto* pluralist world and consider the importance of attempting to arrive at universally applicable values. In the third section, I examine some of the ambiguities in the doctrine of the distinctness of persons and attempt to cast some doubt on its acceptability. In the fourth section, I argue, in the light of preceding considerations, that materiality deserves a central place in formation of social identity.

Broadly, what I try to do is call attention to the constraints, arising from our nature as interconnected individuals and individuals embedded in collective entities, which we ought to respect if we are to form rational conceptions of our social identity. Many important questions lie beyond the scope of this paper, including the question of just what form of significance we should attach to our materiality if I am right in my contention that materiality is central. The argument proceeds at a very abstract level, at some distance not only from concrete events like those at Auschwitz but also from an explicit addressing of racism and nationalism as such. This reflects my belief that our understanding of these phenomena rests on much more general assumptions which themselves need to be examined first.

Pluralism and Autonomy

In deciding who we are, what we value and how we ought to act (in deciding 'our identity and values' for short), the explicit or implicit assumptions we inevitably make about ourselves and the world around us may be more or less reasonable and plausible. At the most general level, what plausible assumptions of the requisite kind might we make in the contemporary context? One is that in making these decisions about identity and values we shall get considerably less help than we need from the world itself. Our age is characterized by the loss of any belief that we can simply infer what is right, and how we should be, from a set of premises about the social order. The long term reason for this arises from the way in which people in the last couple of centuries have ceased to live in some all-embracing community which provided their perspective on the world and a perception of their own place within it. The more immediate reason lies in the break-up, in comparatively recent times, of small-scale communities and the loss for many people of their associated traditions, their absorption into a much wider and more amorphous world. These small-scale communities were already considerably less than all-embracing and their inhabitants lived parts of their lives in other (not necessarily geographical) spheres, but they did nevertheless provide a general orientation for those who lived within them.

The upshot is that, generally speaking, we no longer believe that we can derive our own moral meanings simply from a consideration of our place in the social order. An appeal to 'my station and its duties'[1] as the source of identity and norms of behaviour would for many people simply raise the prior question of how one was to decide what one's station was. In consequence we are thrown back on our own resources in constructing moral meaning.[2]

One possible response to this situation is to make a virtue of necessity, to take the view that the need to create one's own identity and values is not a predicament, but something which is itself of enormous moral value. That response occurs in our culture in the form of bestowing importance – for many liberals the highest importance – on *autonomy*. I use the term here very broadly to describe the view that in some substantive sense we have to *decide* on our values, rather than being able to infer them from data amassed about the world without any original input of our own. For a proponent of autonomy in this sense, choosing our own forms of identity and behaviour is seen not as something we are stuck with but something which gives us our dignity as moral beings, something to be prized. After all, it might be said, endorsing a certain identity and certain values in the light of critical reflection and consideration of alternatives is far more worthy than merely finding oneself attached to them by accident of birth, or whatever other circumstance.

A distinct part of the wider background of contemporary life consists in *de facto pluralism*, by which I mean simply the coexistence of a plurality of conflicting values embraced by different people: I have spoken of 'our' culture, but someone might well ask who 'we' are. For it is a fact of contemporary life that there are many competing cultures and values, many different ways of living and behaving which different people find acceptable or unacceptable. Is it acceptable or unacceptable to publish pornography, to eat meat, to hang criminals, to wear a skirt in the street, to abort foetuses, to teach children about customs and values different from those they are growing up with? Very different answers are given to such questions. The existence of the conflicting values and practices which the different answers represent may not be a new phenomenon, at least on a world scale; but what is new is, first, our unprecedented accumulation of knowledge of other cultures and their differing values, and, second, the extent to which different cultures have interpenetrated geographically. Spatial proximity has made much more pressing the question of how to handle widely varying views on acceptable behaviour, since the people holding those widely varying views are much more likely than in previous times to live, literally, next door to one another.

What is the connection between *de facto* pluralism and autonomy? On a very optimistic view of the process of the autonomous choice of values, I suppose it might be thought that autonomy would encourage convergence on the same values, with the result that the problems associated with *de facto* pluralism might be reduced. That does seem excessively optimistic, however; and perhaps a more plausible view would be that autonomy encourages a healthy divergence. Divergence might be held to be healthy on a number of quite different grounds: *either* that we should let a hundred flowers bloom, that experiments in living will lead us to a deeper understanding of what is truly valuable; *or* that there just is a plurality of potentially conflicting but genuine and authentic values (a kind of *normative* pluralism); *or* (a more radically sceptical view) that there are no objective, non-relative values, and therefore there can be no transcultural reason to favour some against others.[3]

There are several reasons for doubting whether proponents of autonomy can make light of *de facto* pluralism in these ways. First, bear in mind that they will not believe just in autonomy: they will also subscribe to a particular set of substantive values. But it will then be much harder simply to take an indulgent attitude towards those whose substantive values conflict with theirs. The examples I gave earlier of competing values are meant to illustrate that. If you think that people who perform abortions are murdering human beings, your abhorrence of murder will be such that you will think it wrong simply to allow them to do so. If, on the contrary, you think that they are aiding a person to maintain control of her own body, you will not. In either event you may subscribe to the importance of autonomy, but it is the divergence of other values which causes the problem. Second, it has to be borne in mind that from some points of view within *de facto* pluralism, an attachment to autonomy will itself be the expression of just one value among others. It will not be a neutral, uncontroversially procedural matter, and the encouragement to exercise autonomy will not have the backing of any privileged second order status. From those points of view, what was described earlier as 'endorsing ... values in the light of critical reflection and consideration of alternatives' might be redescribed as allowing the rot to set in by exposing people to wicked ways, the very exposure to which will corrupt and lead them away from true virtue. I do not say that we should accept those points of view; I do say we need to take them into account where autonomy is embraced in the context of *de facto* pluralism. Third, and connectedly, where people live in a culture which is heterogeneous with regard to values at this level of generality, there is a particular problem about settling conflicts. There are many people who regard the celebration of the autonomous agent as subscription to a dangerous myth: instead they adopt a politics of identity, privileging their race or nationality as being definitive of who they are. That fact is important because it is likely to play a fundamental role in fixing the rules they accept and are responsive to in the first place. In consequence, settlement of conflicts by appeal to some commonly accepted set of rules is problematic in *de facto* pluralism. A certain kind of conflict which might previously have been expected *between* societies will now be much more frequent *within* societies. Fourth, it will be more difficult in *de facto* pluralism to sustain familiar, restricted versions of the celebration of autonomy, according to which our construction of our own identity and values is subject to the qualification that we may not do so in a way which harms other, or infringes on their liberty, or their rights, and so on. That qualification will itself be a matter of especially deep, rather than merely surface, controversy, for some of the reasons already given. The whole idea of harm, and not merely which particular cases are instantiations of it, will be a matter of deep dispute. In addition to this, the interconnected nature of human life, which I explore in the third section ('The Distinctness of Persons'), suggests further problems for the attempt to circumscribe the sphere in which autonomy is to operate.

So far in this section I have made the point that conclusions about identity and values cannot simply be read off from truths about our position in the world, and that decisions about them must be made in a particularly diverse and conflictual world. In these circumstances it is at once more pressing and more difficult to find *shared* values and identities, rather than those like race and nationality which divide people. However, even though the conclusions that we reach on these matters are not *determined* by considerations about ourselves and our world it would be premature to take the view that they cannot be *constrained* by them. Indeed, despite *de facto* pluralism, it would be premature even to take the view that no conclusions can be reached which have a universal validity. Yet that is the tenor of much recent theorizing, even where the theorizing is quite diverse in other respects.

For example, Michael Walzer criticizes what he takes to be the universalizing tendency of most philosophers who have written about justice, and in particular their contemporary representatives, Rawls, Habermas and Ackerman:

> [E]ven if they are committed to impartiality, the question most likely to arise in the minds of the members of a political community is not, What would rational individuals choose under universalizing conditions of such-and-such a sort? But rather, What would individuals like us choose, who are situated as we are, who share a culture and are determined to go on sharing it? And this is a question that is readily transformed into, What choices have we already made in the course of our common life? What understandings do we (really) share? (Walzer, 1983, p. 5).

But of course there has been an interesting shift in Rawls's own aspirations over the years. He no longer seeks universal principles of justice which all reasonable people could be got to agree to, but rather principles for a specific kind of society; and he now makes the assumption that in their wider views, people are bound to go on disagreeing, that we cannot expect anything other than such disagreement, and that it is reasonable for them to go on holding widely divergent views. There is similarly a withdrawal from any attachment to a comprehensive liberalism or autonomy in favour of narrower, political versions of them (Rawls, 1993, pp. 36–40, 99–101, 199–200).[4]

It is not within the scope of this paper to assess the implications of Walzer's position, or to determine whether Rawls can safely insulate political liberalism from more comprehensive doctrines and whether the result is any more attractive if he can. They are both concerned specifically with theories of justice, and although my topic overlaps with theirs it is also wider, taking in values in general (which may not even necessarily be moral values). My claim is that we should not give up too quickly on the possibility of universal constraints on conclusions about values in that wider arena. It may well be that there can never be uniformity across all cultures, and it might be highly undesirable if there were; but there is room for change in practical attitudes and there is room for critical assessment of the practical aspirations and decisions that people currently attach themselves to. The fact that a given culture holds a given set of values (whether our own culture or some other) is no reason in itself for allowing that those values are acceptable, tolerable or even sensible. That is always a matter for further investigation. Charles Taylor has persuasively argued in that connection that to assume at the outset that all cultures are equally valuable is not to pay respect, but to condescend. There will certainly be a presumption that any culture which has animated a large number of human beings over a long time will have something important to say to all human beings; but assessment of a culture as valuable must follow, not precede, a critical examination of its values (Taylor, 1992, pp. 66–70).

The point of this section, therefore, has been to call attention to the nature of the circumstances in which people must make decisions about who they are, what they value and how they ought to act, and to indicate the implications which those circumstances carry for how these decisions might be reached. The actual diversity of values is something which must be taken into account, but should not itself be taken as an unalterable given, beyond the reach of critical assessment. Nothing alterable by human decision and action should have that status. In the process of making that kind of assessment it is then worth aspiring to a certain kind of universalism. It is worth asking whether there are any facts about human agents and their circumstances which are invariant, which hold good across all particular contexts, and which ought to exercise an influence over the identities, values and courses of action which those agents adopt if their adoption is to be reasonable. In answering that question we should not shrink from examining quite obvious and familiar facts which hold good of all people. Facts can be perfectly familiar and obvious while it is far from obvious what further conclusions they license or proscribe.

But if we are to arrive at any universally compelling constraints along those lines, we need to take care, in two respects, in conducting such an enquiry. First, we need to ensure that any features of our situation which we think dictate such constraints really are universal features, rather than historically or geographically local ones. We need to show a decent regard for the range of evidence which can be turned up by historical and anthropological studies, rather than assuming that human beings everywhere are more or less just like us. Secondly, it will be an advantage if we can express any relevant putatively universal truths in terms which are themselves not purely local. Debates on these matters are often confined to *moral* conceptions, and that is not necessarily an advantage. For example, some theorists have tried to argue from universal facts about the nature of human agency to conclusions about individual rights.[5] They may or may not be right to do so, but when the language of individual rights represents one (contentious) option in the stock of concepts of one (relatively local) culture it will require further argument to justify any conclusions couched in that particular way. An alternative approach, which I prefer, is to investigate whether any universal features of the human situation necessarily give everyone practical reasons, whether moral or non-moral, for embracing particular identities, values or actions. The concept of having a reason for action is itself closer to being a universal one, and is therefore more readily available in a relatively culture-neutral way as compared with strictly moral concepts.

The Distinctness of Persons

Frequent appeal is made, in the liberal tradition but also well beyond it, to the distinctness of persons, a doctrine which formally speaking has some of the features of the universality described in the previous section. I raise two broad questions about it here: how exactly the doctrine is to be understood, and what is thought to follow from it. I distinguish a number of interpretations of the doctrine and a direction of dependency among them, and I raise questions about the conclusions which are thought to follow from them. Generally, what I want to emphasize is a rival idea which might be termed the indistinctness of persons: the fact that human lives intermingle in two ways, by virtue of causal connection and by virtue of collective membership.

The idea of the distinctness of persons has its origin in Rawls and Nozick. Rawls had argued in *A Theory of Justice* for the need to give priority to individual liberty over aggregate increase in social welfare, and he criticized classical utilitarianism for supposing that all the desires of different people could be summed into one system and their satisfaction then measured. To do that 'fails to take seriously the distinction between persons' (Rawls, 1971, p. 187); and 'the plurality of distinct persons with separate systems of ends is an essential feature of human societies' (ibid., p. 29). Nozick, in *Anarchy, State, and Utopia*, had in a similar vein resisted any analogy between an individual sacrificing something for the sake of an overall greater good in their own life and the sacrifice of some individual for a greater social good. For, he said, 'there is no *social entity* with a good that undergoes some sacrifice for its own good. There are only individual people, different individual people, with their own individual lives' (Nozick, 1974, p. 33; italics in original).

This idea of distinctness might plausibly be construed in at least the following four different ways, D1 to D4. Each of them might then be used to support some conclusion of the kind embraced by Rawls and Nozick about how persons are appropriately and inappropriately to be treated. But it is far more difficult than is sometimes supposed to know what conclusions concerning the appropriate treatment of persons actually follow from each interpretation.[6]

(D1) *Qualitative distinctness: persons considered as a species of entity are distinct from **other entities***. Thus, persons are distinct from inanimate or collective entities in certain relevant respects. They exhibit a range of properties which are specific to them, making it appropriate for them to have certain expectations about how they could reasonably be treated. For example, they have intentions, desires, wishes, feelings and wills in a way that other entities do not. From this it might be thought to follow, for example, that only persons are fully qualified members of the moral realm. Kymlicka argues (1989, p. 242) that 'groups just aren't the right sort of beings to have moral status. They don't feel pain or pleasure. It is individual, sentient beings whose lives go better or worse, who suffer or flourish, and so it is their welfare that is the subject-matter of morality' (see also Pettit, 1993, pp. 287–8).

(D2) *Distinctness as separateness: persons considered individually are distinct from **one another***. They each live a separate life, with their own separate thoughts, memories, experiences and aspirations. As well as all sharing these properties as members of a species, each of them instantiates them individually in their own fashion. Bernard Williams (1985, pp. 201–2; italics in original) expresses the 'optimistic belief ... in the continuing possibility of a meaningful individual life, one that ... is enough unlike others, in its opacities and disorder as well as in its reasoned intentions, to make it *somebody's*'. From this it might be thought to follow that people should be left free to regulate their own personal lives according to their own conceptions of how they should be lived (see Nagel, 1987, pp. 238–9). It might also be thought to follow that there is nothing wrong with caring more about one's own projects than about other people's (see Scheffler, 1982).

(D3) *Distinctness as integrity: persons are distinct in forming a unity*. They have an internal psychological integrity which supports the individuation we make into separate human lives. It is not just bodily discontinuity which gives the rationale for distinguishing between persons in the way that we do but also the metaphorical hiatus between one person's life and another's. This might be thought to endorse 'our everyday conception of persons as the basic units of thought, deliberation and responsibility' (Rawls, 1993, p. 18, n. 20) or the idea that 'any moral duties to larger units (e.g. the community) must be derived from our obligations to individuals' (Kymlicka, 1990, p. 235).

(D4) *Distinctness as uniqueness: persons are distinct in being unique*. The concatenation of one person's memories, thoughts and aspirations is always in many respects different from any other person's. As Hannah Arendt puts it, 'each man is unique, so that with each birth something uniquely new comes into the world. With respect to this somebody who is unique it can be truly said that nobody was there before' (Arendt, 1959, p. 158). And, we might add, nobody is there afterwards, or at least not *that* person. This might be thought to explain why any person's death is a tragedy. People are not just replaceable one by another, and when someone dies a unique point of view and set of experiences disappears with them.

Consider now the links among D1–D4, and the difficulties in drawing inferences from them. The point about uniqueness expressed in D4 is perfectly correct, but in itself that suggests nothing about why a person's death might matter to us, why they might be valuable or how they should be treated. It is as true that every bicycle pedal is unique as it is that every person is unique, but nothing of any importance follows from the former fact. It is the nature of the beings as much as their uniqueness that matters to us: it depends on what it is uniqueness *of*. In that way, any significance attaching to D4 is parasitic on the significance attaching to D1.

The security of D3 can be questioned in a number of ways. From a psychoanalytic direction, it might be argued that the unity of persons is not all it appears. An individual may have a unified ego, but there will also be an unconscious which is unruly and unintegrated into the personality, and that may temper the picture of unity originally embraced. Derek Parfit's work on personal identity has also raised deep questions about the unity of a person over time and doubts about the importance which we attach to it (Parfit, 1984). Against this, it might be replied that whatever surprising truths might come to light about the internal structure of a human life, we know enough already about the hiatus between one person's life and another's, the way one person's memories and aspirations are distinct from another's, to justify according separate importance to each individual person in the way that we do. Any significance attaching to the idea of integrity expressed in D3 would then turn out to be parasitic on the significance attaching to D2.

But if we then focus on D1 and D2, the inferences drawn from them are equally problematic. It is perfectly true that we can preserve the qualitative distinctness of persons claimed in D1 by drawing up a compendious list of the relevant properties (sentience, intentions, wishes, etc.) and arguing that no other entities possess that list in its entirety. But other entities will certainly share *some* of the properties on the list, properties which are highly germane for entry into the moral realm. The least controversial example would be non-human animals possessing sentience, whose status makes moral claims on us for that reason. More controversial and more pertinent for liberal ideas of autonomy and identity is the example of collective entities. Committees, for example, possess properties such as the power to deliberate, to decide and to act on decisions. They are capable of acting in ways which are morally untoward and the responsibility for which lies with the collective rather than with any individuals (except in so far as the individuals are themselves considered *as* members of the collective entity). That is, there are non-human entities which enter the moral realm as moral agents (collectives), as well as non-human entities which enter that realm as moral patients (non-human animals).[7] This is sufficient to cast doubt on any inference from the truth of D1 to the conclusion that the qualitative distinctness of persons gives them sole occupancy of the moral realm.

A similar problem attends D2. No doubt it is true that my life is not your life and my thoughts are not your thoughts. But what follows about how far you are entitled to live your life according to your own aspirations? Some of our thoughts and some of our life are shared and we sometimes have joint aspirations, and that already raises complications for any conclusions that might be thought to follow from the distinctness of persons. Even where there is not that complication, there is one universally recognized way in which lives fail to be separate, and that is that any action is connected by causal links to lives other than the agent's. That is the problem acknowledged even by John Stuart Mill in his attempt to distinguish the area where interference in someone's life against their wishes is not justified. Mill's position is not that there is a class of acts which have no connection with others' lives but that there is a class of acts where the nature of any adverse effects is not sufficient to justify interference (Mill, 1983, pp. 136–7).

However, the fact of causal links has wider implications than usually thought. On a simple interpretation this is merely a matter of the effects which *follow* from any action. The argument would then be that the distinctness of persons is complicated by the causal effects which proceed from virtually any significant human action. But on a more complex interpretation it is a matter of the causal *preconditions* of any action too. For example, my decision to buy a cheap computer doesn't just have effects on others; it requires that others' lives should already have taken a particular course. It is arbitrary to take only causal effects and not casual preconditions into account when judging how far one person's life is distinct from another's. When causal preconditions of action are taken into account too, then the extent to which persons' lives are not separate but interconnected is much greater. It will be correspondingly more difficult to draw conclusions about people's regulation of their own personal lives. No act will be 'purely my business' if the causal preconditions for performing it require that other people's lives should have taken a particular course, and if that course involves something demeaning or injurious to them, then it is at best not obvious that I should be justified in pursuing it.[8]

When we think of persons, then, even at the most general and abstract level, our idea of their distinctness must be tempered in two respects. First, part of their existence consists in their being constituents in numerous collective bodies: families, neighbourhoods, churches, committees, classes and so on. Second, any person stands in relations to an indefinite number of other individuals in a complicated causal network stretching through space and time. Adoption of values takes place in the light of this collective membership and causal interconnection, and every and any choice will carry implications for other persons' lives.

Now, when we come to think of persons in more specific and concrete terms, it can easily seem that ideas like individual choice and autonomy cease to have any application. Part of what I do I do as a component in a parents' association, a club or some social movement. What I do as a parent, neighbour or cyclist both affects those around me and require others to have acted in certain ways for me to be able to act as I do. Considerations of that kind prompt the familiar communitarian objection that I do not choose my identity but discover it. Thus Alasdair MacIntyre says (1981, pp. 204–5): 'I belong to this clan, that tribe, this nation. Hence what is good for me has to be the good for one who inhabits these roles'; and Michael Sandel (1982, p. 179) refers to 'loyalties and convictions whose moral force consists partly in the fact that living by them is inseparable from understanding ourselves as the particular persons we are – as members of this family or community or nation or people ...'. Certainly one can readily see how race and nationality may seem non-negotiable parts of someone's identity.

But we should not suppose that we must choose *either* the liberal *or* the communitarian position here. Both have a portion of truth here, and it is important to recognize and preserve both portions. It is true, for example, that any individual person is part of a multiplicity of communities and collective agents, and that the identities, values and loyalties that they manifest can be traced back to those communities and collectives. That is what licenses communitarian talk of the individual being embedded or encumbered. But the possibility of critical reflection is crucial here. The important insight in liberalism is just that I can always distance myself from any such particular encumbrance, at least in imagination, and in that sense take up an endorsing or a critical stance towards it. Moreover, I can in some cases divest myself of encumbrances – not merely in imagination but in practice. I can cease to be what I am. Accordingly, it is inaccurate to say that my encumbrances, as such, *determine* my identity and my values. Of course some encumbrances may have that determining role, because some encumbrances I cannot rid myself of: there is a limit to how far I can distance myself from what I am. Features of myself and my situation over which there is no control constitute *constraints of necessity* (see Graham, 1996, pp. 137–40). They set a limit to the autonomy I have in embracing or rejecting values and it is important to acknowledge them for that reason. It is important to own, so to speak, what you cannot change.

Are race and nationality constraints of necessity? Race falls clearly into that category, since it comprises a set of features which cannot be altered. Nationality, however, is more ambiguous. Where it is defined by reference to place of birth, then this too constitutes a constraint of necessity; but where it is defined by reference to citizenship, then that is something which I may choose to change (and even where I do not make that choice, I may still resolve not to identify with my nationality). Of course, the idea of a constraint of necessity has been specified in a purely formal way and there will be many examples of this constraint which are of no practical significance: it will be a matter for empirical investigation which constraints are as a matter of fact of any importance. And there could be little doubt that race falls into the important category. Notice, however, that there are two interestingly different ways in which such a constraint can acquire its significance. We might label them *independent* and *reactive*. A constraint assumes independent significance where I choose to endow it with such: I make the decision to value and celebrate (or, as it may be, to revile and deplore) some ineradicable feature of myself. A constraint assumes reactive significance where I am forced to regard it as significant irrespective of whether I think it actually has intrinsic significance or not. For example, I might be forced so to regard it because of the actions and attitudes of others. The difference between independent and reactive significance would then be illustrated by the difference between my choosing to become part of a Black Pride movement and my needing to regard my race as significant in the construction of my values as a means of protecting myself from white racists.

Materiality

Decisions about values have to be made, and I have argued that they have to be made in recognition of the indistinctness of persons and under constraints such as that of necessity. Where theoretically and practically feasible, decisions to embrace or reject parts of one's identity will depend on a variety of factors, including the particular aspirations and projects which one has embraced, either as an individual or as a member of a collective, and the vagaries of fate in the form of the attitudes directed at one. That makes it plain that the decisions will depend on factors which are contingent, socially variable and attitude-dependent, factors which are therefore not a matter of brute, but of social, fact. Will they also depend on any factors which are *not* socially variable? Is there anything in the nature of human life itself, regardless of the social attitudes, beliefs and conventions obtaining in a particular situation, which places any kind of constraint around the decisions concerning identity and values that someone could reasonably adopt? Recall the context in which the issues discussed in this paper are raised: a pluralist world in which socially variable factors create problems for people living in proximity to others. It would be significant if there were a socially-invariant factor to which individuals with very different sets of values must pay attention, on pain of irrationality if they do not.

I want to suggest that the fact of human materiality is such a factor, and one carrying great significance. It requires subscription to no particular set of values, no particular or contentious way of looking at the world, to recognize that we are material creatures with material needs. What is distinctive of the constraints arising from our materiality is that they are of enduring significance at all times and places, and their significance is not dependent on social attitudes or conventions. Their significance is there whether we like it or not, and however we theorize (or fail to theorize) about it.[9] Any way of theorizing about oneself or about the world which ignores that fact is immediately convicted of error.

My reason for claiming this special role for our materiality is that the constraint of having to satisfy one's material needs is not just formally speaking a constraint of necessity as defined in the previous section, but one of enormous practical importance. Imagine creatures like human beings in most respects, but capable of settling the satisfaction of their material needs in the first 15 seconds of their existence. They no longer have to concern themselves with nourishment, providing sheltered habitation or clothing to protect themselves against the elements, and they can simply go on to give their life a chosen shape free of all those concerns. In that respect at least they are so different from human beings that they remind us of something so obvious that we can miss its full significance. The constraint of material necessity is absolutely central in our lives, and in a number of respects. It is a constraint which is *recurrent* rather than once-and-for-all as in the imagined example. It makes itself felt for however long a lifetime may be, since life literally ceases if material needs go unmet. It is also therefore what I have elsewhere called a *constraint of precondition*: it constrains absolutely *any* other aspirations or activities which a human being might conceive of (Graham, 1996, pp. 140–3). It is, further, central in the sense that for most people the activities they must engage in in order to satisfy these needs are themselves central in their lives. The activities often take the form of having to take employment to gain the resources necessary for their satisfaction or having to enter into a relation of dependence with someone who can provide the resources. (If you possess a sufficiently large fortune, however, the material constraint will not be central in your life in these ways.) It would be erroneous to suppose that these considerations were peripheral to most people's lives.

It might be objected that such considerations are nevertheless peripheral to questions of value. There is so much more to human beings than their materiality, it might be said, and it is everything else about them which is intrinsically important. There is a need for recognition, aspirations of artistic and spiritual kinds, and so on. Isn't all this more important than mere material existence? My answer is that if it is, then that indicates precisely why it is a mistake to ignore our materiality. Our material relations exercise an enormous influence over what we can do with that part of our lives which is not concerned in one way or another with securing material needs, in terms both of the time remaining for other aspirations and of the sort of people we have become as a result of the social relations defining our material activity. If we wish to endow these aspects of human life with greater intrinsic importance we cannot afford *not* to develop a theory of material relations. I leave open the question what form such a theory should take. For example, it is not clear whether it could be adequately couched in terms of social class. The concept of class is an ambiguous and theoretically contested one and it has sometimes been drawn in excessively narrow terms. Everyone has to do *something* to meet their material needs, and what they have to do can have momentous consequences for their lives; but what they do is enormously varied. It need not involve anything as particular as work in an industrial location or directly paid employment of any form. An adequate theory of material relations would have to do justice to all of those facts.[10]

What would a comprehensive theory of the rational construction of social identity look like? It would have to include as sources at least (1) considerations which people themselves (rationally) place significance and value on; (2) considerations whose significance is imposed on them by the actions and attitudes of others; and (3) considerations whose significance is a matter of brute fact. Generally speaking, (1) and (2) are addressed much more thoroughly in discussions of pluralism and the politics of identity than (3). There are good reasons for that kind of concentration, not least the kind of reactive significance mentioned at the end of the previous section. If you want to arrive at a rational view of yourself it is vital to take into account the view which others have of you. Yet the considerations under (3) are also vital in making us who we are and in raising questions for decisions about whether we should continue to be who we are in those respects. Meeting the material needs of life involves us in social activity on a colossal scale, puts people into groups experiencing similar conditions of life which stand in marked contrast to the conditions of life enjoyed by other groups, calls forth relations of subordination and exploitation and generally results in grossly unequal circumstances of life. Any social theory which ignores all of this is bound to be radically incomplete. We live, moreover, in an unprecedentedly self-conscious era and as a result tend to theorize about social identity in terms of our own self-conceptions. An emphasis on materiality is a useful corrective to this, reminding us of facts whose importance is independent of our thinking about them. It is useful to be reminded that, before everything else, being somebody is a matter of being some body.[11]

Notes

1   Bradley (1962, p. 198, n. 5) said that 'collisions of duties are avoided mostly by each man keeping to his own immediate duties, and not trying to see from the point of view of other stations than his own'. More recently Strawson (1961, p. 33) reported: 'A certain professor once said: "For me to be moral is to behave like a professor."'

2   For comments on the impact of the loss of these beliefs, see Sandel (1982, pp. 175–6) and Scheffler (1992, pp. 14–15).

3   Mill might be taken as a representative sponsor of the first ground, Berlin of the second and Walzer of the third. See Mill (1983, pp. 114–31), Berlin (1991, pp. 79–80) and Walzer (1983, p. 6).

4   Although Rawls is explicit that a political conception of justice may not apply to all societies, he resists the suggestion that this makes it relativist or historicist. See Rawls (1989, p. 286, n. 46).

5   For such attempts, see Gewirth (1994) and Steiner (1977). For scepticism about taking rights as a starting point, see O'Neill (1996).

6   This is reflected in the fact that, although Rawls and Nozick formulate the distinctness of persons in a similar way, the conclusions they reach about how persons are to be treated are very different. Rawls uses the distinctness of persons to dismiss utilitarianism, but Nozick uses it to dismiss just the kind of redistributive welfarism favoured by Rawls.

7   I have argued for the ineliminability of collectives from our view of the social world in two different contexts: see Graham (1986 and 1992). Whether collectives can enter the moral realm not solely as agents, but also as patients, in the sense that we could reasonably care what happened to them, is a more difficult question. I try to answer it in 'The Moral Status of Collective Entities' (unpublished).

8   I elaborate on these claims in 'Are all Preferences Nosy?', a paper read at *Utilitarianism Reconsidered*, a conference of the International Society for Utilitarian Studies, New Orleans, March 1997.

9   This is not to deny that the *form* which that significance takes will vary crucially from one historical period to another: a society where the main option for gaining access to material resources is that of assuming the status of chattel slave is different from one where the main option is that of assuming the status of wage-worker or housewife.

10   I persist in my belief that the writings of Marx, when stripped of 100 years of misinterpretation, are one useful source for an adequate theory. See Graham (1989 and 1998).

11   The original draft of this article was prepared while I was a visiting fellow at the School of Advanced Study at the University of London. For extremely helpful comments and conversations at various stages I am grateful to David Archard, Alison Assiter, Chris Bertram, Ed Brandon, Katrin Flikschuh and Ross Poole.

References

Arendt, H. (1959), *The Human Condition*, Doubleday Anchor, New York.
Berlin, I. (1991), *The Crooked Timber of Humanity*, Knopf, New York.

Bradley, F. H. (1962), 'My Station and its Duties' (1876) in his *Ethical Studies*, 2nd edn, Wollheim, R. (ed.), Oxford University Press, Oxford.

Gewirth, A. (1994), 'Is Cultural Pluralism Relevant to Moral Knowledge?', *Social Philosophy and Policy*, Vol. 11, pp. 22–43.

Graham, K. (1986), *The Battle of Democracy*, Wheatsheaf, Sussex.

Graham, K. (1989), 'Class – A Simple View', *Inquiry*, Vol. 32, pp. 419–36.

Graham, K. (1992), *Karl Marx, Our Contemporary*, Harvester, Hemel Hempstead.

Graham, K. (1996), 'Coping with the Many-Coloured Dome: Pluralism and Practical Reason' in Archard, D. (ed.), *Philosophy and Pluralism*, Cambridge University Press, Cambridge.

Graham, K. (1998), 'Digging up Marx' in MacKenzie, I. and O'Neill, S. (eds), *Reconstituting Social Criticism*, Macmillan, London.

Kymlicka, W. (1989), *Liberalism, Community and Culture*, Clarendon Press, Oxford.

Kymlicka, W. (1990), *Contemporary Political Philosophy*, Clarendon Press, Oxford.

MacIntyre, A. (1981), *After Virtue*, Duckworth, London.

Mill, J.S. (1983), *Essay on Liberty* (1859), Dent, London.

Nagel, T. (1987), 'Moral Conflict and Political Legitimacy', *Philosophy and Public Affairs*, Vol. 16, pp. 215–40.

Nozick, R. (1974), *Anarchy, State, and Utopia*, Basil Blackwell, Oxford.

O'Neill, O. (1996), *Towards Justice and Virtue*, Cambridge University Press, Cambridge.

Parfit, D. (1984), *Reasons and Persons*, Clarendon Press, Oxford.

Pettit, P. (1993), *The Common Mind*, Oxford University Press, New York.

Rawls, J. (1971), *A Theory of Justice*, Oxford University Press, Oxford.

Rawls, J. (1989), 'The Domain of the Political and Overlapping Consensus', *New York University Law Review*, Vol. 233, reprinted in Goodin, R. and Pettit, P. (eds) (1993), *Contemporary Political Philosophy: An Anthology*, Blackwell, Oxford.

Rawls, J. (1993), *Political Liberalism*, Columbia University Press, New York.

Sandel, M. (1982), *Liberalism and the Limits of Justice*, Cambridge University Press, Cambridge.

Scheffler, S. (1982), *The Rejection of Consequentialism*, Clarendon Press, Oxford.

Scheffler, S. (1992), *Human Morality*, Oxford University Press, Oxford.

Steiner, H. (1977), 'The Natural Right to the Means of Production', *Philosophical Quarterly*, Vol. 27, pp. 41–9.

Strawson, P.F. (1961), 'Social Morality and Individual Ideal', *Philosophy*, Vol. 36, reprinted in his (1974), *Freedom and Resentment*, Methuen, London.

Taylor, C. (1992), *Multiculturalism and 'the Politics of Recognition'*, Gutman, A. (ed.), Princeton University Press, Princeton.

Walzer, M. (1983), *Spheres of Justice*, Martin Robertson, London.

Williams, B. (1985), *Ethics and the Limits of Philosophy*, Fontana Press, London.

13 Recognizing Multiculturalism

SIMON THOMPSON

A number of writers have recently commented on the importance of the idea of 'recognition' in contemporary politics. For Daniel Salée (1995, p. 278), '[t]he will to recognition, to have one's identity universally acknowledged and respected, has become perhaps one of the most significant determinants of the sociopolitical dynamics of contemporary modern societies'. Even more strongly, Nancy Fraser (1995, p. 68) contends that '[t]he "struggle for recognition" is fast becoming the paradigmatic form of political conflict in the late twentieth century'. From this perspective, it may be possible to cast light on a number of features of contemporary multicultural politics. For example, certain types of nationalism, anti-colonialism, organizations of linguistic and cultural minorities, and indigenous and aboriginal peoples can all be seen as groups engaged in struggles for recognition (Tully, 1995, pp. 2– 3). While these political formations are very various in character, they at least share a desire to secure appropriate acknowledgement of their identity and a revaluation of the cultural traits associated with that identity.

An acknowledgement of the importance of this phenomenon has led to the development of a body of political theory based on the idea of recognition. Probably the most widely known contemporary exponent of this approach is Charles Taylor. In his essay on 'The Politics of Recognition', first published in 1992, he develops a political theory that issues in the claim that all members of a multicultural society should be given due recognition.[1] The principal aim of this chapter is to undertake a critical examination of this sort of political theory. For a number of reasons, the argument will focus primarily on Taylor's essay. First, he is the theorist most closely associated with the politics of recognition at present. Second, he offers a subtle and complex account of such a politics; in particular, his theory has a number of resources that rival theories lack. Third, he develops a fairly general theory of recognition; that is, it would not be too difficult to expand it to cover cases he does not discuss. Thus, while Taylor's work cannot be taken as fully representative of the entire body of political theory that deploys the notion of recognition, for our purposes it can serve as an exemplar of this approach.

Taylor's politics of recognition has already been criticized on a number of different grounds. Consider three particular charges. First, while multiculturalism is defined as a situation in which there is a plurality of cultural groups, this theory offers too simplistic an account of the notion of 'culture' that is intended to identify the relevant groups. Taylor has a tendency to assume that each group is an isolated unit characterized by a separate and homogenous culture. But, as James Tully (1995, p. 10) – among others – has argued, cultures are always internally complex, overlapping, interactive and internally negotiated. Second, it is argued that Taylor's politics of recognition offers too 'cultural' an account of cultural groups. That is to say, little or no reference is made to the broader social and economic context in which these groups exist. As a consequence, Taylor's practical proposals are also over-cultural in that they neglect issues of redistributive justice necessary at least to supplement cultural revaluation. Thus Amélie Rorty contends (1994, p. 156) that, given '[t]he mutual permeability of the various dimensions of culture', 'cultural survival cannot be assured by respectful recognition: it also requires far-reaching political and economic self-determination'. Third, Taylor's politics of recognition has been criticized for not distinguishing between the very different natures and needs of the various groups – from nations, through cultural minorities, to women – to which it has been applied (Habermas, 1994a, pp. 116–19).

All of these highly pertinent points certainly must be taken into account in any attempt to develop an adequate politics of recognition. However, this chapter will be rather more narrow in focus. One aspect of Taylor's theory has not been subject to the same critical scrutiny as those already mentioned. This concerns the account he offers of the conception of recognition itself. Since this must form the keystone of his (or indeed of *any*) politics of recognition, it is vital to get this right if the political theory itself is to be successful. It is for this reason that attention will be focused here on the conception of recognition that underlies Taylor's theory. It will be argued that, while he is right to claim that a multicultural society should give due recognition to all its members, Taylor relies on too simplistic an account of the conception of recognition, and that as a consequence his political theory is unable successfully to meet the objectives it sets itself. Although beginning with, and framed around, a critique of Taylor, this chapter will also make a start on a more constructive endeavour. Drawing particularly on the work of Jürgen Habermas and Axel Honneth, the argument will work toward a more sophisticated account of the conception of recognition, and some hints will be offered about what a political theory based on this conception might look like.

The argument to be defended is founded on an intersubjective account of identity formation, according to which there are three dimensions of human selfhood that, although interrelated, must be distinguished. Corresponding to each of these dimensions is a different pattern of recognition, and these patterns in combination determine the necessary structure of a coherent and defensible multicultural politics. The argument advances in two principal stages. First, a distinction is made between *autonomy* and *identity*, and their corresponding forms of recognition. While Taylor is aware of this distinction, he fails fully to work out its implications for his political theory. Then a further dimension of human selfhood – and its correlative form of recognition – are introduced. Following R.D. Laing (1965, p. 39), this will be referred to as '*ontological security*'. Although Taylor does makes a fleeting reference to this idea, he does not make it part of his political theory.

The importance of this argument is that it is only on the basis of a suitably sophisticated conception of recognition that a successful politics of recognition could be formulated. In this chapter, while there will be insufficient space to describe such a politics in any detail, it will be possible at least to hint at its main outlines. In brief, the tripartite conception of recognition to be developed here points to a politics that combines three corresponding elements – of rights, solidarity and love.[2] Only such a politics could provide all individuals and groups with full recognition, and hence only such a politics could make a just and stable multicultural society a real possibility.

Taylor's Politics of Recognition

Before embarking on the critique of Taylor's conception of recognition, it is first necessary to consider the principal features of his conception, and of the politics of recognition that he constructs on its basis. Taylor's theory is based on an intersubjective account of identity. He stresses that the 'crucial feature of human life is its fundamentally *dialogical* character'. Thus, to discover 'my own identity' is to 'negotiate it through dialogue, partly overt, partly internal, with others' (Taylor, 1994, pp. 32, 34). It follows, he argues, that a failure of recognition or an act of misrecognition by those others can do me harm, oppress me, imprison me in 'a false, distorted, and reduced mode of being', and even saddle me 'with a crippling self-hatred' (ibid., pp. 25–6; cf. Honneth, 1995, pp. 131–2).

Taylor then considers the political implications of this account. Here a particularly pressing question is whether the demand for recognition can be met by recognizing citizens as individuals, or whether, given that their identity is to some significant extent formed by their membership of groups, these groups must themselves enjoy some form of recognition (cf. Habermas, 1994a, pp. 107–8). Taylor considers both of these options by setting up a contrast between two rival theories: a 'politics of universalism' and a 'politics of difference' – both of which seek to secure due recognition for all persons in a multicultural society. But while both these forms of politics are grounded in a commitment to show all citizens 'equal respect' (Taylor, 1994, p. 43), their understandings of what this commitment implies for politics are at considerable variance.

The Kantian politics of universalism believes that it is as a result of '*a universal human potential* for rational agency that we deserve respect' (ibid., p. 41). From this, a politics follows that centres on 'the equalization of rights and entitlements' for all individuals (ibid., p. 37) under the aegis of a neutral state (ibid., pp. 56–7). By contrast, the politics of difference holds that the 'universal potential', in light of which respect is due, is 'the potential for forming and defining one's own identity' (ibid., p. 42). It follows that individual and group distinctiveness should be recognized, and political forms should be devised that encourage and foster the development of particular identities. At a practical level, while exponents of the politics of universalism give strong priority to individual rights, their rivals allow certain collective goals – in particular, cultural survival – to override fundamental individual rights. For example, while the former theory would refuse ever to allow the individual's right to freedom of religious worship to be overridden by reference to the need to protect an established religion, the latter could conceive of circumstances in which this would be justified.

Having set the problem up in this way, Taylor tries to find a *via media* between these two politics. He rejects a purely procedural liberalism since it is 'inhospitable to difference'; in particular, 'it can't accommodate what the members of distinct societies really aspire to, which is survival' (ibid., pp. 60–1). But he seeks also to avoid a politics of difference that is prepared to override fundamental rights and thus to abandon the goal of equality between individuals. Taylor's solution is a political theory that he refers to as a 'nonprocedural' form of liberalism. It is nonprocedural since it does not claim to be neutral between different ways of life; in fact it is 'grounded very much on judgments about what makes a good life – judgments in which the integrity of cultures has an important place' (ibid., pp. 61–3). To be specific, while such a politics would stand by the liberal commitment to defend certain fundamental rights, these would be distinguished 'from the broad range of immunities and presumptions of uniform treatment that have sprung up in modern cultures of judicial review'. These latter *may* sometimes be overridden, Taylor argues, and thus the goal of uniform treatment abandoned, in the name of 'cultural survival'. To take a particular case, he argues that, within the framework of the 'Charter of Rights' that protects all Canadians' basic rights and freedoms, it is possible to recognize Québec as a distinct society. On such a model, Québec governments could, for example, take certain measures to protect the French language (education, commercial signage, etc.) so long as these such measures did not violate citizens' fundamental rights (ibid., pp. 58–61). In this way, Taylor hopes, the recognition of individual autonomy can be rendered compatible with the recognition of the identity of distinct cultural groups.

Autonomy and Identity

It seems that for Taylor an individual or group is given recognition if treated with respect. A necessary condition of this sort of recognition, he believes, is for all citizens to be guaranteed certain fundamental rights. As long as this condition is met, the state can then pursue policies which promote a particular national culture without this pursuit undermining respect for citizens with different cultural identifications. For example, Christianity can be given the place of an established religion so long as non-Christians' right to freedom of religion is preserved.[3] Does Taylor's theory provide an adequate basis for a politics of recognition in a multicultural society? And, of particular concern in this chapter, is the conception of recognition this theory employs a suitable foundation for such a politics?

First, note that, at a practical level, the Canadian case with which Taylor is most concerned offers scant support for his position. At Meech Lake, the constitutional debate reached a complete deadlock. Some English-speaking Canadians rejected the accord since they saw it as an attempt to legitimate Québec's collective goals (Taylor, 1994, pp. 54–5). Many Québeckers rejected it since they believed that it sought to impose an alien form of liberal society on them, one to which they could not have accommodated themselves without losing their distinct identity (Laforest, 1994, pp. 202–5; Taylor, 1994, p. 60). Indigenous Canadians rejected the 1982 constitutional reform on very similar grounds, contending that it was based on what they saw as an alien conception of individual rights (Laforest, 1994, pp. 196–7; Tully, 1995, pp. 11–12). It could be argued that this deadlock can be explained historically, by seeing mutual suspicions as the result of past betrayals. While this may explain part of the problem, however, it will now be argued that the very way in which this struggle has been conceptualized has contributed significantly to the intransigence of the rival parties.

Consider how this standoff occurs in Taylor's theory. By setting up the politics of universalism and the politics of difference as the twin poles around which his analysis revolves, his nonprocedural liberalism becomes an unstable compromise between the two. In particular, it presents us with a zero-sum game in which the goals of universalism can be advanced only at a cost to the goals of difference, and vice versa. Thus the protection of individual rights can be guaranteed only by resisting demands to further collective goals; and if collective goals are promoted, it is individual rights that must suffer.[4] In terms of recognition, every call by a group for recognition will be seen by others as an attack on their demand to be valued as individuals, while any defence of a system of purely individual recognition will be seen as a slap in the face to those seeking acknowledgement as members of groups.[5] A precarious balance between these two objectives is struck at the point at which Taylor distinguishes fundamental from non-fundamental rights. As a result, his theory is located on an unstable fault-line between a politics of individual rights and a politics of collective protection. The Canadian situation replicates the problem in practice. The conflict over the constitution has been seen as a battle between two politics that correspond to Taylor's politics of universalism and of difference. While the politics of individual rights and of collective cultural protection can both be seen to be based on a conception of recognition, they lead to wholly incompatible objectives. Thus the parties involved are put at odds, and any possibility of a just and stable solution is rendered remote. The result is a continuing standoff between these two forms of politics that weakens the legitimacy of the multicultural polity.

The argument to be developed here is that the source of instability both in Taylor's theory and in Canadian practice can be traced directly back to the conception of recognition that he employs. He fails to realize the significance of a distinction between two separate patterns of recognition that correspond to two distinct forms of appraisal: aspects of selfhood, and types of political goal. Only by making these sets of distinctions explicit will it be possible to specify a form of politics that can do justice to both individual rights and cultural affirmation, and thus help to establish the foundations of a successful multicultural politics.

To begin with, recall that, after starting from the premise that all individuals must be shown respect, Taylor distinguishes between autonomy and identity as alternative grounds for such respect. However, it will now be argued, he fails to realize that, while the autonomy is conceptually tied to the notion of respect, identity is not. That is, although it is plausible to say that an individual earns respect on the basis of his or her capacity for rational agency, it would be stretching the notion too far to say that just the same sort of respect is also due to that individual in light of his or her unique and irreplaceable sense of identity. For this reason, a second, distinct form of appraisal must be introduced: in the terms used here, it is necessary to distinguish between *respect* and *self-respect*, on the one hand, and *esteem* and *self-esteem*, on the other.[6]

In order to see why it is necessary to distinguish between these two forms of appraisal, consider what is implied by their absence. You show me lack of respect if you treat me paternalistically or deny me my rights. A number of groups are characteristically treated in these ways – including children, the senile and the mad. They may be treated with kindness, but they are not respected in the specific sense used here. But even if you do show me respect, you may still not hold me in esteem. You can regard me as an entirely responsible agent, but think that who I am or what I do is not worthy of your praise. In an extreme case you may judge my character, my qualities as a person, to be contemptible. Here, to say I chose to make of myself what I did, to hold me responsible for who I am, is actually to sharpen the criticism that I am unworthy of your esteem. Now consider how these two modes of appraisal are applied reflexively. People lacking in self-respect do not mind having their wishes ignored, or their rights flouted, or being treated in ways that others would find degrading (Sachs, 1981, p. 350). But even someone who *does* have self-respect may nevertheless lack self-esteem. As David Sachs comments, such a person says 'he has his pride', but then adds 'that that is nothing of which to be proud' (ibid., p. 352). We may believe that it is our own fault that we have fallen short of standards we have set ourselves, and may therefore not believe that we are worthy of others' praise.[7]

The importance of this analysis here is that the contrast between these two separate modes of appraisal corresponds to the distinction that Taylor makes between two different aspects of our conception of selfhood. Thus, while respect and self-respect are due to individuals in virtue of their autonomy, their capacity for rational agency, judgments of esteem and self-esteem are based on individuals' identities, which include their character, abilities, achievements and so on. By contrast, Taylor, having failed to distinguish respect from esteem, loses sight of the distinction between autonomy and identity.[8] It is for this reason that his theory seeks to trade off the protection of the one aspect of the self against the protection of the other in order to achieve the single goal of equal respect.

It will now be argued, against Taylor, that respect and esteem must be seen as distinct but complementary, rather than alternative and competing, forms of appraisal. The best way to see this is to consider how these different forms of appraisal, directed toward these two distinct aspects of the self, are expressed in two contrasting patterns of recognition. Here both Habermas and Honneth make the relevant distinction. Both identify a first type of recognition in which a subject is accepted by others as being autonomous in the sense of being rationally accountable for his or her judgments and actions. For Habermas, this recognition occurs in a moral discourse in which each participant advances norms that he or she hopes all persons will accept as universally valid. Here I am recognized as autonomous when others see me as a suitable partner in such a discourse (see, e.g., Habermas, 1993, pp. 12–13; and cf. Cooke, 1994, p. 90). Honneth's account includes the corresponding case of 'a condition of mutual recognition in which the individual learns to see himself from the perspective of his partners to interaction as a bearer of equal rights', and hence as an autonomous agent. In this way, an individual develops the 'positive attitude' of 'self- respect' (Honneth, 1994, p. 194). Habermas argues that the second form of recognition occurs in an ethical discourse when the subject is recognized by others as making judgments and taking actions that are ethically right for a specific individual in the context of a particular horizon of strong evaluations (see, e.g., Habermas, 1993, pp. 11–12; and cf. Cooke, 1994, pp. 91–2). Similarly, Honneth identifies 'a relationship of recognition that can aid the individual in acquiring ... *self-esteem*'. This is 'a condition of solidarity with, and approval of, unconventional life-styles' which 'would enable the subjects to find recognition based on mutual encouragement given their special characteristics as persons whose individuality has been formed by their specific biographies'. Thus individuals come to see themselves as unique and irreplaceable beings (Honneth, 1994, p. 195; see also Cooke, 1995, pp. 344–5).

The distinction between these two patterns of recognition leads both Habermas and Honneth to defend a politics that possesses two distinct aspects. First, a political order must enable citizens to develop self-respect by treating them as autonomous agents - and this requires guaranteeing them certain fundamental rights. This is the aspect of a normative order that Habermas and Honneth refer to as 'justice'.[9] In addition, since citizens develop self-esteem when they are publicly acknowledged to follow ways of life that are unique and irreplaceable, such a political order must at the same time protect those ways of life. Here Habermas and Honneth talk of a politics of 'solidarity'.[10]

How can rights and solidarity be brought together in one coherent politics? At this point, there is a parting of the ways. Habermas, drawing on his account of deliberative democracy,[11] argues that, if an effective public sphere is put into place, 'then the democratic process of actualizing equal individual rights will also extend to guaranteeing different ethnic groups and their cultural forms of life equal rights to coexistence' (Habermas, 1994a, pp. 128–9). In other words, under the institutional conditions he specifies, a multicultural politics would be able to attend equally to the demands of individual freedom and cultural survival. Honneth, for his part, argues that this dichotomous account of recognition implies a politics that requires both the establishment of a system of rights that protects citizens' fundamental freedoms and the creation of an 'intersubjectively shared value-horizon' (Honneth, 1995, p. 121) which ensures that all citizens' distinct identities are valued.

Within the confines of this chapter, it will not be possible to assess the validity of these rival proposals. But enough work has been done here to support the following conclusions. The first is that two sets of interrelated notions must be kept distinct: in one, a complex relation is established between self-respect, autonomy and rights; and, in the other, self-esteem, identity and solidarity are entwined together. It is within the two patterns of recognition in the forms of rights and solidarity that flows of respect and esteem help to generate and protect autonomy and identity respectively.[12] The second conclusion is that Taylor's position on this issue is inadequate. In contrasting the politics of universalism and of difference, he is certainly aware of the way in which two different modes of recognition focus on two distinct aspects of our conception of the self (Taylor, 1994, p. 41). However, since he overlooks the distinction between respect and esteem, Taylor fails to keep autonomy and identity apart. As a result, his politics of recognition regards the protection of these two aspects of the self as competing rather than complementary goals. It follows that, for as long as Taylor fails to make systematic use of the series of corresponding distinctions – between respect and esteem, autonomy and identity, rights and solidarity – developed in this section, his theory will continue to sit on an unstable fault-line between a politics of individual rights and a politics of collective protection. Without a conception of recognition that can encompass these distinctions, his theory will not be able to provide a suitable basis for a politics of recognition in a multicultural society.

Ontological Security

Two distinct aspects of recognition have now been identified: the respect given to autonomy in the form of rights, and the esteem given to identity in the form of solidarity. Whether we follow Habermas' or Honneth's specific proposals thus far, could this dichotomous conception of recognition provide a suitable foundation for a politics of recognition capable of underpinning a just and stable multicultural society?

It can doubtless be argued that such a conception of recognition has certain strengths that will help it to achieve this goal. First, the existence of a rights-system that protects all citizens' basic freedoms removes the need for the sort of political struggle that has in the past been necessary either to create such a system or to gain access to a system already in place.[13] Second, if all citizens have a chance to secure esteem for their particular cultural identities, this reduces the likelihood of certain political dangers. For example, Habermas suggests that, if a certain group feels that it is not valued, then 'experiences of impotence lead the minority struggling for recognition to take a regressive position'. If, by contrast, they feel esteemed, it is less likely that such a group's 'tendencies to self-assertion' will 'take on a fundamentalist and separatist character' (Habermas, 1994a, p. 118).

In spite of these considerations, it will now be argued that a politics of recognition based on this modified conception of recognition still has significant shortcomings. Let us look briefly at two accounts of problems that may occur even in a multicultural society governed by a politics that combines elements of rights and solidarity. First, consider part of Amy Gutmann's account of what she calls the 'challenge' of multiculturalism for political theory. She observes that '[m]embers of different cultural groups may share the same standards of justice, but nevertheless act unjustly out of hatred or distrust of others, or because they believe that justice is less important than solidarity' (Gutmann, 1993, p. 171). Here Gutmann identifies two distinct problems that may beset a multicultural society: in the first case, justice is outweighed by hatred; and, in the second, it is outweighed by solidarity. Now consider Maeve Cooke's development of a Habermasian theory of social integration. In the course of this account, she effectively expands on Gutmann's remarks by offering an explanation of the problem of solidarity in terms of the problem of hatred. According to Cooke's theory, social integration in modern pluralist societies would be ensured if respect-based solidarity were able to override esteem-based solidarity – roughly, if loyalty to the fellow citizens of one's nation state took precedence over loyalty to one's own particular group.

However, as Cooke rightly points out, respect-based solidarity may be too weak to do the job asked of it: 'it may not be *sufficient* as a socially binding and bonding mechanism' since, in particular, it may be outweighed in practice by different esteem-based solidarities. Her explanation for this situation is that, since forms of esteem-based solidarity are rooted in 'affectivity', and forms of respect-based solidarity in 'cognition', the former have a tendency to outweigh the latter (Cooke, 1995, p. 351).[14] On this account, then, the problem of solidarity is caused by the problem of hatred.

Unfortunately, the solutions Gutmann and Cooke propose to these problems are entirely inadequate. First, having described the challenge of multiculturalism, Gutmann goes on to conceive the task of political theory in these circumstances as one of specifying 'standards of social justice' on which all can agree (Gutmann, 1993, p. 171). But, *ex hypothesi*, given that agreement on justice is not enough to prevent unjust action – including action driven by 'hatred' and 'distrust' – this task will not and cannot meet the challenge that multiculturalism presents. Cooke, for her part, places her faith in 'learning processes'. Thus, with regard to respect, she hopes that citizens might learn to give greater weight 'to universalist principles of respect'. As evidence of this, she offers the case of 'the institutionalization of citizenship' from the Enlightenment onward. And, so far as matters of esteem are at issue, she hopes that a group that ignores and disparages others can learn to accept that they may be enriched by their encounters with those previously despised (Cooke, 1995, pp. 352–3). But such hopes seem wholly unrealistic. First, while the status of citizenship may provide an individual with certain resources for self-determination and hence for the acquisition of self-respect, it will be argued presently that it does nothing to facilitate the development of the sort of self-confidence that may help rationality to outweigh affectivity. Second, with regard to esteem, Cooke makes no attempt to specify the conditions under which encounters with others could generate empathy and enrichment rather than horror and violence. The problem in both cases is that, since learning processes are cognitive rather than affective, they are peculiarly ill equipped to deal with the problem in hand. Since the problem is precisely that affectivity has a tendency to override rationality, how could it be solved by invoking rational considerations?

The lesson to be drawn from this analysis is that these political theories are unable to account for and hence to deal with *affect* – the emotional dispositions that every subject has to the field of objects around it. In the particular circumstances of a multicultural society, these theories have no resources with which to conceptualize and respond to the loves and passions, hatreds and fears that the condition of multiculturalism generates in people's daily lives. In this case, solutions to the problem of multiculturalism which propose forms of rational agreement and understanding will always risk being scuppered by the passionate allegiances that individuals have to particular groups, and by their hatred and distrust of others.

The implication of this argument is that any political theory that seeks to identify the structure of a just and stable multicultural society must have some account of the psychological dispositions that individuals need to possess if affective problems are not undermine such a society. Does it follow from this argument that political theorists must become social psychologists? The thesis of this chapter is that, if they do not *become* social psychologists, political theorists must at least *draw on* social psychology in order to render their theories viable. While it is obvious that the full redemption of this claim would require a great deal of work, it will be possible in the rest of this section to sketch one way in which a small part of this thesis – that concerned specifically with the conception of recognition – could be worked out.

The argument to be made here is that, in addition to the two aspects of recognition already identified, it is necessary to introduce a third aspect that occurs in relations of emotional attachment to significant others (Honneth, 1994, p. 193). In introducing this final form of recognition, note that Taylor himself is well aware of its existence and significance. He makes a distinction between types of recognition that occur in two different spheres: 'in the public sphere', as we have already seen, 'a politics of equal recognition' has become increasingly influential. In addition to this, there is also the form of recognition that occurs 'in the intimate sphere'. Here 'we understand the formation of identity and self as taking place in a continuing dialogue and struggle with significant others'. However, while Taylor acknowledges the importance of this latter type of recognition, he makes no attempt to build it into the structure of his political theory. Its importance is detailed like this:

> [W]e can see how much an original identity needs and is vulnerable to the recognition given or withheld by significant others. It is not surprising that in the culture of authenticity, relationships are seen as the key loci of self-discovery and self-affirmation. Love relationships ... are the crucibles of inwardly generated identity (Taylor, 1994, p. 36).

But, in spite of these observations, the rest of Taylor's essay focuses exclusively on public recognition: as he says, 'I want to concentrate here on the public sphere, and try to work out what a politics of equal recognition has meant and could mean' (ibid., p. 37).

There are, however, a number of reasons why it could be argued that what can be called 'emotional' recognition should be brought fully into the picture. First, since it is a vital aspect of the general phenomenon of recognition, any complete account must include it in its analysis. In reply, of course, Taylor could and does say that a comprehensive account of recognition is not within the scope of his ambitions. Second, given that emotional recognition is essential for the formation of self-identity, a political theory like Taylor's – which claims to be based on an intersubjective account of identity formation – must make room for this aspect of recognition. For since Taylor's theory is committed to securing the recognition of social identities, it is highly inadvisable for him to try to proceed without an account of how such identities are actually forged.[15]

A third reason for including emotional recognition in our analysis, and perhaps the most important for our current purposes, is that it may help us to identify at least some of the necessary psychological prerequisites of a stable multicultural society. This argument will be made by drawing on the work of the object relations school of psychoanalysis.[16] The claim will be that successful emotional recognition leads to the individual's development of what will be called *ontological security*. This condition – which Honneth (1994, p. 193) calls 'body-related self-confidence'[17] – may help individuals to deal successfully with the affective challenges of a multicultural society. Before embarking on this argument, however, it is necessary to sound a couple of notes of caution. First, the account to be offered here will be simplified and perhaps even idealized; the intention is simply to suggest why a comprehensive account of the social psychology of multiculturalism is necessary, and to indicate one particular form that such an account might take.[18] Second, ontological security is probably best seen neither as a necessary nor a sufficient condition for selves to be able to live well in a multicultural society. The claim is only that individuals' possession of ontological security may increase the likelihood that they can live with the affective demands of multicultural life.

First, consider how ontological security comes about. Here the key relationship of recognition is that between an infant and its primary caretaker – where it is generally assumed that this means the mother. As Laing says (1965, p. 116), 'a necessary component in the development of the self is the experience of oneself as a person under the loving eye of the mother'. From an initial state of symbiosis with the mother, the infant gradually becomes separated from her. While this separation inevitably generates anxiety for the infant, psychoanalysts such as D.W. Winnicott have shown that this process can be managed successfully through the use of 'transitional objects' and the emergence of 'potential space'.[19] In this way, infants come to trust their mother: when she is absent, they are confident that she will return. This idea of basic trust plays an essential part in the argument. According to Anthony Giddens, such trust 'is the main emotional support or *protective cocoon* which all normal individuals carry around with them as the means whereby they are able to get on with the affairs of day-to-day life' (Giddens, 1991, p. 40). It forms a basic layer of self-confidence that an individual carries into adult life.

If this process of recognition goes well, the individual successfully develops ontological security. To see what this condition is like, consider Laing's description of 'a basically ontologically secure person': such a person has 'a sense of his integral selfhood and personal identity, of the permanency of things, of the reliability of natural processes, of the substantiality of natural processes, of the substantiality of others'. For such a person, 'his identity and autonomy are never in question'; he has 'an inner consistency, substantiality, genuineness, and worth' (Laing, 1965, pp. 39, 41).[20] For the purposes of the current argument, two aspects of this picture are of particular importance: first, ontologically secure individuals have a firm sense of their own identity; and, second, they exhibit confidence in their interactions with other individuals. Let us very briefly consider some of the most relevant implications of these features.

The ontologically secure individual, having successfully acquired a robust sense of self, is able to become an integrated and autonomous self. This achievement can be divided into two parts. First, such a self, when faced with the potential dangers and threats of an unstable environment, will not resort to rigid routines of behaviour that exclude the possibility of flexible adaptation to such an environment. Here Giddens, following Mihaly Csikszentmihalyi, describes an 'autotelic' self who 'is able to translate potential threats into rewarding challenges ... to turn entropy into a consistent flow of experience'; for such a self 'risk is confronted as the active challenge which generates self-actualization' (Giddens, 1994, p. 192; and see Csikszentmihalyi, 1992). Second, such a self will not need to construct an inflexible sense of his or her own identity that depends on the strict exclusion of all others. For example, such selves will not need continually to emphasize the purity of their heterosexual identity by being homophobic. Instead they are able to tolerate – and perhaps to enjoy – the ambivalences and uncertainties that permeate their sense of self.[21] Following on from this point, while an ontologically insecure individual may disparage and ridicule others' ways of life, and, at worst, may engage in violence against them, the autotelic self is able to trust others. Here Giddens describes (1994, p. 192) a self 'with an inner confidence which comes from self-respect, and one where a sense of ontological security, originating in basic trust, allows for the positive appreciation of social difference'. Rather than regarding different others as threats to themselves, such a self is able to celebrate the differences between themselves and others, to learn from them in productive dialogue. In light of these features of the ontologically secure self, it should be clear why it could be seen as the basic building block of a multicultural society.

Conclusion

The central thesis of this chapter has been that a successful politics of recognition for a multicultural society must be founded on an adequately complex conception of recognition. Three aspects of such a conception were distinguished: first, individuals must be respected as autonomous agents; second, they must be esteemed as unique beings; and, third, they need to acquire the self-confidence that comes from being loved by significant others. It is possible to argue that this tripartite conception of recognition lays down certain general requirements for any politics of recognition suitable for a multicultural society. In particular, certain fundamental rights must be protected; cultural identities must enjoy public esteem; and individuals need to live in conditions in which they can acquire ontological security. Of course, a fully elaborated theory of recognition would need to provide answers to many specific questions. For example, which rights should be regarded as fundamental? Might these include group rights?[22] Following on from this, how are citizens' identities to be protected? How are the relevant 'intersubjectively shared experiences and life contexts' (Habermas, 1994a, p. 129) to be identified? Finally, how is it possible to establish the conditions in which ontological security could develop? For instance, could this require political intervention in family life? The formulation of answers to these questions will have to await another occasion. The hope must be that, by clarifying the required structure of the conception of recognition, these answers will be much easier to work out than would otherwise be the case. The final claim to be made here is that, if a politics of recognition managed successfully to combine the three elements of recognition specified in this chapter, the result would be a just and stable multicultural society. In Habermas' terms, such a society could be described as one in which 'political integration' is secured in the form of 'loyalty to the common political culture', while, at the same time, 'sub-political' integration is guaranteed as the 'different forms of life coexisting within a multicultural society' receive due recognition (Habermas, 1994a, p. 134; and see 1992, p. 7).[23] To this it is necessary to add that citizens must also be 'emotionally' integrated; that is, they must possess the ontological security that is the necessary prerequisite of both political and sub-political integration in a multicultural society.[24]

Notes

1   Note that references are to a later, expanded edition (1994) of the collection in which the essay first appeared.

2   Here the analysis follows Honneth (1995, p. 195).

3   For the principle, although not for this example, see Taylor (1994, p. 59).

4   In the course of his argument for the protection of minorities, Rickard (1994, p. 164) admits that, since the defence of such minorities' freedom will inevitably decrease the freedom of the majority, 'the potential for conflict is ever present'.

5   For simplicity's sake, putting the problem this way ignores an additional dimension of conflict in which the recognition of one particular individual or group is seen to diminish the recognition accorded another individual or group respectively.

6   It should be noted that in everyday language people may sometimes talk of respect and self-respect when, in the terms deployed here, they mean esteem and self-esteem. This doesn't weaken the argument so long as it can be shown that, although people may not use exactly these terms, they do make the distinction introduced here in some shape or form. See Sachs (1981, p. 346).

7   Compare Darwall's distinction between 'recognition self-respect' and 'self-esteem' (1978); and Honneth (1995, pp. 133–4). More generally, see phenomenological and psychoanalytical theories that offer corresponding contrasts between dignity (and its opposite, humiliation) and pride (and its opposite, shame). In psychoanalytical terms, while the former pair are feelings originating in the superego, the latter pair crop up in relation to ego-ideals. See Giddens (1991, pp. 67–8); and Honneth (1994, p. 199).

8   Note that elsewhere Taylor (1989, p. 15) does make a closely related distinction between 'active' respect and 'attitudinal' respect. While the former is due to an individual in virtue of their autonomy, the latter involves 'thinking well of someone, even looking up to him'. But Taylor does not make use of this distinction in the essay we are considering, and this is where he needs to use it in order to overcome the problems we have identified here.

9   It should be noted that, for Habermas (1990, p. 239), questions of justice are not exhausted by questions of subjective rights since justice also concerns matters of distribution.

10   For further explication of the claims summarized in this paragraph, see Habermas (1990, p. 244).

11   For a brief summary, see Habermas (1994b).

12   In his chapter in this volume, Jonathan Seglow develops a very helpful account of how authenticity (the term he uses for what is referred to here as identity) is distinct from autonomy.

13   On this subject, see Honneth (1995, pp. 115–8), for a summary of T.H. Marshall's history of the development of rights.

14 Note that, in this analysis, affect is conceived exclusively as a problem of self-esteem. But it must be possible, at least in theory, for it also to concern self-respect. For example, an individual could be too proud to cooperate with others, or to fit in with the norms of his or her own cultural group.

15 Since personal identity is partly and importantly formed in relation to cultural groups, this also relates back to the first criticism of Taylor mentioned in the introduction – namely, that he fails to provide an adequate account of the cultures that make up cultural identity.

16 For a general survey of this school, see Greenberg and Mitchell (1983).

17 Note that in this paper Laing's term is generally preferred to that of Honneth. This is partly because the term 'ontological security' places emphasis on the bodily character of this aspect of the self, and partly because in everyday language 'self-confidence' is too often entwined with notions of self-respect and self-esteem.

18 Alterative approaches could take a variety of forms. For example, one could draw more directly on the work of Melanie Klein. See Alford (1989) and Bird (1994).

19 For a useful selection, see Winnicott (1986).

20 For a corresponding description of the ontologically insecure individual, see Laing (1965, p. 42).

21 Compare Fraser's ideal of a society characterized by fields 'of multiple, debinarized, fluid, ever-shifting differences' – although note that, going beyond the argument developed in this paper, she argues that socialist political economy plus cultural deconstruction are necessary to produce this condition. (See her 1995, pp. 83, 89.)

22 Seglow's analysis of the relation between individual and cultural authenticity in his chapter in this volume would be of considerable use in answering this question.

23 To be more precise, only those forms of life espousing what Rawls (1993, p. 60) calls 'comprehensive views that are not unreasonable' are to be tolerated.

24 I received a number of helpful comments when I presented earlier versions of this chapter at the Politics Departments of the Universities of Bristol, Southampton and the West of England. I also received very useful written comments from John Bird, Bob Brecher and Kate Nash.

References

Alford, C.F. (1989), *Melanie Klein and Critical Social Theory*, Yale University Press, London.

Bird, J. (1994), 'Bodies, Boundaries and Solidarities: A Psychoanalytical Account of Racism and Ethnic Hatred' in Weeks, J. (ed.), *The Lesser Evil and the Greater Good: The Theory and Politics of Social Diversity*, Rivers Oram, London.

Cooke, M. (1994), 'Realizing the Postconventional Self', *Philosophy and Social Criticism*, Vol. 20, No. 1/2, pp. 87–101.

Cooke, M. (1995), 'Selfhood and Solidarity', *Constellations*, Vol. 1, No. 3, pp. 337–57.

Csikszentmihalyi, M. (1992), *Flow: The Psychology of Happiness*, Rider, London.

Darwall, S. (1978), 'Two Kinds of Respect', *Ethics*, Vol. 88, No. 1, pp. 36–49.

Fraser, N. (1995), 'From Redistribution to Recognition? Dilemmas of Justice in a "Post-socialist" Age', *New Left Review*, No. 212, pp. 68–93.

Giddens, A. (1991), *Modernity and Self-Identity: Self and Society in the Late Modern Age*, Polity, Cambridge.

Giddens, A. (1994), *Beyond Left and Right: The Future of Radical Politics*, Polity, Cambridge.

Greenberg, J.R. and Mitchell, S.A. (1983), *Object Relations in Psychoanalytic Theory*, Harvard University Press, Cambridge, Mass.

Gutmann, A. (1993), 'The Challenge of Multiculturalism in Political Ethics', *Philosophy and Public Affairs*, Vol. 22, No. 3, pp. 171–206.

Gutmann, A. (ed.) (1994), *Multiculturalism: Examining The Politics of Recognition*, Princeton University Press, Princeton.

Habermas, J. (1990), 'Justice and Solidarity: On the Discussion concerning Stage 6' in Wren, T.E. (ed.), *The Moral Domain*, MIT Press, Cambridge, Mass.

Habermas, J. (1992), 'Citizenship and National Identity: Some Reflections of the Future of Europe', *Praxis International*, Vol. 12, No. 1, pp. 1–19.

Habermas, J. (1993), *Justification and Application: Remarks on Discourse Ethics*, Polity, Cambridge.

Habermas, J. (1994a), 'Struggles for Recognition in the Democratic Constitutional State' in Gutmann, A. (ed.), *Multiculturalism: Examining The Politics of Recognition*, Princeton University Press, Princeton.

Habermas, J. (1994b), 'Three Normative Models of Democracy', *Constellations*, Vol. 1, No. 1, pp. 1–10.

Honneth, A. (1994), 'Integrity and Disrespect: Principles of a Conception of Morality based on the Theory of Recognition', *Political Theory*, Vol. 20, No. 2, pp. 187–201.

Honneth, A. (1995), *The Struggle for Recognition: The Moral Grammar of Social Conflicts*, Polity Press, Oxford.

Laforest, G. (1994), 'Philosophy and Political Judgement in a Multinational Federation' in Tully, J. (ed.), *Philosophy in an Age of Pluralism: The Philosophy of Charles Taylor in Question*, Cambridge University Press, Cambridge.

Laing, R.D. (1965), *The Divided Self: An Existential Study in Sanity and Madness*, Penguin, Harmondsworth.

Rawls, J. (1993), *Political Liberalism*, Harvard University Press, Cambridge, Mass.

Rickard, M. (1994), 'Liberalism, Multiculturalism, and Minority Protection', *Social Theory and Practice*, Vol. 20, No. 2, pp. 187–201.

Rorty, A. (1994), 'The Hidden Politics of Cultural Identification', *Political Theory*, Vol. 22, No. 1, pp. 152–66.

Sachs, D. (1981), 'How to distinguish Self-respect from Self-esteem', *Philosophy and Public Affairs*, Vol. 10, No. 4, pp. 346–60.

Salée, D. (1995), 'Identities in Conflict: The Aboriginal Question and the Politics of Recognition in Québec', *Ethnic and Racial Studies*, Vol. 18, No. 2, pp. 227–314.

Taylor, C. (1989), *Sources of the Self: The Making of Modern Identity*, Cambridge University Press, Cambridge.

Taylor, C. (1994), 'The Politics of Recognition' in Gutmann, A. (ed.), *Multiculturalism: Examining The Politics of Recognition*, Princeton University Press, Princeton.

Tully, J. (1995), *Strange Multiplicity: Constitutionalism in an Age of Diversity*, Cambridge University Press, Cambridge.

Winnicott, D.W. (1986), *Home Is Where We Start From: Essays by a Psychoanalyst*, Penguin, Harmondsworth.

14 The Philosophy of Cultural Recognition

JONATHAN SEGLOW

Introduction

Minority cultures which strive to assert their identity, secessionist demands made by nations in multinational states, the struggle for survival of indigenous peoples, special privileges demanded under the banner of religion: these and similar demands have acquired a new and urgent salience in recent years. They all turn on the issue of recognition. What minority groups demand is to have their specific identity recognized and affirmed on the public political platform. That is why modern liberalism, with its focus on the autonomous self-sufficient chooser of ends has had so much difficulty in accommodating them. But I shall not rehearse the arguments over liberalism's (in)ability to confer recognition here. I want instead to consider Charles Taylor's essay 'The Politics of Recognition' (1994) which addresses the question directly. Taylor proposes a notion of cultural authenticity whose recognition demands measures which challenge the freedom of liberalism's autonomous subject. This essay has attracted much comment and criticism, most of it focusing on whether cultural authenticity does indeed justify restrictions on freedom. I will set out that criticism below. My main interest here, however, is the prior question of whether the notion of cultural authenticity makes sense at all: what does 'authenticity' really mean?; can it be applied to cultures?[1] These are very important questions, important because the demands for recognition of the kind I mentioned at the outset are made in terms of the authentic identity of a group. If group identities are more problematic than their proponents politically concede then the whole plethora of demands for recognition needs to be rethought.

I shall argue that there is indeed a valid notion of individual authenticity, but that its transfer to cultures is problematic. This of course bears directly on liberalism, because if 'cultural authenticity' is invalid then the meta-status of autonomy in the political domain seems unchallengeable from that direction.

211

But things are not as simple as that, and I end with a suggestion about how the needs of cultures might properly be integrated into political structures.

Two aspects of Taylor's philosophical outlook deserve mention at the start.[2] The first distinctive feature of Taylor's work is his profound conviction that the moral sources which we follow – nationalism and communitarianism among them, but also religion, ecocentrism, individualism – are indeed goods of value, not to be theorized away by some meta-theory of a Kantian or utilitarian kind. Any good which is coherently, clairvoyantly and consistently held by human agents is, on that account, a genuine good. It is the fate of us moderns to live in an age of plural goods, but neither that nor the fact that we can never attain a perspective outside and beyond the goods which move us betoken relativism. Thus Taylor holds fast to Berlin's insight that no imaginable social order can possibly realize all that we cherish. Taylor's second major theme is that we are self-interpreting agents. We are not rational pursuers of contingent preferences, but rather live inescapably in networks of interpretation about what goods and values we ought to pursue. Human agents are strong evaluators who assess their wants and desires by second-order reflection about who they are and what they want to be. These evaluative stances give us moral identities and orientation. They may change, but it is a slow evolution over time.

It is easy to see how, if one subscribes to this pluralism of evaluations, cultural authenticity can become a valid self-interpretation which challenges the liberal icon of autonomy. In 'The Politics of Recognition' Taylor accepts the validity of both of these and attempts to find a political settlement between them. The practical context is the demand by citizens of Quebec to maintain their distinct Francophone culture. But the philosophical implications are far wider and it is these which are our interest here. Taylor's brief, clear, elegant sentences, animated by a humane reasonableness, contain some bold theses about the human condition: that authenticity is something valuable and distinctive, that authentic cultures have value in and of themselves, and that our politics must confer, and not deny, their proper recognition.

'The Politics of Recognition'

To clarify Taylor's vision, and give us a basis from which to approach his interlocutors, I'll begin by setting out the argument of his essay below as a rough list. Laying out the components of an argument in this quasi-deductive way is not Taylor's style, which is typically conversational and takes us on a journey around the good. My purpose is only to help us identify what is more controversial and what is less so.

0 In order to be a fully formed human being you need recognition from others. That is a human universal. Recognition means that others affirm your worth as a person. This is achieved through dialogue and the dialogic formation of human identity is a central truth of the human condition. By affirming others' worth and receiving their affirmation of our own, transmitted in dialogic context, we come to realize ourselves as properly formed identity-bearing persons – and we come to see our own worth[3] (pp. 25–37).

1 The first interpretation of human worth is autonomy. What is recognized here is the universal capacity for moral autonomous agency. Such an agent is self-sufficient: she directs her life by principles she has chosen as her own. That is a moral ideal. It is not realized in everyone and consequently what is recognized is the potential for doing so. We owe respect to others not for what they are but for what they could be, or what they are morally. What is recognized is not the individual person but personhood (p. 41).

2 The second interpretation of human worth is authenticity: 'There is a certain way of being human that is *my* way' (p. 30). Each of us has our own unique, particular, original accent on the human condition. We each have a personal potential which must be nurtured through dialogue and recognition. Our identities are negotiated through our own evolving articulations, and others' interpretations of them. This is also true of cultures, so that, as Herder believed, each culture has its own particular, unique worth or measure. A people should try to be true to themselves, should live up to their own potential. Cultures too require recognition. The attitudes of outsiders are internalized: others' esteem can help realize a culture's identity; negative attitudes tend to interiorize a demeaning collective self-image (pp. 28–37).

3 Interpretation (1) gives us the Politics of Equal Dignity. Political morality expresses the equal respect owed to persons as such, and that is founded upon their moral autonomy. Political principles exist to protect and enable citizens' autonomy: classical liberal rights (such as free speech) are the archetype. Partial principles might promote one person's autonomy, but only at the expense of that of others, and that violates our equal dignity.

Hence all principles demand universal application (p. 41, pp. 56–8).

4   Interpretation (2) gives us the Politics of Recognition. Political morality expresses recognition of the worth of actually evolved (not potential) groups and persons. Political principles exist to protect the collective expression of certain authentic cultural identities (for example, laws regulating permissible language in public life). Hence principles will be partial; they will promote some identities over others. This is justified when societies recognize that some collective goals – such as maintaining an authentic cultural identity – are of such importance that some discrimination elsewhere is justified. On this model, the promotion of certain collective identities must entail some curtailment of citizens' autonomy (pp. 58–61).

5   The principles of interpretation (2) come into play when we recognize the worth of authentic cultural identities. That is what many oppressed (non-recognized) cultures demand. But moral worth cannot flow merely from a whim of the will. Granting worth to all evolved cultures from the outset undercuts the very notion of what attributing worth means. What we can do, however, is presume that cultures which have animated and given meaning to human societies over a considerable time do have objective moral value (p. 66, p. 72).

6   We approach our study of other cultures with a 'presumption of equal worth'. That presumption can be sustained only through engagement with that culture. Through interchange and mutual learning we experience a 'fusion of horizons' which for both sides brings a new vocabulary of comparison with which to make judgments of worth. Thus the moral worth of cultures, both granted and received, depends on recognition and dialogue (p. 67). This takes us back to (0).

Except that it doesn't. We began by talking about how individual *persons* need to be recognized through dialogue and we have ended by affirming the dialogic origins of authentic cultural worth. Within claim (2) authenticity moves from being a predicate of individuals to something true of cultures. Let's first look at the structure of the argument and then return to this point.

Claim (0) is Taylor's Hegelian starting thesis. It tends to be denied by liberals who want to separate the universal premise of moral personhood from whatever self-understandings agents happen to have. Rawls' (1971, pp. 440–6) communitarian liberalism grants 'self-respect' as the most important primary good but it is not clear how – or whether – its social bases are secured other than through the principles of justice themselves. Honneth (1995, pp. 71–139), by contrast, argues that the self-respect of being a rights-bearing moral person, and, as a separate matter, the self-esteem of being an individual with a distinct identity, are each dependent on the recognition of others. In the former case, we recognize the universal which inheres within each person; in the latter we are asked to recognize others' particular moral worth. These two dimensions of recognition differ over whether worth flows from what I share with all agents – the inherent dignity of humanity – or whether, as in the case of self-esteem, from those attributes which I, uniquely, possess. Claim (4) (the first dimension) encapsulates Rawls' liberalism, Habermas' more radical discourse ethics and the many who write in their wake. On this procedural view moral principles provide a framework which more specific everyday political argument can never go beyond. In Habermas' case citizens may certainly express some shared conception of the good or other ethical pattern within their legal order (Habermas, 1994, pp. 122–8): but that specific order itself exists within a Kantian theory of basic rights by which citizens are collective – yet autonomous – authors of their constitution. The Kantian theory sets out the universal basis of interaction between moral persons (ibid., p. 122), which interaction should be institutionally enshrined in a reflexive public sphere. But, by contrast with a society's legal code, the universal theory cannot itself be abrogated because it is a condition of abrogating, extending or in any way modifying all possible legal codes.

This is the root of Habermas' dispute with Taylor.[4] As we saw in the introduction, Taylor subscribes to a philosophical pluralism which precludes him from promoting any general moral scheme which trumps existing argument. There are only our self-interpretations. Under claim (4) – the politics of recognition – he seeks to give expression to the political demands of Quebecois nationalism. Using the lever of cultural authenticity, Taylor seeks to restrict *some* of the (non-fundamental) rights and immunities attached to individuals in order to guarantee the *survival* of Quebec culture. Outlawing non-Francophone schools for French-speakers comes under this category as do regulations on the language of advertising and signage (pp. 52–3). Such collective goals introduce a substantive conception of the good into liberalism. But, *pace* Habermas, there is no over-arching moral framework in which this restriction of freedom may be justified. It is true that actual judgments of worth (claim (5)) may emerge from a fusion of cultural horizons within a multicultural state (6). If citizens have an attitude of openness, such a fusion may indeed give culture promoting measures some legitimacy in the eyes of those not of the culture. That must be the main point of (6). But it is a mistake to regard it as a model of democratic public reason on Habermasian lines. This kind of universalist basis for regulating moral life is simply not available to Taylor. He thinks that survival policies may be justified for two more prosaic reasons: first, because fundamental liberal rights such as free speech and freedom of religious conscience remain protected (p. 59); and second, the positive reason, that the survival of Quebec's Francophone culture simply is a collective goal of supreme importance. Here are some remarks Taylor makes under the banner of claim (4):

> [I]t is axiomatic for Quebec governments that the survival and flourishing of French culture in Quebec is a good. Political society is not neutral between those who value remaining true to the culture of our ancestors and those who might want to cut loose in the name of some individual goal of self-development (p. 58).

> Quebeckers, therefore, and those who give similar importance to this kind of collective goal, tend to opt for a rather different [i.e. non-neutral] model of the liberal society. On their view a society can be organised around a collective definition of the good life, without this being seen as a depreciation of those who do not share this definition (p. 59).

And on the politics of equal dignity, i.e. claim (3):

> I call it inhospitable to difference because it can't accommodate what the members of distinct cultures really aspire to, which is survival. This is ... a collective goal which ... will inevitably call for some variations in the kinds of law we deem permissible from one cultural context to another, as the Quebec case clearly shows (p. 61).

This last claim is what really rankles Habermas and other Kantians. They cannot accept that the rights to which a person is subject can rest upon something so contingent as a judgment of cultural worth (Habermas, 1994, p. 129; Wolf, 1994, p. 79). It is true that rights to welfare and the like are only claimable by those who occupy a certain role. But unemployment, say, is a circumstantial role which any person may enter: it is not like being a cultural member which you either are or aren't. As they see it, the equal dignity of free persons is offended if cultural and other group affiliations become the basis of special legal rights. On this view, the legal promotion of collective goals cannot but discriminate against those outside the collective. Universal human rights occupy all the moral space that there is.

Taylor, on the contrary, thinks that Quebeckers' desire to sustain their authentic Francophone culture simply is a collective goal of sufficient importance to trump some of the rights which flow from the liberalism of equal dignity. In doing so he appeals to authenticity, as a concept which escapes the lexicon of liberalism and its procedural cousin, discourse ethics. Authenticity is the self-interpretation where one prizes what is unique, particular, distinct about oneself. Only recognition by others enables one to value one's identity in this way. Taylor then moves to claiming that cultures, too, are unique and distinctive. Thus they require political recognition in order to realize their collective self-interpretation. Individual autonomy remains a good, but it must now be balanced against the demands of cultural authenticity. There are two controversial claims on the way to this conclusion. The first is how authenticity (2) differs from autonomy (1). The second is the internal move noted earlier within (2), from individual to cultural authenticity, since there are many other ways of understanding cultures. In order to sustain his political argument that the survival of cultures is a collective goal of such moral worth that equal rights may on occasion be legitimately trumped, therefore, Taylor has to defend authenticity as an ideal separate from autonomy and to show that it is authenticity that best renders what cultures are about. The first claim breaks the moral monopoly of autonomous agency so that, *pace* liberalism, other sources of moral value are equally admissible. The second says that cultures bear that value because they are, so to say, the authentic bearers of authenticity. Once the first claim is accepted, the second makes the fate of cultures a matter of legitimate political concern.

I will discuss these two claims in a little depth below. Before doing so, however, it's worth asking why Taylor adopts this two part strategy in the first place. If you want to defend collective cultural goals there are more straightforward ways of doing so than through the apparatus of authenticity and recognition. The main normative point – that Quebec culture is crucial for Quebeckers – could be established more simply by a general communitarian argument about the importance of a secure cultural identity for a sense of belonging, solidarity and so on. This is in fact the sort of strategy employed by defenders of nationalism and appears consistent with Taylor's general philosophical outlook. Thus, for example, David Miller's *On Nationality* (1995) and Yael Tamir's *Liberal Nationalism* (1993) defend principles of nationality from a broadly communitarian position and their articulation of nationality is quite coherent, even forceful. It is of course fortunate for Miller and Tamir that, in drawing on the public culture of their own nations (Britain and Israel), some liberalism can be extracted too: but their account does not stem from that. Even if Taylor thought it was Quebec's distinctiveness from Canada that placed it under the special political rubric of the politics of difference, the communitarian position evidently has the resources to deal with multinational states, with self-determination within a larger state, and even secession (Miller, 1995, pp. 81–118; Tamir, 1993, pp. 57–77). So the question remains, why get to the Canadian case only via the more complex concepts of authenticity and recognition?[5]

The answer is that while nationalism, and for that matter individual freedom, are contingent goods (not valued in all times and places), recognition, by contrast, is a human universal. To be recognized as a person is simply a precondition of realizing any identity at all. This is a claim Taylor makes at some length in *Sources of the Self*, along with the idea that we are oriented to the good. Individual autonomy is one such good: the form of recognition it takes is respect. Authenticity, which comes from the Romantic movement, and not the Enlightenment, is another good. Here we seek, not freedom for its own sake, but to realize our true selves. These are the two main meta-goods of modernity and we feel the pull of them both. Neither can therefore be denied without doing violence to many people's self-interpretations; and that is something which Taylor's philosophy can never allow. We have to start, not with any good in particular, but with the person trying to realize her identity through networks of recognition and then seeking to integrate the goods she faces into a single life. Simply to give authority to Quebecois nationalism, or indeed any communitarian or individualistic values, denudes from the start the power of other demands which must also be acknowledged. Taylor devotes much space to authenticity, not because it is more important than autonomy, but because, for reasons we saw above, it tends to be eclipsed by it. Authenticity is a distinct ethical paradigm and cultural authenticity is one crucial form of it. In an era of pluralism, authenticity is neither an unproblematic starting point, nor something to be dismissed as an archaic premodernism. Rather, it is no less valid for being distinct from autonomy.

Autonomy and Authenticity

In the remainder of this paper I want to explore the constellation around authenticity and cultural authenticity, and assess whether they have the moral purchase which Taylor claims. Before looking at the cultural question, we must begin by addressing the first question I raised above: does authenticity really differ from autonomy? Unless that can be answered in the affirmative, we relapse back into the politics of equal dignity and Interpretation (1) above.

On the face of it, it does not. Both are modern ideals which suppose that individual persons can look inward and reflect on their own lives, rather than taking their compass from religious or other authoritative horizons (pp. 28–31). The notion that I own my life is the seedbed of both autonomy and authenticity. And if we recognize this, then it's not clear whether there are really two distinct modes of self-direction – as opposed to one mode animating two accidental types. Taylor himself says that Mill appealed to 'something like the ideal of authenticity' in chapter 3 of *On Liberty* when he wrote that 'his own mode of laying out his existence is best, not because it is best in itself but because it is his own mode' (pp. 30–1, n. 7). But the Mill of authenticity is the same Mill whose ideal of individual freedom is rarely distinguished from autonomy. Or again, a recent collection of essays on autonomy, John Christman's *The Inner Citadel*, (1989) has ten references to authenticity in the index. Gerald Dworkin's contribution, 'The Concept of Autonomy' – a condensation of his influential book on the subject (1988) – defines the 'full formula' for autonomy as 'authenticity plus procedural independence' (Dworkin, 1989, p. 61). 'A person is autonomous', he writes, 'if he identifies with his desires, goals and values and such identification is not itself influenced in ways which make the process of identification in some way alien to the individual' (ibid.). Or, finally, in a very recent paper, Maeve Cooke (1997, p. 261) distinguishes between a strong and a weak reading of authenticity. On the weak reading, authenticity refers to 'the equal *potential* of every individual (and culture) to form and define her or his own identity'. But since, as potential, the uniqueness of each fully realized individual is left open, authenticity, in this weak sense, amounts simply to the ability to determine one's good, and this is scarcely distinguishable from autonomy. On a stronger reading, Cooke argues, we must attend to what a person has made of her autonomy, her distinct identity. But if distinctiveness is to have moral significance, it must be by reference to moral standards independent of the will. (With this idea Taylor would agree and it is encapsulated in claim (5) above.) The problem for Cooke is that in a plural, or as she says (ibid., p. 264), 'postmetaphysical world, no metastandards appear to be available for adjudicating between rival conceptions of the good life'. Without such standards, however, there is no guarantee that what the 'inner voice' of authenticity says is right or good. Either authenticity is not distinct from autonomy; or, if it is distinct, it cannot possibly be a standard of evaluation in the public sphere – as Cooke (ibid., p. 266) requires it to be in the case of cultural authenticity.

It doesn't seem that these writers are using 'authenticity' in some radically different way from Taylor. The basic idea of making one's life one's own seems to be equally well captured by both autonomy and authenticity. So is it really distinct? And is it morally coherent?

Against the conflationists, I believe that authenticity is distinct from autonomy, and in a morally relevant way. In order to substantiate this I want to make a brief detour from Taylor's essay and explore some recent work by a writer who has done much to promote authenticity as an alternative ethical ideal to autonomy, Alessandro Ferrara (1992, 1993, 1994). Ferrara agrees that authenticity and autonomy are both ideals of modernity. Both are investments in the self and represent a move away from the external logos and inward towards the subject. In this sense, authenticity presupposes an autonomous subject (Ferrara, 1994, pp. 241–2). But while the autonomous subject discovers in her self a universal – the generic capacity for moral autonomy – the authentic subject – conducting the same enquiry, finds that truth, standard or calling which is uniquely hers. The moment of individuation stops at the individual and is not (or only later) reconnected with the moral law or, for that matter, with communal mores. Authenticity is thus realizing the capacity to be oneself (ibid., p. 245). This has repercussions for both social action and moral theory. Commenting on the generalized accountability demanded by Weber's value-rational and purposive-rational action, Ferrara writes (ibid., p. 243):

> [A]uthentic conduct has the quality of being somehow connected with, and expressive of, the core of the actor's personality. It brings into play the actor's uniquely personal, as opposed to culturally or socially shared identity. If I am insensitive to my deepest needs, if I betray them, or if I inscribe my action into a life-plan which in turn fails to fit with who I am then I may act in a purposive-rational or value-rational way inauthentically.

Luther's 'Here I stand, I can do no other' is an archetype of authentic conduct. Authentic action is thus about putting one's own unique stamp upon the world, inscribing the self onto existing social relationships (Ferrara, 1993, p. 148). The ethics of authenticity challenges the Kantian view that submitting one's emotional, affective being to self-imposed principle is the essence of morality. Rather, 'we must not deny or try to suppress, but rather acknowledge the urges which deflect us from our moral principles, while at the same time continuing to orient our conduct to the moral point of view' (Ferrara, 1994, p. 244). But if we do seek to be authentic, why should we monitor our moral orientation at all? This question leads Ferrara (1993, pp. 114–17) to distinguish two kinds of authenticity, earlier called 'ethical' and 'aesthetic', but now rendered as the integrated and the antagonistic modes (Ferrara, 1994, pp. 247–9). Antagonistic authenticity rails against all order within the self: temporally, when we give a coherent narrative to our lives; or spatially when we try – along the ethical lines suggested above – to reconcile our true selves with external normative demands. Antagonistic authenticity sees all role-bound institutional orders as disciplinary mechanisms which cannot but constrain the self. Against the chaotic anti-structuralism of this postmodern reading, seekers of integrative authenticity desire to construct for themselves a unique yet coherent, narratable, identifiable life-project, using the roles and expectations of the external world as symbolic material with which to do so. Authentic integrated selves seek to balance, to bring into harmony, normative principles with the moments of their person, to unite these under their aegis of their own life-project without suppressing either side (Ferrara, 1994, p. 249). These two modes of authenticity also suggest different political readings. Collective actors who seek to secure for themselves an authentic communal identity within the existing public arena of a larger society (and who therefore acknowledge the latter's normative demands) clearly espouse an integrated authenticity. Their aim is to bring their own way of life into some sort of harmony with the existing social order. By contrast, groups who exist to subvert, resist or undermine the public normative order exhibit antagonistic authenticity– radical feminism is Ferrara's example (ibid., p. 249).

In preferring integrative to antagonistic authenticity – because it seems to capture the predicament most of us perceive we face in modernity, unless we unthinkingly submit ourselves to all external expectations (inauthenticity) or unflinchingly resist them all (antagonicity) – I'm perhaps just reintroducing my own liberalism. But however that may be, political authenticity, in the sense Taylor uses it and as I've followed here, seems clearly to enjoin the integrative kind. Integrative authenticity is, in this sense, inherently liberal: it seeks to bring order to the individual's relation with society.

This takes us to the social aspect of authenticity. Like Taylor (see claim (0) above), Ferrara is sure that only an intersubjective matrix can generate authentic selves (ibid., pp. 259–66). Selves emerge from social processes, but they are not its mechanical result. Rather the process of identity-building is a dialectic one where the social formation of persons finds an antithesis in each individual's particular, unique perspective on the social world. Personal identity thus emerges through the interplay of social recognition and a reflective self-consciousness. No one can have a wholly unique, individual personal identity – this fiction ignores the social constitution of human agency. In any case, in order to be recognized as a generic person involves possessing those emotional, social and cognitive traits which we associate with personhood. On the other hand, we have to start somewhere. Recognition must have a subject. That subject is the individual person who reacts to others' individuality as they react to hers. Recognition is a dynamic process and the human will is its motor. From the collective network of individual wills and powers of recognition, each person's identity is created. Sometimes we struggle against others' interpretations, rejecting their view of what we are, in an effort to assert our authentic identity (1994, p. 263; Taylor, 1994, pp. 34–7). Creating identity, therefore, is an ongoing process of negotiation as agents reciprocally mediate between their own and others' view of themselves, modifying these views as they do so.

On the intersubjective origins of individual authenticity, Taylor and Ferrara agree – though Taylor stresses in particular how recognition is specifically transmitted through dialogue. What I think Ferrara's expansion more specifically explains, however, is how authenticity differs from autonomy, which was our first critical question.

Ferrara's work suggests that there are two key differences. First, few if any defenders of autonomy view recognition as central to the achievement of autonomous agency. On the contrary, all social attitudes are apt to be seen as potentially coercive interventions in the process of self-government: Dworkin's call for procedural independence can, for example, be seen in this light. To be autonomous is to be, precisely, autonomous from one's surroundings – no one was more keenly aware of this than Mill (cf. Mendus, 1989, pp. 53–5, pp. 97–102). The most which can be conceded is that society actuates a capacity for autonomy which is latently there. Or it might be argued that recognition is a bonus, an icing on the cake of identity, which adds a sheen of self-worth to that which an autonomous person would do anyway. The autonomy perspective cannot appreciate how authenticity and recognition are reciprocally related – how each conceptually requires the other. Only the first half of that reciprocal – the individual will – is present for the autonomy view. It cannot appreciate how, for integrative authenticity, the symbolic material of the social world is not there to be adopted or rejected, but rather constitutes the very identity of agents.

The second difference between autonomy and authenticity is that autonomy underplays how we seek to mould our lives around our particular calling; how we seek to make a narrative which is especially ours, a life-project with our stamp. Some defenders of autonomy do indeed consider it an occurrent, rather than a dispositional notion (e.g. Young, 1986, pp. 8–9). But the tendency is still to think, considering our lives in light of the choices we have made, how at each fork in the route we were not coerced by others. It does not see the wholeness of that route as something uniquely ours, the externalization of our internal needs. (This is so for integrated authenticity; antagonistic authenticity might well be seen as internal heteronomy.) Bernard Williams (1981, p. 12) complains that the liberal notion of a plan of life 'seems to me ... to imply an external view of one's own life as something like a given rectangle that has to be optimally filled in'. Authentic rectangles have a temporal dimension, just as we inhabit the centre of our own lives and do not merely manipulate the causal levers which happen to operate on our ends. Moreover, authenticity is about expressing our deepest needs: and that means (to continue the spatial metaphor) that we worry first about what shape our life should have before considering whether it tessellates with others. On Ferrara's integrative model we have to acknowledge both sets of demands – our own and other people's – before we can seek some balance between them. This reveals, I think, what is wrong with Cooke's strong reading of authenticity. Her problem was that the worth of distinct authentic identities presupposes transcendent moral standards, and these were not available. This seems to me to put the cart before the horse. We live in an era of plural goods: that (as Taylor sees very clearly) is our condition. Cooke is quite right to say that there's no guarantee that what our authentic voice says is true or good: but then a competition between claims to goodness is exactly where we cannot avoid starting from. Ferrara's integrative model enjoins us to bring our voice into harmony with others. Taylor's presumption (not conclusion) of equal worth – claim (5) – and method of fused horizons – claim (6) – similarly enjoins us to test each other's particular claims to moral worth. Cooke's preferred meta-value of autonomy provides principles of adjudication by looking only at the equal potential of all agents. In doing so it abstracts from that network of self-interpretations which makes our lives our own.

Individual and Cultural Authenticity

Authentic identities, therefore, are unique; require recognition; and raise a claim to moral worth. Can the same be said of cultures? That is our second question. Unless it too can be answered in the affirmative, Taylor's survival argument will fail to go through.

Let us go back to the rather complex phenomenon of recognition. We know that it is crucial to the formation of identity: but this seems to be true in two quite distinct ways. There is a collective level of recognition which fixes on generic labels like culture, race and gender. These generic labels inhere in particular individuals. This must be true or else these notions would make no sense to us. Collective labels are recognized and reaffirmed by seeing their impersonal instantiation within each individual. When we see a person we recognize what she shares in common – her race, say – with similar others. No one who is a member of some oppressed group would deny the salience of this collective level of recognition. Yet this logic works in a very different way from authenticity as we've discussed it so far. We were concerned before with achieving an authentic understanding of ourselves within the network of others' interpretations. Here, however, the symbolic material of our culture (and race and gender) is put to our own use and what we want to be recognized for is the stamp we have put on it, as well as our purely individual needs. The generic category of the person is, on closer inspection, particular. There are thus two modes of recognition:

> (a) recognizing the dignity and worth of another person from the standpoint of what that person *shares in common* with the other members of a culture and (b) recognizing the dignity and worth of that person from the standpoint of what distinguishes her from everybody else and makes her unique (Ferrara, 1994, p. 264, emphasis in original).

This is indeed a conflict – one experienced by all those who seek to construct authentic lives for themselves – between the recognition of an individual's authentic identity and the recognition of the cultural and other collective modes which inhere in the self. This is resolved in a different way by each of us. Few seekers of integrative authenticity would want to abjure entirely those symbolic resources made available by the cultural communities they inhabit. Cultural, national and similar labels help constitute the very media through which recognition of worth is transmitted and it is natural, therefore, that they should become part of our best self-understanding. Only an antagonistic hyper-authentic individualist would want to reject them *tout court*. The unchosen nature of culture makes it an unproblematic and secure constituent of individual identity: culture removes some of the struggle out of achieving an identity in modernity. On the other hand, it is inconceivable that blanket labels such as 'Quebecois' and so on can express the authentic self-understanding that any individual person strives for. They miss the subtleties, the special interpretation, that each of us wants to make of our authentic identities. Moreover, terms like Quebecois are not defined across large parts of the role identities we play:

being a Quebecois does not tell us how to be a good parent or employee. This absence of definition gives space for individual exploration of our own best self-interpretation. (Being authentic, we could say, involves constructively using role conflict, not being a captive of it.) But those self-interpretations are conducted against a background or horizon provided by, among other things, our culture (cf. Taylor, 1991, pp. 31–40).

Ferrara's two modes of recognition, therefore, have a dynamic relationship. But the conflict between them – between individual and cultural authentic identity – is a conflict which goes in on within each person. It centres on whether our best self-interpretation takes a more inner-directed form or is referenced to the wider culture of which we are members. There is no resolution to this conflict other than what each of us can work out for ourselves. Yet if this is the case, it causes a grave problem for Taylor's cultural authenticity argument. That argument championed cultural authenticity against autonomy and called for a politics of difference to express it. But now it would appear, rather, that there is an internal politics of difference within each seeker of authenticity where our cultural inheritance is tested against our best understanding of ourselves, and each is reinterpreted in the light of the other. Both must be given their due. We are now less concerned with politics in the public domain, and more with the dialectical relation within the self.

I suggested earlier that Taylor's argument works only if collective authenticity is conceived of as a sufficiently weighty goal sometimes to restrict some of the rights and freedoms of the politics of equal dignity. But now we have seen that there is no goal of collective authenticity *per se*. Collective authenticity is one aspect in which individuals want to be recognized. And this denudes it of its moral power as an unproblematic, pre-interpreted and vital constituent of persons' identities. In reality, cultures simply aren't as homogenous as Taylor's survival argument requires.

In fact, several writers have complained that Taylor underplays the inner pluralism of cultural identities (Rorty, 1994, pp. 156–9; Dumm, 1994, p. 171; Digeser 1995, pp. 188–9). Susan Wolf, in her 'Comment' on Taylor's essay (1994, p. 85), calls for the 'conscientious recognition of cultural diversity: … we might even say that justice requires it'. K. Anthony Appiah notes that collective social identities supply life-scripts, 'narratives that people can use in shaping their life plans and in telling their life stories', where, '[t]he story – my story – should cohere in the way appropriate by the standards made available in my culture to a person of my identity' (1994, p. 160). And so '[i]n order to construct a life with dignity, it seems natural to take the collective identity and construct positive life-scripts instead' (ibid., p. 161). But, Appiah argues, the recipients of recognition might object that it is not they who are receiving it, but just some attribute of theirs – first language, skin colour – which they themselves invest with no special significance. What a person wants is to be recognized as the free individual that she is. The recognition offered to cultures, therefore, offends the individuality of those who are labelled with that social tag. 'It is at this point that someone who takes autonomy seriously will ask whether we have not replaced one kind of tyranny with another' (ibid., pp. 162–3). Life scripts with no 'interpretive space' leave little room for individual discretion. Appiah's argument contrasts collective authenticity with personal autonomy. The emphasis is therefore different from that of the argument I've just put, but the direction of the critique of Taylor is the same.

I began this paper by comparing Taylor's approach with the liberal proceduralist one which is so familiar to us. Proponents of that paradigm don't like the way Taylor eschews an overall moral framework within which the demands of cultures must be accommodated. But nor does Taylor take the contrary position of celebrating cultures or nations *per se*. There is indeed an argument of sorts for cultural promotion which simply appeals to the need for community, solidarity and belonging. By itself, this is hardly liberal. It is also not Taylor's argument: his is more sophisticated; he wants to say instead that the authentic self-understanding of cultures calls for a balance between individual freedom and measures to protect distinct cultures like Quebec. Enquiring into what authenticity meant, we were led away from collective notions and back towards the self. Distinct from autonomy we discovered a separate paradigm of selfhood which enjoined us to express the unique persons we found ourselves to be. Although self-determining freedom is a good, it is with authenticity that Taylor's sympathies lie. Culture is certainly relevant here. But it is indebted to us, so to say, and not we to it. Cultural authenticity, therefore, can no longer be defended as a goal of such inestimable importance that it can do the moral trumping work required of it.

Conclusion

We are left with a dilemma. To transfer authenticity from the individual to the collective is to commit something like the fallacy of composition. This leaves, first, the procedural view, the politics of equal dignity. Here all that is real are autonomous individuals. Cultures consist of no more than contingent agglomerations of individual wills. It may be lamentable if certain cultures wither away but it is not a matter for political action. Second, there is the communitarian view. Now we can appeal to particular cultures, since politics consists of just particular reasons. But unless we are fortunate enough to live in a liberal society there is no reason why citizens' autonomy has to be respected since there simply are no universal reasons. And autonomy is, we should recall from Taylor, also a good. Still, the political demands made in the name of cultural preservation are real enough: rights of language use; distinct educational curricula; restrictions on majority citizens' buying land in minority areas (as with the Aboriginal people in Canada); privileges on clothing, holidays and the slaughter of animals to maintain a religious way of life. It is simply that, between universalism and communitarianism, there is no coherent notion of cultural authenticity to do the necessary philosophical work.

What is needed here are some general conditions for the flourishing of cultures. Against the procedural view, this would enable us to enter cultures as such into the lexicon of moral justification. But since they would be *general* conditions, pertaining to all cultures, we would not relapse into an over-particularist communitarianism which denied the other goods which move us. In his 1992 paper, 'Postmodern Eudaimonia', Ferrara offers a fourfold typology for a good life for persons which can suitably amended to apply to collectives too. *Coherence* refers to the solidarity, cohesion, temporal continuity, and determinate boundaries which collectives will ideally possess (Ferrara, 1992, pp. 397–401). *Vitality* means that culture-reproducing practices are carried out spontaneously and earnestly, not ritualistically, and hence stimulate the identities of those taking part (ibid., pp. 401–3). The consequent self-esteem means that members are ready to accept change when necessary. *Depth* designates a group awareness of just what practices are crucial for reproducing collective identity over time (ibid., pp. 403–5). Members have a reflective awareness of how, for example, group integration can be sustained, or how children should be socialized. Finally, a collective with *maturity* is one with a healthy degree of rationalization and disenchantment (ibid., pp. 405–6). Jettisoning belief in their own magical omnipotence, mature collectives are pragmatically aware of their own limitations and can shape their conduct flexibly.

The role of these guidelines is to serve as a reference for the wellbeing of cultural identities. Will state action make a culture more or less cohesive, stimulate or rob it of vitality? Will it deepen members' self-understandings and enable them to practise collective autonomy? Criteria such as these allow us to factor cultural flourishing into public deliberation. Cultural fulfilment becomes a valid part of political justification – but without resorting to a naïve communitarian ethics. Naturally, Ferrara's guidelines require further refinement and clarification. It is true also that they can come into conflict with the principles of liberal individualism. We do well to remember the central message of Taylor's philosophy: in an age of pluralism, conflicts between goods can never simply be theorized away. My claim is merely that, since culture is a good for so many, some general criteria of cultural wellbeing deserve to be introduced into the moral justification of political arrangements. It is then up to agents whether or not they make culture a part of their authentic self-interpretations.

Notes

1   My interest in Taylor's essay parallels that of Simon Thompson in this volume, inasmuch as we are both concerned somewhat more with the assumptions governing Taylor's setting out of the problem of recognition than with his suggested solution. Certainly a full treatment of Taylor's position would require to be informed by Thompson's critique.

2   For Taylor's approach to moral philosophy see Taylor (1989, chs 1–4 and 25). See also Seglow (1996), which explores this outlook in greater depth.

3   All page references hereafter are to 'The Politics of Recognition' unless otherwise specified.

4   Compare Thompson's treatment – from a somewhat different angle – of this dispute (esp. pp. 197 ff in this volume).

5   I also omit from consideration Will Kymlicka's argument for cultural preservation in his *Multicultural Citizenship* (1995). This book deserves a paper of its own. Briefly, I think Kymlicka's work is ambiguous between a communitarian defence of particular cultures (in which case it's liable to the problem of over-particularism and denying other goods) and a universalist defence which can't address the needs of particular cultures. See Danley (1995), Tomasi (1995) and Levey (1997), who accuse Kymlicka of tending towards one or the other side of this dichotomy.

References

Appiah, K.A. (1994), 'Identity, Authenticity, Survival' in Taylor, C., *Multiculturalism: Examining 'The Politics of Recognition'*, Gutmann, A. (ed.) (2nd edn), Princeton University Press, Princeton.

Christman. J. (ed.) (1989), *The Inner Citadel: Essays on Individual Autonomy*, Oxford University Press, Oxford.

Cooke, M. (1997), 'Authenticity and Autonomy: Taylor, Habermas, and the Politics of Recognition', *Political Theory*, Vol. 25, No. 2, pp. 258–88.

Danley, J. (1995), 'Liberalism, Aboriginal Rights, and Cultural Minorities', *Philosophy and Public Affairs*, Vol. 20, No. 2, pp. 168–85.

Digeser, P. (1995), *Our Politics? Our Selves?*, Princeton University Press, Princeton.

Dumm, T. (1994), 'Strangers and Liberals', *Political Theory*, Vol. 22, No. 1, pp. 167–75.

Dworkin, G. (1988), *The Theory and Practice of Autonomy*, Cambridge University Press, Cambridge.

Dworkin, G. (1989), 'The Concept of Autonomy' in Christman, J. (ed.), *The Inner Citadel: Essays on Individual Autonomy*, Oxford University Press, Oxford.

Ferrara, A. (1992), 'Postmodern Eudaimonia', *Praxis International*, Vol. 11, No. 4, pp. 387–411.

Ferrara, A. (1993), *Modernity and Authenticity*, State University of New York Press, Albany.

Ferrara, A. (1994), 'Authenticity and the Project of Modernity', *European Journal of Philosophy*, Vol. 2, No. 3, pp. 241–73.

Habermas, J. (1994), 'Struggles for Recognition in the Democratic Constitutional State' in Taylor, C., *Multiculturalism: Examining 'The Politics of Recognition'*, Gutmann, A. (ed.) (2nd edn), Princeton University Press, Princeton.

Honneth, A. (1995), *The Struggle for Recognition*, Polity Press, Cambridge.

Kymlicka, W. (1995), *Multicultural Citizenship*, Oxford University Press, Oxford.

Levey, G.B. (1997), 'Equality, Autonomy, and Cultural Rights', *Political Theory*, Vol. 25, No. 2, pp. 215–48.

Mendus, S. (1989), *Liberalism and the Limits of Toleration*, Macmillan, London.

Miller, D. (1995), *On Nationality*, Oxford University Press, Oxford.

Rawls, J. (1971), *A Theory of Justice*, Oxford University Press, Oxford.

Rorty, A. (1994), 'The Hidden Politics of Cultural Identification', *Political Theory*, Vol. 22, No. 1, pp. 152–66.

Seglow, J. (1996) 'Goodness in an Age of Pluralism: On Charles Taylor's Moral Theory', *Res Publica*, Vol. 2, No. 2, pp. 163–80.

Tamir, Y. (1993) *Liberal Nationalism*, Princeton University Press, Princeton.

Taylor, C. (1989), *Sources of the Self*, Cambridge University Press, Cambridge.

Taylor, C. (1991), *The Ethics of Authenticity*, Harvard University Press, Cambridge, Mass.

Taylor, C. (1994), *Multiculturalism: Examining 'The Politics of Recognition'*, Gutmann, A. (ed.) (2nd edn), Princeton University Press, Princeton.

Taylor, C. (1996), review of W. Kymlicka, *Multicultural Citizenship, American Political Science Review*, Vol. 90, No. 2, p. 408.

Tomasi, J. (1995), 'Kymlicka, Liberalism, and Respect for Cultural Minorities', *Ethics*, 105, April, pp. 580–603.

Williams, B. (1981), 'Persons, character, morality' in his *Moral Luck*, Cambridge University Press, Cambridge.

Wolf, S. (1994), 'Comment' in Taylor, C., *Multiculturalism: Examining 'The Politics of Recognition'*, Gutmann, A. (ed.) (2nd edn), Princeton University Press, Princeton.

Young, R. (1986), *Autonomy*, Croom Helm, London.

Contributors

David Archard was educated at Oxford University and the London School of Economics, and is currently Reader in Philosophy at the University of St Andrews. He has published books on Marxism and existentialism; consciousness and the unconscious; and children, rights and childhood, as well as numerous articles and chapters. His most recent book on sexual consent is shortly to be published. He is currently working on issues of community, the family and the nation.

Alison Assiter is Professor of Feminist Philosophy and Head of Social Studies at the University of Luton. She has been in this job for two years. Prior to that, she spent four years in a job at the University of North London that set out to introduce equality of career opportunity to students from 'non-traditional' backgrounds. She has published a number of books, including *Bad Girls, Dirty Picture*, with Avedon Carol (Pluto Press, 1993) and *Enlightened Women* (Routledge, 1996). She lives in London, with her partner and their nine year old son.

Bob Brecher is Principal Lecturer in Philosophy in the School of Historical and Critical Studies at the University of Brighton and Editor of *Res Publica*, a journal of legal and social philosophy. His publications include *Anselm's Argument: the Logic of Divine Existence* (Gower Press, 1984); *Getting What You Want? A Critique of Liberal Morality* (Routledge, 1998); and articles in *Health Care Ethics*, *Journal of Medical Ethics*, *Radical Philosophy*, *Philosophy*, etc. and in various collections. His main interests are in moral and social philosophy and its applications.

Fernne Brennan is a Senior Teaching Fellow at the University of Essex. She lectures in the law of the European Community, criminal law, human rights and race discrimination. Her research interests include racism, European law, criminology and criminal justice. She has completed research on the relationship between British criminal law and European Community law with Janet Dine, with whom she was coauthor of a critique of the *Cadbury's Report* *on Corporate Governance.* She has a background in sociology, local and central government.

Claude Cahn is the research coordinator for the European Roma Rights Center. Following a BA from Oberlin College and an MA from the Central European University, he has conducted field research into, and written on, the situation of Roma in Albania, Austria, Macedonia and Ukraine, as well as contributing to ERRC publications on Romania and Slovakia. He compiles the ERRC newsletter *Roma Rights.*

Gideon Calder is working on a doctorate at the University of Wales, Cardiff on the implications (philosophical and political) of Richard Rorty's more recent writings. He teaches part-time both in the Philosophy Department and in the Continuing Education Department at Cardiff. His publications include reviews in *Radical Philosophy* and *Res Publica,* and a critique of Rorty's theory of metaphor in *Philosophical Writings.* Thesis apart, his research and teaching have been centred on political and social philosophy, Continental philosophy since Kant, and issues in literary theory and the philosophy of language.

John Edwards is Professor of Social Policy at Royal Holloway, University of London. His work has focused on the morality of group practices such as affirmative action and preferential treatment in Britain and the United States. In recent works he has concentrated on questions of group rights in liberal states. His recent book, *When Race Counts,* won the Gustavus Myers Award for outstanding scholarship in the field of human rights in America.

Edward Garrett is a research student at Middlesex University. His thesis explores the margins of liberal justice, with particular focus on the Criminal Justice and Public Order Act 1994 as a means of marginalization in a liberal society. He has published 'All Done with Mirrors' (1997), a review of Alan Haworth's Anti-Libertarianism, *Res Publica,* Vol. III, No. 1 (1997).

Keith Graham is Professor of Social and Political Philosophy at the University of Bristol. He was educated at the Universities of London and Oxford and has held visiting research fellowships at the Universities of Manchester, St Andrews and London. He is the editor of *Contemporary Political Philosophy: Radical Studies* (Cambridge University Press) and his books include *The Battle of Democracy* (Wheatsheaf and Barnes and Noble) and *Karl Marx: Our Contemporary* (Harvester Wheatsheaf and Toronto University Press). He has published numerous articles in philosophy and politics journals and is currently working on a book about practical reasoning in a pluralist world.

Jo Halliday is Head of Academic Standards and Audit at Anglia Polytechnic University. Her main research interest concerns how liberal ideology permits public policy to be defined in particular party political terms and she is currently working towards a PhD on the erstwhile Tory government's higher education policies. Her publications include 'Maoist Britain?', in *Curriculum Studies* (1993) and 'Maoist liberalism? Higher education in contemporary Britain' in B. Brecher and O. Fleischmann (eds), *Liberalism and the New Europe* (Avebury, 1993).

Irina Khmelko is a doctoral student at Indiana University, USA. She also holds the position of research fellow at the Ukrainian National Academy of Sciences. Her publications include 'Liberal Education in Practice' in B. Brecher, O. Fleischmann and J. Halliday (eds), *The University in a Liberal State* (Avebury, 1996). Her other interests include public policy, with particular reference to institution-building in newly-established Eastern European democracies.

Klára Kolinská teaches English language and literature at Charles University, Prague and at J.E. Purkyně University, Ustí nad Labem. Her main research interests are in Canadian literature, with particular emphasis on issues of ethnicity and multiculturalism and she is currently working towards a PhD on contemporary Canadian fiction.

Ross Poole is Associate Professor and Head of Philosophy at Macquarie University, Sydney, Australia. Since *Morality and Modernity* (Routledge, 1991) he has published a number of articles on nationalism, multculturalism, indigenous rights, identity and related topics. With luck, a monograph, *Nation and Identity*, will be published by Routledge in 1998. He has also written on Nietzsche, practical reason and persons. His next project will concern globalization, citizenship and democracy.

David Ricci is Professor of Political Science and American Studies at the Hebrew University in Jerusalem. He has been a fellow at the Woodrow Wilson Center in Washington, DC, the Institute for Advanced Study in Princeton, New Jersey and the Brookings Institution in Washington, DC. His books include *The Tragedy of Political Science: Politics, Scholarship, and*

Democracy (Yale, 1983) and *The Transformation of American Politics: the New Washington and the Rise of Think Tanks* (Yale, 1993). He is currently researching the subject of American citizenship as a sense of belonging and commitment to the civic community.

Jonathan Seglow has taught political philosophy at the Universities of Manchester and Liverpool. He is the author of 'Seven Types of Perspicuity: on the liberal/communitarian controversy' in R. Lekhi (ed.), *The State of the Academy* (1995); 'Richard Rorty and the Problem of the Person', *Politics* 16/1 (1996); and 'Goodness in an Age of Pluralism: On Charles Taylor's Moral Theory', *Res Publica*, Vol II, No. 2 (1996).

Simon Thompson is Senior Lecturer in Politics at the University of the West of England, Bristol. His current research interests in contemporary political philosophy are in the fields of theories of recognition, deliberative democracy and the relationship between politics and psychoanalysis. Recent publications include 'The Agony and the Ecstasy: Foucault, Habermas and the Problem of Recognition' in D. Owen and S. Ashenden (eds), *Foucault, Habermas and Political Theory* (Sage, 1997) and 'Postmodernism' in A. Lent (ed.), *New Political Ideas: An Introduction* (Lawrence and Wishart, 1998). He is currently coediting a book for Polity Press on Richard Rorty and political theory, due for publication in 1998.

Lubica Učník was born in Czechoslovakia, and worked as a TV producer in Czechoslovak Television in Bratislava. She studied journalism at Komenský University, Bratislava but left before completing her final year of study to emigrate to Australia with her daughter, in 1980. In 1992, she completed a degree in Communication Studies at Murdoch University, Western Australia. She is now writing a PhD thesis in Philosophy at Murdoch University and teaching part-time.